Late and Close

Late and Close

A History of
Relief Pitching

by Paul Votano

McFarland & Company, Inc., Publishers
Jefferson, North Carolina, and London

Library of Congress Cataloguing-in-Publication Data

Votano, Paul, 1929–
    Late and close : a history of relief pitching / by Paul Votano.
       p.   cm.
    Includes bibliographical references and index.

    ISBN 0-7864-1162-7 (softcover : 50# alkaline paper)

    1. Pitching (Baseball)—United States—History.   2. Relief
pitchers (Baseball)—United States—History.   I. Title.
GV871.V68 2002
796.357'22'0973—dc21   2002000285

British Library cataloguing data are available

Cover photograph ©2002 Corbis Images

Manufactured in the United States of America

*McFarland & Company, Inc., Publishers
  Box 611, Jefferson, North Carolina 28640
    www.mcfarlandpub.com*

Table of Contents

Introduction

No other major sport has experienced the number and variety of changes that major league baseball has seen since its arrival in America more than a century and a half ago. While football, basketball, track and field, soccer and other athletic pursuits still compete essentially as they always have, baseball has endured countless reforms, and none more so than in the domain of relief pitching.

This book discusses how relief pitching has evolved—from the early days of baseball when, for the most part, a pitcher would be replaced only when injured or when another pitcher was used in a "mop-up" role, to where it has become a managerial tool crucial to the outcome of games.

Not all fans are thrilled with the comings and goings of pitchers today, but regardless, interest in the game of baseball has never been higher. With few exceptions, record crowds are attending baseball games day and night— and not just in the major leagues. There has been a boom in the minor leagues as well. New teams and ballparks are springing up everywhere and communities from coast to coast are reveling in this marvelous transformation. Merchandising has reached record breaking proportions.

Baseball is being introduced in more countries around the world all the time, and players from other countries are on the rosters of more major league teams than ever before. Consider the number of countries that sent teams to compete in the 2000 Summer Olympic Games in Sydney, Australia. Can a true "world" series be far behind?

What makes the metamorphosis in relief pitching over time so captivating is how the changes, which have had such a dramatic effect on how managers utilize their bullpens, were instituted and why. Much has had to do with the way the game's fan base felt about it at any given point in time. Were too many runs being scored? Not enough? Did pitchers have adequate arsenals to counter the advantages that batters perceived them to have? Could rules changes, the dimensions of the ballparks, the equipment, the playing surfaces, and all of the many other variables that have gone into this great game have resulted in a better product? Perhaps. All of these issues and more have been addressed at various times in the history of baseball to contribute to the how the game is played.

But before any of these innovations could have been instituted, leaders with vision and exceptionally talented players had to enter the arena and make their presence felt. Babe Ruth, Branch Rickey, John McGraw, Jackie Robinson, Joe McCarthy, Bruce Sutter, Leo Durocher, Kenesaw Mountain Landis and scores of others had a profound effect on baseball at the time they were each active.

As you read this book, you will discover various periods or eras in baseball that were noted for what they bestowed upon the national pastime and how each logically advanced baseball to the next level. Baseball fans are known for their strong feelings about the game they love with such passion. No other game in the history of American sport numbers such devoted fans.

There has been no attempt here either to soft-pedal or to convince anyone that a particular theory regarding strategy and, in particular, the tremendous growth of relief pitching has improved the quality of baseball. Most everything presented herein is historical in nature and details a natural progression to where the game is now. We can either like it or not. The intensity of baseball fans cannot be rivaled. The arguments that rage daily about this and that in the game are legendary. Just listen to any radio sports talk show at any time of day.

These "discussions" are often directed at the use of relief pitchers by managers and why the moves were doomed to failure. A manager usually has only a split second to make a decision, while those in the sanctity of their dens, living rooms or neighborhood bars can speculate over the course of an evening or entire day about how they would have approached it. Again, that is the beauty of sport, but baseball especially is in a class by itself when it comes to the "second guess."

The history of relief pitching has afforded me a marvelous opportunity to examine the entire range of the glorious game of baseball from its earliest days. I have seen clearly what it means to so many people every day of their lives, not just in the baseball season but in the so-called "hot stove" league or off-season as well. Whether or not you agree with how relief pitching has developed, after you read this book you will have to concede that the craft has taken a leading position in the excitement and appeal that surrounds today's game of baseball.

◆ *Chapter 1* ◆

The Early Years
(1845–1899)

In the beginning of the nineteenth century, a ball-and-stick game at various times called "town ball," "base" and even "base ball" started to become increasingly popular in this country. Originally based on the English game of rounders, the game inspired even small towns to form teams to play it, while the large cities established what were called base-ball clubs.

By the 1840s, a number of different versions of the game began to emerge, mostly from Massachusetts and New York. The Massachusetts brand used an irregular four-sided field with four bases at fixed and uneven distances from each other. The batter or "striker," as he was called at the time, was actually away from home base. Fielders or "scouts," as they were identified, were able to make putouts by fielding batted balls either on the fly or on one bounce, or by hitting a runner with a thrown ball.

The New York–style game that was being played by members of that city's Knickerbocker Club was created by a surveyor and amateur athlete named Alexander J. Cartwright and it was growing even more renowned than the Massachusetts type. Cartwright's version included an infield that was in the shape of a diamond with bases 90 feet apart, just as they are today. The pitching distance was 45 feet and the ball had to be delivered underhanded in a stiff-armed manner.

Three strikes were required to record an out, and a batter could also be put out by a fielder catching a ball on the fly or on the initial bounce, or even with a fielded ball reaching first base on a throw before the runner. Cartwright also set the number of players on a side to nine and the number of outs to three in order to close out a time at bat for each team.

Obviously, this version eventually became the model for the game as it is now played.

It was on June 19, 1846, that the first recorded contest, officiated by Cartwright, took place at the Elysian Fields in Hoboken, New Jersey. Cartwright's Knickerbockers were defeated that day by a team known as the New York Baseball Club.

As the game's notoriety and stature increased, more and more amateur teams came into being and a convention was called in 1857 to review the rules and to discuss other pressing questions about the sport. Some 25 teams in the northeast corridor sent delegates to this gathering and the result was that a group called the National Association of Base Ball Players was formed a year later. Among the first rules changes the Association made was the creation of a pitcher's box and establishing nine innings for a complete game. It also began the practice of charging for admission. By 1860, the new league could count 60 teams as members.

While things were looking up for the future of the game, the unrest in the 1860s intervened to substantially reduce the number of teams from that original alliance. However, during the Civil War, Union soldiers, playing baseball during whatever leisure time they had, introduced the game in other parts of the country where they might have found themselves. When the war broke out, Southern teams were excluded from competing and at its conclusion an east-west alignment of teams had materialized and lasted for many years. Even so, when peace came more people were playing baseball than ever before. When the league's annual convention took place in 1868, delegates from over 100 clubs attended.

While the skills of those playing the game had vastly improved, there was neither an organized league nor a playing schedule. Barnstorming teams like the Washington Nationals were adding to the game's growth, but it was evident that structured competition was indeed becoming necessary.

Changes were starting to become evident, thus adding to the enjoyment of the game. For instance, fielders were exhibiting much more dexterity, and sliding to avoid being tagged came into vogue. Also, outs that were charged against a hitter via the one-bounce rule were outlawed. And a pitcher named Arthur "Candy" Cummings came up with a new twist— the curveball that he said he developed after seeing a spinning clamshell curve as it skipped along the water.

Born in Ware, Massachusetts, Cummings, at 5'9" and weighing a mere 120 pounds, pitched for a team known as the Excelsiors of Brooklyn. After many hours of practice he found that he was able to make a ball curve with the wind in his face but not at his back. By the way, he picked up the nickname of "Candy" because in his day the name was synonymous with "best," which many considered him to be during his relatively short-lived (1872–1878) career. Because of his discovery of the curveball, which some historians still dispute, Cummings, despite a losing record, was elected to the Hall of Fame in 1939.

The very first totally professional team—the Cincinnati Red Stockings—was born in 1869. Harry Wright, a jeweler, former English cricket professional and head of a local amateur club, paid $1,200 not only to manage the team but to be its captain, principal recruiter, publicist and center fielder. Harry, who also became known as the "Father of Professional Baseball," and his brother, George, who helped to run the club and played shortstop, saw to it that only the best players in the country would wear their uniform. Not surprisingly, these first-ever paid players went out and won every single game they played against all comers, winding up with a perfect 60–0 record. They traveled over 11,000 miles by rail, ship and stagecoach, and helped bring the game of baseball to people who had never even heard of it, let alone seen it played. More than 200,000 fans attended their games during this monumental cross-country journey.

The Red Stockings finally met their match on June 14, 1870, when they met a local team called the Atlantics in Brooklyn, New York, at the latter's home field, the Capitoline Grounds. Cincinnati went down to defeat, 8–7, in a hard-fought contest that consumed eleven innings before a crowd of 20,000.

The bitter loss wasn't the only thing to go wrong for the Red Stockings that year. Escalating salaries and mounting expenses finally signaled the team's end, but their impact upon the American psyche was undeniable. Were it not for their barnstorming and spreading the news about this great new game, it is difficult to imagine that baseball would have attained its remarkable new-found status.

While there was a great deal of interest in keeping the game on a strictly amateur level, it was well nigh impossible to compete against the professionals. Therefore, amateur teams took a back seat to the professionals and the better players signed on in droves. On March 17, 1871 (St. Patrick's Day), the National Association of Professional Baseball Players became baseball's first all-professional league. The historic event took place, fittingly, in a bar called Collier's Cafe on the corner of Broadway and Thirteenth Street in New York City.

Ten men met that day to become charter members of the new league, which was composed of the Boston Red Stockings, Chicago White Stockings, Cleveland Forest Citys, Fort Wayne Kekiongas, New York Mutuals, Philadelphia Athletics, Rockford Forest Citys, Washington Nationals and

Washington Olympics. Although the Brooklyn Eckfords sat in on the meeting as well, their representatives weren't too sure how the new venture was going to turn out and, consequently, refused to ante up the $10 entry fee. However, they did sign on later when the Kekiongas team folded in August.

The National Association's original nine teams had increased to 13 by 1875. But the life of the league was not to be extended. The presence of gamblers and the sale of alcoholic beverages at games undercut the general public's appreciation of the game and its reputation as a wholesome pastime. It also faced some stiff competition from an upstart league known as the International Association, which consisted mostly of gate receipt-sharing teams. As attendance plummeted, the National Association's influence also decreased and the league was replaced by the National League on February 2, 1876, at a meeting in the Grand Central Hotel in New York City. Now teams that were formerly owned and operated by the players were taken over by businessmen who established the standards and policies for ticket prices, schedules and player contracts.

The game as we know it today was played far differently back then. For example, pitchers had to throw underhanded and a hitter could ask for the ball to be delivered either "high" or "low." A base on balls was issued after nine balls, not four, and the distance from the pitcher's mound to home was only 45 feet. In 1884, pitchers were allowed to throw overhand if they wished and three years later the request for either a "high" or "low" pitch was forbidden. By 1889, the number of balls required for a walk was reduced to four and four years later the distance between home plate and the pitcher's mound was increased to 60 feet, six inches. And not only that, the new rule required the pitcher to deliver the ball with his back foot moored to a rubber slab instead of allowing him to take a skip step inside a 5½ by 4-foot box.

The Boston team, which somehow had remained free of the corruption that hastened its league's demise, unwittingly helped bring on the collapse just by being far superior to its competition. William A. Hulbert, the new league's president and owner of the Chicago Cubs, convinced Boston's Al Spalding to join the National League. Spalding, a right-handed pitcher who in only five years registered 207 wins, in turn brought along some of his teammates. The 1939 Hall of Fame inductee, who won 52 games in 1874 and followed up with 57 more in the following season, also managed the Red Stockings in 1876–1877.

An opposing player that Spalding also induced to come along to the National League with him was a star of the Philadelphia Athletics, Adrian "Cap" Anson, who went on to become one of the game's all-time greats and the first player to collect 3,000 hits. Anson, also inducted posthumously into the Hall of Fame with Al Spalding in 1939, was a player-manager of the Chicago Cubs for 19 years. Primarily a first baseman, he also caught some, and played a little outfield and all the other infield positions on occasion, winding up with a lifetime .334 batting average.

As the Chisox manager and a strict disciplinarian, Anson led his team to pennants from 1880 to 1882 and again in 1884 and 1885. An innovator, he rotated his pitching staff and used signals to his hitters and fielders. Many credit him with being the first manager to platoon his players and to launch pre-season training camps. He was fined continuously by umpires and league officials because of his on-field antics. In fact, at one point in his career, Anson was known as "Baby" (short for crybaby) before he gained some maturity and earned the nickname "Cap" (for captain).

He was extremely tough on his players and used bed checks to keep them in line, but he also got them first-class hotel accommodations. He would also march them onto the field of play in single file before every game. Anson died in Chicago in 1922 at the age of 39.

The National League's president, William A. Hulbert, who was as tough as nails when it came to running things, saw the new league through all kinds of upheavals, including financial reverses, franchise disturbances and scandals, until his death in 1882. In that year, a new league, the American Association (AA), was formed and it not only reduced ticket prices but also played on Sundays. The AA also created new teams in big cities that were not represented in the NL like New York, Philadelphia, Cincinnati and St. Louis. Cincinnati, which had been thrown out of the National League after the 1880 season for playing its games on Sundays and allowing liquor to be sold and consumed during games, was one of the first franchises to join. The AA established a 25-cent admission charge—half of the NL's 50-cent fee—and allowed its teams the privilege of selling liquor and playing on Sundays, if they desired.

It wasn't long before both leagues realized that their interests would be better served by honoring each other's players' contracts, and they reached an agreement in 1883. They also permitted every one of their teams to obligate a select group of players to a "reserve clause" that would allow the clubs to unilaterally renew a player's contract and prevent him from going elsewhere. It also paved the way for the first post-season series between league champions in the following year.

Naturally the players were livid and decided to form their own league, the Union Association, in 1884, with the help of a youthful St. Louis tycoon, Henry V. Lucas, who loved baseball and couldn't have cared less for Sunday games or about how much money could be made from selling beer. Many of the players left their teams for the freedom their new league gave them and encouraged by Lucas, who thumbed his nose at the reserve clause. This caused the conflict to escalate, as there was open warfare between the leagues for players. Of the 12 original franchises in the Union Association, only five made it through the season and it folded up after one year. The only one who profited at the end of the day was Lucas, who joined the National League with what remained of the Cleveland team and moved it to St. Louis.

There is little doubt that the most spectacular event of the 1884 season on the field was Rochester, New York's Charley "Old Hoss" Radbourn's 59 victories for the Providence Grays—aided by a new rule allowing overhand pitching. A man who was not easy to take, Radbourn possessed an extremely suspicious nature that drove him to perform at unbelievable levels. The *Providence Journal-Bulletin* called the hard-drinking right-hander "Lord Radbourn" and labeled him "erratic, capricious and ill-tempered."

In the beginning of the 1884 season, Radbourn and Philadelphia native Bill Sweeney, both right-handers, shared the pitching load. The 21-year-old Sweeney was well liked and this only incensed Radbourn more, who at 29 was already jealous of the youngster. Following a mid-season suspension for "improper conduct " (he threw a baseball at his catcher for dropping a third strike), Radbourn suddenly became the Grays' only pitcher when Sweeney jumped the club and signed on with St. Louis of the new Union Association. "Old Hoss" worked out a plan with Providence's team management to pitch the remainder of the season for a bonus and then become a free agent at the end of the year if they would only drop his suspension. The club didn't have much of an option with Radbourn being their one and only pitcher at the time, and agreed to the terms.

Thereafter, Radbourn performed like a man possessed. While it's true that he did not pitch every game left on the schedule (some position players filled in from time to time), he did pitch in most of them, including a stretch from August 21 to September 15 when the club was in the midst of a 20-game winning streak that eventually earned them the pennant. "Old Hoss" pitched 678⅔ innings, only an inning and a third less than Will White's record-setting pace for Cincinnati in 1879.

Radbourn went on to win all three games in a championship playoff against the American Association's New York Mets, which many call major league baseball's first World Series. His 59 wins in 1884 are six more than any other pitcher has ever recorded, and what's also remarkable about the feat is that most of the victories were turned in during the second half of the season.

Although he continued to pitch underhanded as required because it meant less strain on his arm, the grueling 1884 campaign eventually took its toll on "Old Hoss." Sometimes he couldn't even comb his hair with his right hand. He would wrap his arm in hot towels and then throw an iron ball around. He would follow this routine by switching over to a baseball that he'd throw at progressively longer distances until he could reach home plate. Then he would go out and, somehow, not only pitch but also best his counterpart over nine innings.

Even though he continued to win 20 games or more in the next three seasons, Radbourn was losing almost as many each year and his strikeout totals were decreasing rapidly as well. After calling it a career following the 1891 season, he ran a pool hall and saloon in Bloomington, Illinois. A hunting accident in 1894 cost him an eye and he lived a reclusive existence in the rear of his saloon until his death in 1897.

In 1889, war broke out again in baseball when something called the Players' League was formed. Originally, a group had been set up in 1885 named the Brotherhood of Professional Ball Players, ostensibly to protect and promote players' rights. It was a noble attempt but did little to resolve some of the problems that the players were facing at the time. These included such delicate issues as the reserve clause, a salary cap, arbitrary fines and other matters foisted upon them by the owners that the players felt were unjustified. Frustrated by the events of the day, a lot of the better players joined the Players' League but it, too, could not survive for more than one year.

Even the American Association, which lost a good many of its players and was not strong financially to begin with, could not compete and also called it a day at the end of the 1891 season. Four of its teams—Baltimore, Louisville, St. Louis and Washington—wound up in the National League. Although its life was relatively short, the American Association will go down in history as the league that began Sunday baseball and introduced league control of umpires. It will also be remembered as the league in which some black players participated for a time. However, a segregated Negro League in Pennsylvania in 1889 and all-black independent leagues spelled the end of black players in big league baseball until 1946, when Branch Rickey signed Jackie Robinson to finally break the color barrier.

Although it was the only game in town so to speak, all of the National League's teams with the exception of Boston and Brooklyn were losing money. It was felt that the best way to increase attendance was to change the rules of the game to emphasize offense. In 1892, the league as a whole was batting only .245, down ten points from the year before.

The first thing the National League did in between seasons was to lengthen the pitching distance to 60 feet. This was later enlarged by six inches in 1895. The man most responsible for this radical change was Amos Rusie, who broke in with Indianapolis at the age of 18 in 1889. A power pitcher of the first magnitude, he threw so hard that his first catcher, Dick Buckley, placed a thin sheet of lead in his glove to deaden the impact. Rusie struck out 341 batters in 1890 to lead the league when he joined the New York Giants after his original team, Indianapolis, had folded following his rookie year.

Called "The Hoosier Thunderbolt," the native Indianan missed the entire 1896 season by becoming baseball's first-ever holdout after having a salary dispute with his boss, Arnold Freedman. Despite winning 24 games and leading the league in both shutouts and strikeouts for a ninth-place team, Freedman wanted to cut Rusie's pay by $600. The pitcher wouldn't budge and sat it out for the whole year. He didn't miss a beat when he returned in 1897 and posted a 28–10 record followed by a 20-win season in the next year. However, he had some arm trouble after attempting a pick-off move that year, which turned out to be his last full year in the majors. He was eventually traded to Cincinnati and started two games for them in 1901 but was hit hard both times and called it quits. He was elected to the Hall of Fame in 1977. To illustrate just how good he was considered at the time, Walter Johnson, who arrived in 1907, received the ultimate compliment when he was labeled "another Rusie."

Earlier rules changes—like establishing a uniform strike zone in 1887, permanently adopting the three strikes rule in 1888 and the four-balls walk rule, along with the aforementioned 1893 changes—exceeded the league's wildest expectations. Batting averages increased by the greatest margin in history for a single season—35 points. Almost a thousand more runs were scored. The older pitchers had more trouble with the new rules than the younger hurlers like Cy Young, Kid Nichols and Amos Rusie, all of whom adjusted rather easily. Older pitchers like Boston's Jack Stivetts dropped from 35 wins in 1892 to only 19 in 1893. Other top pitchers fared just as poorly. While earned run averages (ERA) were not compiled in that period, historical statisticians have since computed that the league went from a 3.28 ERA in 1892 to 4.66 in 1893 and jumped even more the following year to 5.32, the highest ever up to that time.

When professional baseball officially began in 1876, most teams had just one pitcher on their rosters. As time went on, the number went up to two, three and even more by 1892. The radical changes in the rules led to more pitchers rather than fewer as the *Spalding Base Ball Guide* suggested. The editor of the publication wrote at the time: "The season of 1892 was marked by the presence of too many pitchers in a majority of the twelve club teams. No less than 48 different pitchers were employed during the season by the six leading clubs of the championship campaign while 54 pitchers took part in the games of the six tail-enders. Three pitchers—two good strategists and a single 'cyclone' twister—would have amply sufficed to take each club through the season. A battery force of five players—three pitchers and two catchers—should be the lowest for 1893. In the spring, when club teams are being worked into good form, it may do to experiment with several pitchers, but when the team has been got into full fighting trim, three pitchers should be amply sufficient for each club's team."

Of course, the rules changes played a significant role, leading to more pitchers being employed rather than fewer. Prior to the 1900 season, the editor of the *Guide*, taking note of the beatings the pitchers were taking as a whole, was prompted to observe: "In the matter of changing pitchers, we advocate the rules being so changed as to allow a pitcher to be put in the box a second time in a game so as to allow him time to recover from a temporary 'rattling' in the box. This is done in bowling, in cricket, and should be a rule in our national game." While this particular proposal was repeated several years later, nothing came of it. If anything, the use of multiple pitchers began to rise with each succeeding year and hasn't stopped since.

The new pitching rules specified that there was to be a rubber slab and not one that would set up in a pile of dirt and produce somewhat of a neutralizing control as pitchers adjusted to the longer distance. The pitcher's best friend then tended to be the groundskeepers at each ballpark, who would try to create a legitimate mound that might compensate for what now amounted to a disadvantage. Nothing seemed to help. In fact, two years after the rules were changed, batting averages soared even higher. The league registered a .309 average as a whole while teams like the third-place Philadelphia Phillies ended up with an unbelievable .349 mark. Baltimore, at .343, and six other teams were over the .300 mark.

Throughout the period 1876–1899, 90 percent of the pitchers who started games finished them. The only team that had more than one or two pitchers was Boston. It had three pitchers and one of them, Jack Manning, started 20 games and relieved in 14 others. The Braintree, Massachusetts, native won four and "saved" five in his relief appearances.

In 1885, believe it or not, complete games attained a record high of 97 percent in the National League and 96.4 percent in the American Association. After the pitching distance was increased in 1893, complete games dropped from 88.1 percent in the National League to 82.4 percent. While the backslide continued for the next couple of years, strangely enough, it

went back up again in 1896 to 86.3 percent as pitchers began to adjust to
the new distance.

Twelve pitchers who toiled in the nineteenth century and compiled
more than 200 starts finished at least 95 percent of their games. New York
City's Jack Lynch, who began his career with Buffalo in the National
League in 1881, had the best record of the group with 215 complete games
out of 217 starts, or a phenomenal 99.1 percent. Although he developed
arm trouble in his rookie year, he was relieved only twice late in the year.
The right-handed Lynch joined the fledgling American Association the following year with New York and finished every one of his starts thereafter.
His 199 consecutive complete games remain a major league record. On
those few occasions when a starter failed to finish a game, the reliever was
actually one of the other starters. Ashland, Pennsylvania-bred Jack Stivetts,
for example, one of Boston's aces in the 1890s, started 333 games but also
relieved in 55 other games, recording 19 wins, seven losses and four saves
in those stints.

None other than Denton True "Cy" Young, who started 411 times
before 1900, actually came in from the bullpen in 53 games (saving 17)
during his 22 seasons in the majors. The man who is unsurpassed in major
league history in total victories as a pitcher with 511, in starts with 815 and
in complete games with 749, needed only a scant 12 warmup pitches before
signaling he was ready to go in any given game.

Born and raised in Gilmore, Ohio, the 6'2", 210-pound Young hurled
more than 400 innings in a season five times and in excess of 300 innings
11 times. He claimed never to have had a sore arm. And this from a man
who took the ball every three days. "Once I pitched every other day for
eighteen days," he said. Young got his nickname while pitching for Can-
ton of the Tri-State League. He was originally called "Cyclone" (later
shortened to Cy) after a few of his warmups shattered the outfield fence.
Producer of three no-hitters, he got his last one as a 41-year-old in 1908.
He was voted into the Hall of Fame in 1937.

Charles "Kid" Nichols was the "saves" leader in the nineteenth century. In addition to his 440 starts, he relieved 49 times and had a won-
lost record of 13–6 with 16 saves. Called "Kid" because of his slight build
and youthful countenance, Nichols won 361 games and yet is barely mentioned today. He had as many complete games as Walter Johnson (531)
and no pitcher had more 30-win seasons—seven. In the decade of the
1890s, no other pitcher in the majors was more effective than Nichols,
who won more than 25 games nine years in a row. Nichols did not wind
up when he pitched and never used a curveball, yet he was able to change
speeds with alarming dexterity. The Madison, Wisconsin, native led his

team to five pennants and became the youngest pitcher—only 30 years of age—to win 300 games.

Nobody could outwork Nichols. He threw for more than 400 innings a year in his first five seasons in the big leagues, and 300 or more innings during that first decade. His record of 12 years for pitching in excess of 300 innings still stands and probably will never be broken. Late in 1892, he performed a feat that can only be described as incredible—he pitched three winning games on three consecutive days. He picked up another nickname—"Nervy Nick"—for defeating the Orioles twice in three days to win the 1897 flag for his team.

After his retirement following the 1906 season, Nichols returned to his adopted Kansas City, Missouri, home and coached some amateur teams. One of his players was Charles Dillon "Casey" Stengel. Nichols was obviously a very durable and energetic athlete who won his city's bowling championship at the age of 64. In fact, he continued to bowl competitively well into his seventies. Nichols entered the Hall of Fame in 1949 and died in Kansas City four years later.

After acquiring the remaining four teams from the American Association following the 1891 season, the National League felt the world was their oyster. The owners truly believed that profits from their now-12-team league would roll in continuously. What they didn't—and probably couldn't—figure on was the impact that factors like a national recession, the Spanish-American War of 1898 and the imbalance of their own league would have on their unconstrained glee. Nothing could stop the reverses the club's owners were facing. They tried everything from salary caps to the division of gate receipts. Nothing worked and, as the situation worsened, the infighting among the teams got out of control as well.

Desperation moves, like stocking NL teams with minor league farm-hands to reduce expenses and acrimonious penalties in vain attempts to halt unruly player behavior, failed. After the 1898 season, agreements were made to transfer the better players from one team to another, which only made for a complete fiasco in the National League. Finally, by agreeing to scuttle the Cleveland, Baltimore, Washington and St. Louis franchises for 1900, the NL returned to its more manageable eight-team format.

The fact remains that professional baseball in the 1890s along with its growing pains and resultant problems did bring some semblance of maturity to the game. The major rules changes were augmented by other important modifications such as player substitutions, adopting the infield fly rule, calling foul bunts strikes, establishing a pentagon-shaped home plate and defining bunts and sacrifice flies.

Before 1889, a pitcher could be replaced only if he was hurt. Otherwise, he was expected to pitch all nine innings—or more. Up until then, substitutes could only be brought in if a regular starting player was seriously hurt as defined by the opposing team's captain. Under these conditions, captains would, therefore, often have backup or "change" pitchers playing in the outfield. Sometimes all that would happen was that the players would be permitted simply to change positions.

Uniforms had improved and most players wore gloves. Originally, these gloves were nothing more than a flimsy piece of leather that fit over the player's palm with five holes cut out to allow room for the fingers to protrude. By this time, though, gloves began to resemble the type that fielders use today, only they were much, much smaller.

The fingers of the gloves were short and the main purpose was merely to stave off injury to the palm and fingers. However, most players would cut a big hole in the palm of the glove so that they could get a better grip on the ball once they fielded it. Catchers used the big "Decker" mitt and wore masks and chest protectors.

The field of play was nothing like we know it to be today. They were not that well maintained and balls could take some pretty horrific bounces thanks to pebbles on the infield and the unevenness of the outfield ground. The ball took crazy bounces due to being somewhat lopsided. And if that wasn't enough for a pitcher to endure, with only two or three balls used in most games, balls got to be rather difficult to manipulate late in the game.

Only one umpire was employed per game to handle the entire field right up until the turn of the century, which posed more than its share of problems for everyone concerned. This sole umpire would call balls and strikes from behind the catcher until someone reached base. Then he would have to work from behind the pitcher, which would cause the fielders to try all sorts of shenanigans to divert the umpire's attention.

Play did improve, though, as signs were employed, infielders began setting up to turn the double play and outfielders were coached to use backups, hit the cutoff man and work relays. And offensively, bunting, sacrificing, sliding, stealing and the hit-and-run were beginning to become integral parts of the game.

◆ *Chapter 2* ◆

The Turn of the Century Brings Changes (1900–1919)

As the twentieth century began, pitchers, for the most part, continued to throw complete games. In the National League, hurlers were finishing more than 80 percent of their starts until 1906, while the new "junior circuit," the American League (AL), fell below that mark in the following year. The AL, formerly a minor league, was taken over in 1894 by a 29-year-old sportswriter named Byron Bancroft "Ban" Johnson and his close friend, the 33-year-old manager of the Cincinnati Reds, Charlie Comiskey. The name of the league was changed from the "Western League" to the "American League" in 1900 to give it more of a national flavor. Comiskey had purchased the Sioux City franchise and moved it to St. Paul after his contract with Cincinnati had expired. He and Johnson immediately started planning for further expansion.

A Cincinnati native and former sports editor of that city's *Commercial-Gazette*, the burly Johnson tried to talk to the National League about these moves, but they ignored him. So he simply "forgot" about the national agreement whereby players could move about freely from club to club and took his chances from there. He governed his league with an iron fist and soon had its umpires enforcing the rules against players' rowdyism, a big problem at the time in the older NL. His organization was becoming recognized as the best-run league in the country and the national press declared it so. The AL games were looked upon as family entertainment since violence and obscene language simply weren't permitted. Attendance at league games jumped. At the same time, the NL's image was decreasing steadily as chaos reigned supreme.

After a successful 1900 season, and fully aware that the national agreement was set to expire anyhow, Johnson declared the AL to be a major league. Obviously, this meant war between the two leagues. Johnson had picked up a number of good players from the NL for the 1901 season and placed competing franchises in NL cities like Philadelphia and Boston. They already had teams in previous NL cities such as Baltimore, Washington, Cleveland and Detroit. The AL also offered higher salaries to NL players and these raids cost the older league more than a hundred players.

A couple of rules changes that were adopted were going to present major league hitters with more problems than they were prepared to handle. One was changing the size of home plate in 1900 from a 12-inch square to a five-sided, 17-inches-across design. Now pitchers had 200 more square inches of the strike zone with which to work. The other change—drafted by the NL in 1901 and the AL in 1903—counted the first two foul balls as strikes, whereas before then hitters could foul pitches off indefinitely without worrying about striking out. Strikeouts jumped immediately by more than 50 percent and batting averages, slugging percentages and runs per game plummeted. But it wasn't just the rules changes that were kicking in to contribute to this dramatic falloff. Soft, discolored balls, altered by players who would deliberately tarnish them either by spitting tobacco juice on them or by rolling them around in the dirt, also made it increasingly difficult for batters to see the ball.

Make no mistake about it, though, improved fielding and the increased use of relief pitchers during this so-called "dead ball era" were other important factors in the lessening of offense in baseball at the time. In 1901, relievers were called on to "save" games only 32 times but by 1909 that figure jumped to 110.

Nevertheless, the game's popularity was increasing steadily as evidenced by the rise in attendance figures. The return to two leagues, as it was in the 1880s and sparked by the World Series of 1903, certainly helped as did broadened press coverage and motion pictures with baseball as their central theme. Of course, the introduction of the song "Take Me Out to The Ball Game" in 1908 helped too. The boom in the sport led to the construction of new ballparks in cities like Chicago, Boston and Detroit, among others, each of which accommodated 30,000 fans or more. Baseball was on the move in this era of prosperity.

It was Manager John McGraw of the New York Giants who, more than any other manager after 1904, began to call pitchers out of the bullpen to help his team win games. Earlier, managers Frank Chance of the Chicago Cubs and Clark Griffith of the Washington Senators had also begun using their better pitchers to complete the victories for their second-tier hurlers.

But it was McGraw more than anyone who started tinkering with the system and began venturing with employing pitchers almost exclusively in relief.

It was to be years and years before those pitchers who would come to be called relief "specialists" would come into vogue. When a starter was to be replaced in the early 1900s, he would merely make way for just another starter. No manager would dare risk holding onto a lead to a seldom-used bullpen occupant when he had one of his starters available to bring in.

With no league president and torn asunder by internal strife, the older National League decided it was time to sit down with the new upstart American League in early 1903. A National Agreement was drawn up and signed, by which

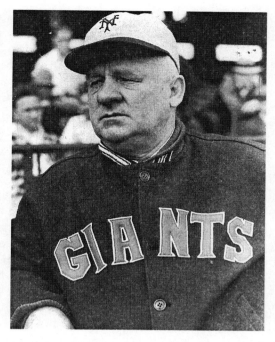

Feisty John McGraw of the New York Giants was the first manager to regularly call in pitchers from the bullpen to help him win games. (Courtesy National Baseball Hall of Fame Library, Cooperstown, N.Y.)

the leagues would operate separately but as equals and be bonded by similar playing rules and non-threatening schedules in addition to recognizing each other's territories and player contracts. A tremendously painful and harmful period of league and franchise uncertainty had ended at long last.

The formal beginning of the new mutual agreement came with the establishment of the first World Series in 1903. Peace did not make it through the next season, however, as no World Series took place in 1904 when the Giants and the feisty John McGraw refused to play the AL champion. The following year was one of reconciliation for the good of the game, not to mention each other, and both associations went forward from there. In order to keep the peace, a National Commission was created to interpret and enforce the newly signed National Agreement. Violators were to be punished by fines and suspensions.

In the first decade of the 1900s, the game of baseball continued to be one of strategy. The so-called "dead ball" era saw very few home runs hit. It was a time of contact hitters and the hit-and-run. Bunting and base stealing were still the order of the day. Rules changes like limiting the height of the pitching mound to 15 inches above the baseline level were adopted. Also the infield fly rule and recording an out via a foul bunt on a third strike were invoked, and earned run averages (ERA) were included in pitchers' records.

Rarely were new balls ever put in play, so pitchers ruled the roost by using the spitball and scuffing up balls by various and sundry means. Consequently, an ERA of 3.00 or less was quite common as was a .250 batting average. Hitters were also affected by the newer, larger ballparks that were being built then along with the adoption of better gloves by fielders.

Pitchers themselves were becoming more intimidating to the hitters just because of their increased sizes. During this period most of the top pitchers were becoming bigger and stronger. In 1894, a typical major league pitcher might weigh about 168 pounds, or four pounds less than the average hitter, and stand around 5'10" tall, which was basically the same size as the normal batter. However, by 1908, pitchers at 5'11" not only stood an inch-and-a-half taller than opposing batters, but also averaged nine pounds more at 180, as opposed to 171 pounds for the typical hitter.

To offset the rules changes and other factors that were seeing baseball games decided on a "one-run-at-a-time" basis, managers were employing tactics such as the hit-and-run, bunting, base stealing and the like disdaining the long ball that was as rare as hens' teeth. Any home runs that were hit were usually of the inside-the-park variety as more hitters were choking upon the bat and just punching balls out over the infield. Just how rare were home runs? In 1908, the Chicago White Sox hit a total of three and the following year, John "Red" Murray of the Giants led the NL with seven.

Nevertheless, complete games began a descent that saw the National League's total fall under 60 percent in 1910, while the American League reached that same percentage in 1913. Despite this trend, some pitchers continued to finish most of what they had started. Jack W. Taylor with Chicago and St. Louis in the National League from 1900 to 1907 finished 234 of his 242 starts during that period, for a remarkable 96.7 percent, including 188 complete games in a row. This is the same guy who finished all 44 of his starts in 1898–1899. At the same time though, future Hall of Famer Ed Walsh of the Chicago White Sox became the first pitcher to relieve in 100 games. He reached that figure in 1912. Otis "Doc" Crandall tied that mark shortly after while Mordecai "Three Finger" Brown and Lew Richie got to it in the next season.

Walsh, who went on to record the lowest earned run average of all time until then with a 1.82 mark, also had the odd distinction of leading the AL with a rather remarkable 1.27 ERA in 1910, yet still lost 20 games thanks to a combination of an anemic offense and a horrendous defense behind him. His club only hit seven home runs that year, batted .211 as a team and committed an astonishing 314 errors.

A spitballer who was also a superb fielder, the 6'1", 193-pound. Walsh won 40 games one year and led the AL in saves five times. He also became the first pitcher in his league to steal home twice. The Plains, Pennsylvania, native, of whom Ty Cobb once said: "When this big moose had his stuff, he was unbeatable," actually helped to design the old Comiskey Park. A fan favorite, he would delight in hitting fungoes into the stands. On a short list of starting pitchers in the period 1900–1919 who relieved in at least 100 games, Walsh made 115 appearances out of the bullpen, saving 28 among the 430 games in which he appeared.

On September 6, 1905, he pitched two complete game wins over the Red Sox and threw 10 shutouts in the following season. He beat his team's cross-town rivals, the Cubs, twice in the 1906 World Series, fanning 12 in the third game, a record that stood for 23 years. Walsh somehow was able to post a 24–18 record in 1907 despite being on the losing end of eight shutouts. His post–1900 record of 464 innings pitched in 1908 still stands. He later won 27 games twice—in 1911 and 1912—but had arm trouble later and was forced to retire in 1917. He was inducted into the Hall of Fame in 1946.

Mordecai "Three Finger" Brown ranks third after Walsh and Addie Joss in lifetime ERA with 2.06. A native of Nyesville, Indiana, his career was all the

Mordecai "Three Finger" Brown of the Chicago Cubs came in to relieve without warming up against the Giants in a 1908 pennant-winning playoff game and shut them out for nine innings (Courtesy St. Louis Globe Democrat Archives at the St. Louis Mercantile Library, University of Missouri–St. Louis.)

more astounding when one considers his physical handicap. He had to have the index finger of his right hand amputated at the age of seven when he inserted it into his uncle's corn shredder. Weeks later he broke his third and fourth fingers while chasing a pig. The hand eventually healed in an ugly, unnatural manner, but it didn't stop him from becoming a baseball player.

Because of his handicap, Brown was able to throw a curve that broke in a rather unusual way, which added to his effectiveness. Originally a semi-pro infielder, he became a pitcher when his team's best pitcher broke his arm. Brown was pressed into service and struck out 14 in his debut. Known as "Miner" when broke in with the Cardinals because he had been a coal miner before he was a ballplayer, he was traded to the Cubs after his rookie year. His manager in Chicago, Frank Chance, called him the "greatest fielding pitcher the game ever had."

At one point in the 1908 season, he posted four shutouts in a row and helped his team finally catch the Giants. He helped immeasurably by winning a double-header against New York on the day before the season ended. Fred Merkle's famous base running gaffe ("Merkle's Boner") enabled the Cubs to tie the Giants and necessitate a playoff game. After the first three Giants hit safely off starter Jack Pfiester, Brown was called in to relieve without warming up. He shut out the Giants from that point on to give the Cubs the flag.

Ty Cobb claimed Moredcai Brown's breaking ball was "the most devastating pitch I ever faced. Christy Mathewson's fadeaway was good, but it was nothing like that curve 'Three-Fingered' Brown threw at you." The Brown-Mathewson matchups were legendary with Mathewson winning 13 games and Brown winning 11. Mathewson was a charter member of the Hall of Fame in 1936 while Brown was elected three years later.

Wadena, Indiana's Otis "Doc" Crandall, who started 131 games in his career but relieved in more—171—could conceivably be considered the first relief specialist of any consequence in the major leagues. Manager John McGraw of the Giants used him almost exclusively out of the bullpen from 1908 to 1913. Earlier McGraw was high on a youngster named George Ferguson and used him to finish out some eventual wins. But the pitcher picked up some bad habits that McGraw eschewed so the assignment fell to Crandall. Before that, the Hoosier had been primarily a utility infielder with a rather respectable .285 lifetime batting average.

Here's what Christy Mathewson wrote about Crandall in his book, *Pitching in a Pinch*:

"Otis Crandall came to the New York club a few years ago a raw country boy from Indiana. I shall never forget how he looked the first spring I saw him in Texas. The club had a large number of recruits and was short of uniforms. He was among the last of the hopefuls to arrive and there was no suit for him, so, in a pair of regular trousers with his coat off, he began chasing flies in the outfield. His head hung down on his chest, and, when not playing, a cigarette dropped out of the corner of his mouth. But he turned out to be a very good fly chaser, and McGraw admired his persistency.

"'What are you?'" McGraw asked him one day.

"'A pitcher,'" replied Crandall. Two words constitute an oration for him.

"Crandall warmed up, and he didn't have much of anything besides a sweeping outcurve and a good deal of speed. He looked less like a pitcher than any of the spring crop, but McGraw saw something in him and kept him. The result is he turned out to be one of the most valuable men on the club, because he is there in a pinch. He couldn't be disturbed if the McNamaras [two radical union leaders who left a bomb at the offices of the *Los Angeles Times*, killing 21 people] tied a bomb to him, with a time fuse on it set for 'at once'....

"His specialty (is) to enter a contest, after some pitcher had gotten into trouble, with two or three men on the bases and scarcely any one out. After he came to the bench one day with the threatening inning behind him, he said to me:

"'Matty, I didn't feel at home out there today until a couple of people got on the bases. I'll be all right now.' And he was. I believe that Crandall is the best pitcher in a pinch in the National League and one of the most valuable men to a team."

Between 1909 and 1913, Crandall relieved in 23, 24, 26, 27 and 32 games respectively. And by 1913 six pitchers were now pitching in as many games in relief as Crandall had in 1913. Something was indeed starting to happen, thanks to John McGraw's unique vision.

The amazing thing about the situation was that while Crandall was doing this, he was also starting some ten to 20 games a year as well as playing second base and pinch-hitting. "During the World Series against the A's that year (1911)," recalled veteran sportswriter and baseball historian Fred Lieb, "he pinch hit in the lead run and then came in to pitch three scoreless innings. Crandall got the name 'Doc' from a writer of the day who called him a doctor of sick ball games."

His teammate on the Giants, Warren, Ohio's Red Ames, chalked up nearly as many relief stints as Crandall—166—but McGraw considered him part of his regular rotation and, consequently, he started at least 25 games a season along with his ten or so bullpen appearances. Crandall ultimately moved on to St. Louis of the Federal League (1914–1915) and pitched thereafter for both the St. Louis Browns and the Boston Braves.

Besides Crandall, the only other pitchers in the first two decades of the new century to pitch in more games in relief than starts were Yancy "Doc" Ayers of the Washington Senators, Dave Danforth, who started only 31 games and relieved in 118 for the Philadelphia Athletics and Chicago White Sox, and Charley Hall, who pitched for the Cincinnati Reds, Boston Red Sox, St. Louis Cardinals and Detroit Tigers during a nine-year career.

While the term "closer" was never used in those days, Mordecai Brown would certainly have qualified for that description. Brown was credited with 49 saves and won 30 more in relief. Only Crandall, with 38 wins, and the immortal Walter "Big Train" Johnson, with 35, had more victories. Altogether 13 pitchers in the period registered more than 20 saves and, as Ralph Horton noted in his book, *Rating Relief Pitchers*, interestingly enough seven of them are in the Hall of Fame.

No event characterized the state of baseball's dead ball era more than the World Series of 1905, the first one truly sanctioned by the respective presidents of the National and American leagues. John McGraw's Giants, with a record of 104–48, had beaten out the Pittsburgh Pirates by nine games. Key roles in the team's success were attributed to a pair of major moves by the manager. One was the installation of Mike Donlin in center field. Donlin, who went on to hit .356, replaced the multi-talented Roger Bresnahan, who was moved behind the plate. A couple of years later Bresnahan gained fame as the man who invented the catcher's shin guards. He went on to become the greatest catcher of his era and in 1945 became the first one admitted into the Hall of Fame.

The Giants' opponents in 1905, Connie Mack's Philadelphia Athletics, were led by Rube Waddell and his 26 wins and southpaw Eddie Plank and his 25 victories. While both Philadelphia and Chicago each recorded 92 wins, the Athletics made it to the series by losing four fewer games.

Although scheduled as a best four-of-seven game set, only five games were played and every one ended up as a shutout. Christy Mathewson blanked the Athletics three times and "Iron Man" Joe McGinnity held them scoreless in the other Giants' victory. The only Philadelphia win came via a 3–0 gem pitched by Charles "Chief" Bender, an American Indian right-hander out of the Carlisle Institute (also made famous by the great Jim Thorpe). Born in Crow Wing County, Minnesota, Bender wouldn't have even been in the rotation had it not been for a shoulder injury to Waddell. The story goes that Waddell hurt it while wrestling with a teammate aboard a train near the end of the regular season. Rumors had been rife that gamblers had gotten to Mack's ace lefty, but the accusations were never proven. More than 100,000 fans took in the series and the winners' share was a whopping $1,142 per Giant based on receipts from the first four games.

What the 1905 series proved without a shadow of a doubt was how much pitchers had adjusted to the 60-foot, six-inch pitching distance created in 1893. New skills and techniques had been adopted and the National League's overall .282 batting average in 1899 fell to .239 by 1908. Also the league was scoring 58 percent less runs than in the previous nine years. Shutouts had increased from 90 in 1899 to 163 by 1908.

While the American League's drop in runs scored wasn't quite as severe as the "senior circuit," it did dip from 5,866 in 1901 to 4,284 in 1908. However, batting averages in the AL came down almost as rapidly as they did in the NL and the number of shutouts shot up considerably as well.

Some could say that although the first two decades of the twentieth century was called the "dead ball" era, the composition of the ball being used hadn't changed. It was still the same cork-centered, yarn-wrapped, stitched horsehide–covered "apple" it had always been since about 1870. And in the mid to late-nineties batters had their way with it as the records clearly show. But other things had changed. For instance, the foul strike rule initiated by the big leagues somewhere between 1901 and 1903 helped pitchers immensely. So did the new five-sided home plate that became a much easier target than the former diamond-shaped, foot-square plate that let umpires call strikes with much more frequency than ever before.

While the irregular bounces of ground balls were still difficult to fathom in some ballparks, the surfaces of others were improving substantially. Gloves continued to be small and fragile compared to those of later years, but the addition of a leather strap between the thumb and the forefinger, and increased padding in the heel, made for a deeper pocket that helped fielders greatly. So much so that between 1899 to 1908, National League fielding averages jumped 19 points and by 20 points in the American League from 1901 to 1908. In 1906, the Chicago Cubs were the first team in history to commit fewer than 200 errors in a single season.

If these adjustments were not enough, pitchers themselves were coming up with newer and better ways to retire batters. Trick pitches were being added to pitchers' repertoires, the most infamous of which was the "spitball." The addition of some form of moisture to the fingers on the ball cut down on the friction and spin of the ball as it was delivered to home plate. The ball actually plunged downward and curved as it approached the plate. Since there was nothing in the rule book forbidding pitchers to apply moisture to the ball, anything went from sweat to damp grass to saliva augmented by substances like chewing tobacco and slippery elm. If a pitcher was relying primarily on his saliva, he could lick the ends of his fingers, cradle the ball in a soaked glove pocket or just spit directly on it.

As is the case today, pitchers were really not permitted to scuff up or even cut the ball by using such substances as belt buckles, razor blades, paraffin, mud or emery boards, all of which could be hidden in their gloves. It is said that Clark Griffith would step off the mound and actually pound the ball against his spikes.

In 1908, Ed Walsh of the AL's Chicago entry was also able to control his spitball. Before adopting the pitch, he had enjoyed a modicum of success. But in 1906 with the spitball, he won 17 games, upping that figure to 24 in the following year and adding an astounding total of 40 victories in 1908. Ironically, Walsh, like Jack Chesbro four years earlier, lost a pennant-deciding game for his team on the final day of the season even though he pitched a four-hitter and fanned 15. However, his opponent, Addie Joss of Cleveland, pitched a perfect game and beat Walsh 1–0, the winning run scoring via a passed ball.

The use of spitballs, doctored balls and, later, knuckleballs gave pitchers an edge over the hitters from about 1902 to 1919. Cy Young, who had won 285 games when batters were dominant, won 216 more after he turned 34. Walter Johnson, who pitched for some very underachieving Washington Senator clubs beginning in 1907, picked up 296 of his 416 career victories before 1920.

Baseball in the dead ball era may not have provided the kind of hitting, base running and scoring as in earlier years but the fans came out to see major league baseball in greater numbers than ever anyway. From 1903 when both the National and American leagues agreed to a kind of peaceful co-existence, attendance increased every year until 1914. The exciting pennant races in both leagues during 1908 brought attendance up past the seven million mark, where it remained for the next six seasons.

Despite its apparent successes, organized baseball had to endure an annoying hiccup in 1913 when still another upstart—the Federal League—came into being. Teams were placed in Chicago, Baltimore, Buffalo, Pittsburgh, Indianapolis, Brooklyn, St. Louis and Kansas City. Offering salary hikes to major leaguers, the Federal League was able to put together a schedule and begin play in 1914. Although it put a crimp in the profits of both NL and AL teams, it barely got through 1915 before throwing in the towel.

Despite the fact that it was awarded $5 million in compensation merely to go away along with franchises for two of its owners, an antitrust suit by the disgruntled owners of its Baltimore club eventually reached the Supreme Court, where it was dismissed in 1922. It marked the last time that major league baseball suffered a potential chink in its armor.

What was significant about this possible incursion was that the name of Kenesaw Mountain Landis was first brought to the attention of organized baseball. During its war upon the establishment, the Federal League attempted to subvert the reserve clause and Landis, a federal judge at the time, listened to arguments from both sides. While Judge Landis never rendered a decision because he didn't really believe that the reserve clause represented that strong a case, the Federal League eventually gave in and settled for the best deal it could get. Actually Judge Landis had saved the game's skin and the owners and officials never forgot it.

A number of factors began to reshape the game of baseball after World War I. At the focal point of the changes that were beginning to assert themselves were the pitchers. And it was to be a former pitcher, and a very good one at that, who helped bring about the most radical changes yet in the big leagues. His name was George Herman "Babe" Ruth, who as 20-year-old rookie in 1915 for the Boston Red Sox won 18 games to help his team attain the world championship. In 1916, he became a 23-game winner and served up a 2–1, 14-inning victory in the World Series against the Brooklyn Dodgers. The left-hander soon was recognized as his club's ace, leading the American League with a 1.75 earned run average in 41 starts and posting nine shutouts. In the following year, he also led the league in complete games with no less than 35. In the 1918 World Series — the last time the Red Sox ever won one — Ruth hurled a 1–0 shutout over the Chicago Cubs in the first game and won for a second time in relief in Game Four. But bigger things were in store for the "Babe" and, as we all know, they did not include pitching.

Ruth was involved in one of the most unusual events in the history of the game. It occurred on the afternoon of June 23, 1917, and could easily be classified as the most famous relief stint of all time. The Babe was the starting pitcher for the Red Sox in a road game against Washington. After walking the first batter, Ruth got into a heated argument with the home plate umpire and was promptly ejected. Ernie Shore, normally a starter, was called in to relieve. The southpaw, in one of the most memorable pitching performances ever, proceeded to mow down every single batter he faced for a perfect game.

The war clouds of 1917 had an unsettling effect on major league baseball as many ball players joined the armed forces. In the following year, the provost marshal declared the sport to be nonessential and the result was a shortened season. Since club owners had lost money because of this, they voted to shorten the 1919 season, but the war ended unexpectedly. They thought they could recoup some of their losses by lengthening the World Series that year to a best-of-nine-game format.

An event that was destined to reshape the direction of the game turned out to be that year's World Series between the Chicago White Sox and Cincinnati Reds. For a change, Cincinnati was not at the focal point of the problem. This time it was another city's team that was the at the core of an ugly situation, as some of the White Sox players had conspired to throw the Series, forever to be known as the "Black Sox Scandal."

As the new year approached, it was evident that the very future of the national pastime was at stake. With a new commission in place, composed of three disinterested public figures with "unreviewable authority" over owners, players and clubs, organized baseball felt there was only one person capable of bringing the game back to where it belonged. Consequently, after a grand jury heard evidence of the 1919 series fix, Kenesaw Mountain Landis was appointed commissioner.

♦ *Chapter 3* ♦

Newer Pitching Strategies Develop (1920–1945)

The aftermath of the "Black Sox Scandal" led the new commissioner of baseball, Kenesaw M. Landis, to only one conclusion: the game had to be cleaned up and fast. And even though the Chicago White Sox players who were accused of throwing the 1919 series against the Cincinnati Reds were eventually acquitted for lack of hard evidence, the autocratic Landis banned them from the major leagues forever. He was convinced that the only way to assure the American public that organized baseball was squeaky clean both on and off the field was by leaving no doubt about its integrity.

There were many who disagreed with his decision, but the sport flourished under his leadership. His was a stern and disciplined method of operating but one that gave fans a clear view of how honest and above board the game was going to be as long as he was in charge. Landis had to face other scandals in the early years of his reign but he dealt with them as swiftly and decisively as he did the "Black Sox Scandal."

"Baseball is something more than a game to an American boy," said Landis. "It is his training field for life work. Destroy his faith in the squareness and honesty and you have destroyed something more; you have planted suspicion of all things in his heart." That was the theme that drove him for the entire 25 years of his regime until his untimely death in 1944, shortly after having his contract extended until 1953.

On the field in 1920, it was the "Bambino," George Herman Ruth, who was deflecting the fans' attention away from the shocking events of the previous year with an unprecedented 54 homers. He actually hit more home runs that year than all but two teams in the American League.

The colorful Ruth had broken his own record of 29 that he had set in 1919, his final season in Boston. That winter, Red Sox owner Harry Frazee, who was strapped for money to support various Broadway productions he was backing, shipped Ruth to the New York Yankees for $125,000 in cash and a $300,000 loan. Frazee proceeded to pay off the loan by sending more players to New York, thanks largely to then–Yankee General Manager Ed Barrow, a former field manager of the Red Sox. The Yankees plucked such players off the Boston roster as pitchers Waite Hoyt, Sam Jones, Joe Bush, Herb Pennock and George Pipgras, as well as catcher Wally Schang and infielders Everett Scott and "Jumping" Joe Dugan. Not bad plucking indeed.

Babe Ruth went on to lead the American League in home runs from 1920 to 1931 thanks in part to a much livelier ball than the one employed in the "dead ball era." Ruth had company too but most of the other sluggers of his time with the possible exception of his teammate, Lou Gehrig, were in the National League. Power hitters like Hack Wilson, Rogers Hornsby, Chuck Klein and Cy Williams were also hitting the baseball out of the park with regularity in the so-called "Senior Circuit."

And did the fans ever love it. A record 9.1 million turned out to watch major league baseball in 1920 and, after falling below that figure in the following three seasons, attendance leaped to an average of 9.6 million from 1924 to 1929, culminating with a total of 10.1 million in 1930.

Although the burgeoning offensive revolution taking place in the game had a lot to do with the game's success, Sunday baseball everywhere but in Pennsylvania, a state famous for its "Blue Laws," was a major contributor. Fans' optimism was spurred by the indomitable spirit brought on by the "Roaring Twenties" and its attendant expanding affluence, rapid population growth in big league cities, additional leisure time as work hours decreased and growing consumer spending. Sports in general were booming with heroes like Ruth, Jack Dempsey, Bobby Jones, Jim Thorpe and Bill Tilden on the scene. And more and more folks were willing to plunk down their hard-earned dollars to see their idols in the flesh.

The decade of the '20s saw batting averages in both leagues exceed the .280 mark with the National League reaching a near astronomical .303 in 1930. Home runs were averaging 540 per year in the NL and 490 in the AL with each team scoring an average of five runs a game. More home runs meant that more new lively balls were being put into play to hammer out. And with fans now being allowed to keep balls hit into the stands, the fresher balls had a better than even chance of leaving the yard.

Then, too, the rules changes that were decreed in 1920–1921 that outlawed the spitball (except for those who were "grandfathered" and exempt like Burleigh Grimes) and other scuffed-up baseballs had a negative effect on the pitching profession. As a result, ERA soared to a point where 4.00 was now considered good. The rules changes, therefore, combined with the revisions taking place in the designs of the parks being built at the time, the continuing improvements in equipment and the escalating awareness on the part of the game's followers, all played significant roles in the heightened interest in the game of baseball. No longer were the stolen base and the sacrifice bunt the focal points of the game on the field.

Obviously, the long ball was going to affect the game of baseball over-all and pitching in particular for years to come. No longer could pitchers use anemic hitters to get their sometime "automatic" outs. These fellows were also now dangerous because they, too, were capable of hitting one out at an inopportune time. The bottom line was that the strategy of the game had to change in order for pitchers to keep pace with the sluggers who were now setting the pace. Home runs and scoring in bunches were now a fact of life in the big leagues and as long as the turnstiles kept revolving, it was something managers and their pitching staffs would have to learn to combat.

In 1901, National League pitchers had completed 976 games or about 90 percent of those played. By 1919, the percentage had slipped down to around 60 percent and in 1922 NL starters finished fewer than half their starts for the first time in history. By 1930, that figure fell to an even lower 43 percent and stayed that way throughout the '30s and '40s in both leagues.

Consequently, with nearly half of the pitchers requiring relief, many starters began to handle both chores. If one were to review the records of pitchers who worked at some point between 1920 and 1945, one would find that 28 of them who had started at least 150 games in their careers also relieved in as many as 150 games or more. Some of the best known of this group included such stars as future Hall of Famers Lefty Grove and Waite Hoyt. In fact, others like Jesse Haines and Dolph Luque, who were originally used as starters, became relief pitchers exclusively several years before they retired. And the reverse could also be true. Witness the fact that Whitlow Wyatt, who went on to become one of the best starting pitchers of his time, actually learned to ply his trade in the bullpen.

The aforementioned Robert Moses "Lefty" Grove of Lonacoming, Maryland, pitched for 17 seasons in the American League. He was noted not only for his flaming fastball but also for his incredibly short fuse, which was not looked upon kindly by some of his teammates. Grove would rip up uniforms, kick water buckets and tear lockers apart early on in his career.

Despite his fiery temper, he still managed to lead his league in strike-outs seven years in a row, in ERA nine times and in victories four times, including 31 in 1931. He won the Most Valuable Player Award that season, just one year after he had led the AL both in games pitched and saves. Grove recorded 55 saves in his career to rank behind only Firpo Marberry, Johnny Murphy, Clint Brown and Joe Heving in the period between 1920 and 1945. The Hall of Famer (1947) was given credit for his three hundredth victory in his very last appearance in the big leagues

With power the order of the day in this 25-year stretch, managers had to look constantly for ways and means to avoid disaster. Rather than having a pitcher deliver a ball "right down Broadway," as the saying goes, hurlers were now being told to "pitch around" certain batters who were capable of hitting it out. Therefore, the intentional, and sometimes even "unintentional," base on balls became an increasingly useful managerial tool. As the years went by, the number of walks began to accelerate with regularity.

The spunky John McGraw, manager of the New York Giants, had always been ahead of his time in the matter of game strategy and it was he who, long before the "Golden Twenties" had gotten underway, had foreseen the role of the relief pitcher as key. By 1919, Oscar Tuero of the St. Louis Cardinals was probably the first relief pitcher to lead the league in total appearances. That year the Havana, Cuba, native pitched in 45 games, 28 of them out of the pen. Hardly anyone noticed, most of all because his team finished in next-to-last place in the NL. However, in 1923 McGraw's pennant-winning Giants had both Claude Jonnard and Rosy Ryan tied for the league lead in appearances with 45 apiece. Although Ryan started 15 times, Jonnard only started once.

In the following year, Fred (Firpo) Marberry of the AL champion Washington Senators appeared in 50 games, only 15 of them as a starter. In 1925, he topped that mark by making 55 appearances and every one of them came as a reliever, breaking teammate Allan Russell's record of 47 established two years earlier. The right-handed Marberry, nicknamed "Firpo" because his dark, scowling look and physique resembled the Argentine heavyweight boxer, Luis Firpo, went on to lead the league in appearances three more times, twice as a reliever and once as a starter.

Although saves did not become an official statistic of major league baseball until 1969, researchers credit the Streetman, Texas–born Marberry with 101 between 1924 and 1934, including a high of 22 in 1926. He is generally acknowledged by baseball historians as the premier relief pitcher of this period.

However, it didn't start out that way for Marberry, as Bucky Harris began to use him pretty much the way most managers used their pitchers in this era—as an occasional starter against the weaker teams and as mop-up men during games that were out of control one way or another. But as time went on, Harris's confidence in Marberry grew and he began utilizing the 6'1", 190-pounder to "save" games, although, as stated earlier, that statistic was not used until decades later.

"Firpo was the type of pitcher who could toss a few in the bullpen, casually saunter to the mound, and then knock the bats out of their hands with his blazing speed," Harris recalled once. Bill James calls Marberry "the first true reliever in baseball history" because he "was the first pitcher aggressively used to protect leads, rather than being brought in when the starter was knocked out…. He was a modern reliever—a hard-throwing young kid who worked strictly in relief, worked often, and was used to nail down victories." With Marberry, the perennial losers, the Washington Senators, won and won big—their first pennant in 1924 and both the American League pennant and the World Series the following year.

Although Marberry's role cannot be denied, he received little credit for his contributions, much the same as today where it appears that the starting pitchers and position players are still accorded much more respect and adulation than teams' relief staffs. More on that later.

The fact is, the 1924 MVP award went to Walter Johnson and in 1925 to the club's shortstop, Roger Peckinpaugh, who, as good as he was, nevertheless did make six errors in the 1925 World Series. Harris, dubbed the "Boy Manager"—he was only 28 at the time—went on to manage for another 25 years in the big leagues based largely upon on the success of his 1924–1925 Senator teams. Marberry? Harris, for some strange reason, did not use him in the seventh and deciding game of the 1925 World Series loss to the Pittsburgh Pirates. He stayed with Walter Johnson despite a 7–6 Washington lead going into the bottom of the eighth inning. The Pirates rallied for three runs and won, 9–7, while Marberry, who had saved Game Three, lingered in the bullpen. Johnson was pounded for 15 hits that day.

The league offered Marberry a job as an umpire toward the latter part of his career in 1935 and he retired from the Detroit Tigers, who were on their way to their second straight AL pennant. He was never assigned to umpire any games involving former teammates. Despite his outstanding record out of the bullpen and as a starter as well—94 wins in his 187 starts, a much better percentage than many Hall of Famers—he has never been selected for enshrinement. His place in baseball history is assured in spite of this slight.

Although complete games continued to decrease during this period in baseball history, tinkering with employing pitchers as relievers on an elite basis terminated with Firpo Marberry after 1925. Throughout the '20s, nearly every pitcher on a ball club would be called upon both to start and relieve.

When the New York Yankees stormed their way through their "1927 "Murderer's Row" season, the guy who got the call out of the bullpen more often than not was a 30-year-old rookie right-hander named Wilcy Moore. He won 19 of the Yankees' then-record-setting 110 victories (13 of them in relief) although he only started 12 games and saved 13 others. The Bonita, Texas, native relieved on 38 other occasions.

Moore was rewarded by being named to start the last game of the World Series that year, which he won to give the Yankees the championship. Although he wandered away from the team for the 1931 season and part of 1932 with the Boston Red Sox, he returned to the club that year to help it win another flag as well as gaining a victory himself in the series against the Chicago Cubs.

Like all other businesses, major league baseball felt the disastrous effects of the Great Depression of the 1930s. With millions of workers unemployed, many even on bread lines, population slowed as did the discretionary dollars that could be spent on recreation. In 1931, the American League felt losses while the National League just about broke even. Though the game provided fans with a chance to temporarily forget the problems of a poor economy, much like motion pictures did, attendance began to fall off drastically. By 1932 only 8.1 million attended major league baseball games and in the following year the numbers really took a nose dive, as only 6.3 million showed up for the games. Thereafter attendance picked up again slowly but it wasn't until 1940 that the leagues combined for a mark of 10 million.

As a consequence, baseball players also felt the results of the economic downturn and their salaries were being cut from a total of $4 million in 1929 to $3 million in 1933. In fact, club payrolls fell behind the 1929 high right up until 1940. The average 1929 salary of $7,500 was reduced to $6,000 in 1933 and only crept up to $7,300 by 1940. Not that this wasn't good money, especially when so many people were either out of work or making a whole lot less. Big league players knew how well off they were compared to the rest of the populace, but their job security wasn't that great either. Most of them realized that if they didn't like the deal, an eager minor leaguer was always ready to take their spot—and at much lower pay.

Most clubs were really feeling the pinch and some, like the lowly St. Louis Browns, were seriously considering a move to the West Coast. Of course, World War II intervened and laid that idea to rest for a time. Other clubs tried promotional schemes like "Ladies' Day" and broadened their concessions in efforts to raise revenues.

The introduction of night baseball in 1935 by Cincinnati Reds General Manager Larry MacPhail was the one idea that appealed to the most fans and it was soon recognized as the way to go, with a lot of teams following suit by 1940. Selling a team's rights to radio broadcasts of its games, also pioneered by MacPhail in Cincinnati with a youthful Red Barber behind the microphone, bode well for future profits. However, World War II came along to shelve some of these more ambitious ventures, including the newest medium, television, as the nation turned its attention to a much more pressing matter.

As in any other industry, manpower took a big hit in the game of baseball during World War II. The majors lost 500 players while the minors were drained of another 3,500. There was much discussion over whether to discontinue play until the war ended, but President Franklin D. Roosevelt felt that the game was a morale booster both on the home front and among our servicemen overseas—and that, it was.

Attendance actually increased to a record 11.1 million in 1945. One idea that was given short shrift during the war was proposed by a young, enterprising minor league promoter named Bill Veeck, who suggested stocking the bankrupt Philadelphia Phillies with a team of players from the Negro Leagues. Commissioner Kenesaw M. Landis, whom some considered to be prejudiced, saw to it that such a proposal never saw the light of day. However, when fair employment practices adopted by the federal government and by some states posed a threat to major league baseball's practice of racial segregation, Branch Rickey seized upon the opportunity the new policies presented to end segregation. He promptly signed Jackie Robinson of the Kansas City Monarchs to a Brooklyn Dodger contract in 1945. He also sent his scouts scurrying into the Negro Leagues for new talent. Judge Landis' death in 1944 had given Rickey just the opening he needed to help develop his plan of integrating the national pastime.

The 25-year period between 1920 and 1945 produced the first significant number of true relief pitchers, many of whom could and would be classified as stars of the game that heretofore considered occupants of the bullpen as necessary, but far from star material. This era changed all of that, as people like the previously mentioned Fred "Firpo" Marberry proved. Another major contributor to this change in thinking was a slender right-handed pitcher out of Baltimore named Allan Russell, who began his 11-year career with the New York Yankees in 1915. In addition to his 110 starting assignments, Russell, who later pitched for both the Boston

Red Sox and Washington Senators, was called on to relieve 235 times before retiring after the 1925 season. He was the first bullpen occupant to pitch in 200 games, a record that stood until Marberry became the first to ever pitch in more than 300 games in relief by 1932.

Paris, Texas' Jack Russell (no relation to Allan), although a starter early in his career with the Cleveland Indians, was made a reliever by the Washington Senators, who acquired him in 1933. In the following year, he became the first full-fledged reliever to make the All-Star team. After leading the American League in saves in 1933, he led it in both saves and games pitched in 1934. He posted a sparkling ERA of 0.75 in two World Series for the Senators and Chicago Cubs. Following his retirement, he relocated to Clearwater, Florida, where he became one of the city's most prominent citizens. In fact, the Philadelphia Phillies, who trained there since 1955, built a new ballpark and called it Jack Russell Stadium.

Some pitchers like Jack Quinn of Jeanesville, Pennsylvania, were able to pitch for many years while doing double duty as both starters and relievers. Quinn, who pitched until the ripe old age of 50 in the majors, was in three World Series with both the New York Yankees and Philadelphia Athletics and led the National League in saves in both 1931 and 1932 while a member of the Brooklyn Dodgers.

The year of 1939 will always be remembered as one of great achievement for the then-growing cadre of relief pitchers in the game of baseball. Clint Brown, a 6'1", 190-pound right-hander out of Backlash, Pennsylvania, who had already made a record-breaking number of relief appearances—53—in 1937 for the Chicago White Sox, set a new standard by coming out of the bullpen 61 times while recording 11 wins and 18 saves. Brown, who also pitched for the Cleveland Indians during his 15 years in the big leagues, relieved in a total of 304 games, winning 41 and saving another 64. He led the AL in games pitched in both 1937 and 1939, and in saves in 1937 with 18.

Although remembered for his relatively short (only six years) but thrill-packed pitching career, Jay Hanna "Dizzy" Dean relieved in some 87 games in this period, saving 30 of them. In fact, in one year (1936), he led the National League in saves with 11. Hit on his big toe by a line drive off the bat of Earl Averil in the 1937 All-Star game, Dean came back before it was fully healed. He could not follow through the way he should have and seriously damaged his arm. He was never the same. Following retirement after the 1941 season, the native of Lucas, Arkansas, went into broadcasting where for 20 years, and despite his limited vocabulary and famed malapropisms, he attained incredible popularity and adulation. He was voted into the Hall of Fame in 1953.

Another Hall of Famer who spent more years (19) as a pitcher with the St. Louis Cardinals than any other in history was Jesse "Pop" Haines. Originally reliant on his smoking fastball, the Clayton, Ohio native later acquired a knuckleball that he had learned from the Philadelphia Athletics' Eddie Ramble. He gripped the ball with his knuckles instead of his fingertips as most knuckleballers did and still do. Haines was the starting pitcher in one of the most famous games in World Series history. In the seventh and deciding game of the 1926 series against the Yankees, he was relieved by Grover Cleveland Alexander, who came in with the bases loaded and two out, and fanned Tony Lazzeri. Haines received credit for the win although Alexander was the big hero that day. The knuckler, which dispenses no strain whatsoever on the arm, allowed Haines to extend his career until the age of 44 while serving as both an effective reliever and spot starter. In his later years, he was extremely generous to his younger teammates, who affectionately called him "Pop." He was voted into the Hall of Fame in 1970 by the Veterans Committee.

Brooklyn, New York–born Waite Hoyt, who had been one of the New York Yankees' top starters throughout the '20s, was always willing to come in to relieve when there might be a need. Even with a 23–7 record in 1928, he led the American League in saves with eight. When he was traded over to the National League for the final seven years of his career, he led that league in relief wins in both 1934 (seven) and 1935 (five). The Hall of Famer (1969) went into broadcasting the same year as Dizzy Dean—1942—and was the voice of the Cincinnati Reds until his retirement in 1965.

Another New York Yankee who came along in 1934 was "Fordham" Johnny Murphy, who is generally considered along with Firpo Marberry as the two greatest relief pitchers of their time. Murphy started half of the 40 games in which he worked in his rookie season. Thereafter, he only started in 20 more games in the remaining dozen years of his career, with only one of those coming after 1938.

While Marberry became the first reliever to notch 100 saves (he did it in 1934), Murphy led in relief wins for the period of 1920 to 1945 with 69, but Marberry was the saves leader with 101. Murphy led American League pitchers in saves in four different seasons. He also pitched in six World Series with the Yankees winning two games, saving three others and being charged with only one earned run for a phenomenal 1.10 ERA in his eight appearances.

The curveballing right-hander, who was also known as "Fireman," "Grandma," and even "Rocking Chair" because he had a motion like grandmother in her rocking chair, Murphy was noted for his pinpoint control. His best season was in 1941 when he recorded 15 saves and posted a 1.98 ERA to go along with his 8–3 won-lost mark. He was often called on to relieve the Yankees' ace, Vernon "Lefty" Gomez. One year in spring training when reporters asked Gomez how many games he expected to win, he replied: "I don't know, ask Murphy."

At this time in baseball history, relievers were not just brought in for an inning or less to nail down a win as are today's "closers." Murphy, for example, after becoming a full-time reliever from 1938 on, would pitch in some 31 or 32 games or more in a given season and throw in better than 77 to 91 innings per year. The numbers would indicate that on occasion he may have pitched in more than three innings per appearance.

The major credit for developing Johnny Murphy into the stellar reliever that he turned out to be has got to go to his manager, "Marse" Joe McCarthy. When he managed the Chicago Cubs before coming to the Yankees, McCarthy did not use his bullpen much at all. As a matter of fact, he had no relief staff to speak of when he came to New York. In 1936, he literally divided his pitching staff into two parts: starters and relievers. He became convinced that the practice of everybody on the staff starting *and* relieving would not continue as long as he was the manager.

The man had foresight, unlike a lot of managers at the time who either would not or could not change their thinking. The leaders of the Yankees' bullpen were Murphy and Pat Malone, another right-hander whom McCarthy had with him in Chicago. That year the Yankees had 21 saves all told, far more than any other American League team. Murphy, who had been successful as a starter up to that time, had to be convinced by the manager that his role would be the equal of anyone in the starting rotation. He became McCarthy's main man out of the bullpen and went on to be considered the first true career stopper in the business.

Another Hall of Famer who did more than his share of work out of the bullpen was the great southpaw of the New York Giants, Carthage, Missouri's Carl Hubbell. Known also as "King Carl" and "The Meal Ticket" with good reason, he was celebrated for a slow, cartwheeling delivery of his famed screwball, a pitch thrown by twisting the arm in the opposite direction from a curveball. As a result of throwing so many screwballs throughout his career, Hubbell's arm was left crooked from his elbow to his wrist forever. In 1934, this workhorse pitched 313 innings, won 21 games with a 2.30 ERA and led the league in saves with eight. The Oklahoman pitched in relief in 104 games, picking up 33 saves. A two-time MVP, he was elected to the Hall of Fame in 1947.

With the passage of time, less importance was being attached to the complete game. However, managers as a group were not that quick to turn matters over to their bullpen during the course of a game. It took the kind of dering-do that Brooklyn's skipper, Leo Durocher, had in the early 1940s to create effective strategies for the use of his bullpen. It was "Leo the Lip," as he was labeled by the media for his loquaciousness, who believed that an "ace" out of the pen in the later innings could snuff out opponents' rallies or relieve a starter who might be running out of gas, or both thereby providing the answer to a difficult problem.

Durocher was a pioneer in that he didn't care if his starters finished games or not, only that his teams won. Consequently, he would often use several pitchers during the course of a game. And he was the first manager to play the percentages, as it were, and bring in a left-handed pitcher specifically to get a left-handed batter out. In 1941, the Dodgers won their first pennant in 21 years, yet the team's starting rotation completed only 66 games.

A laughing stock of the National League for years before the arrival of Durocher, the Dodgers were in contention in the following year as well when their starters only finished 67 games. In the 1940s while other managers used an average of about 120 relievers a year, the "Lip" was using 180. He made Hugh Casey, a hard-throwing and, it is alleged, hard-drinking right-hander out of Atlanta, Georgia, become the first preeminent full-time reliever since the days of Firpo Marberry. He won 20 games and saved another 20 during the 1941 and 1942 seasons. His ERA in two World Series with the Dodgers (1941 and 1947) was a sparkling 1.72 in nine appearances.

A starter in his rookie year, Casey bested the immortal Carl Hubbell, 3–1, at the Polo Grounds before a sellout crowd of 58,000 in his very first major league start. Although Durocher had two capable veteran starters in Whitlow Wyatt and Kirby Higbe, he had little else from which to choose and was fearful of late inning blowups. Although Casey posted 15 victories that season, the manager decided to take advantage of the pitcher's poise in critical situations and converted him into his ace out of the bullpen.

Unfortunately for Casey, he was on the mound when that famous third-strike pitch to Tommy Henrich in the '41 series got away from catcher Mickey Owen. The Yankees went on not only to win the game but also the series on the following day. Owen, who was really an outstanding defensive catcher, became the goat of the series, but some felt that the ball got away from the receiver only because it was a spitter which had been outlawed more than 20 years before.

Casey's six appearances against the Yankees in the 1947 World Series produced an unprecedented effect on the evolving role of the relief pitcher.

Although the Dodgers fell in seven games, he set two records by beating the Bronx Bombers two days in a row and accomplished both by only throwing one ball each time. Ironically, six years earlier, "Hughie" had been the only pitcher up to that time to lose two games on successive days, also against the Yankees. But it was his accomplishments in the 1947 series that began to change the face of relief pitching forever.

A pitcher who truly epitomized the art of relief pitching was Ace (his real name) Adams of the New York Giants. Although some consider him to be strictly a wartime fill-in pitcher, the right-hander led the National League in appearances for three consecutive years starting in 1942. The Willows, California, native also finished more games than any other pitcher in the NL for four straight years.

With 70 appearances (67 of them in relief) in 1943, he set a new record for total appearances by a pitcher and, while at it, eclipsed Clint Brown's previous relief record of 61 appearances set four years earlier. And his 13 saves in 1944 and 15 in 1945 were tops in the NL as well. All told, he saved a total of 437 games and won 37 for the Giants in his six-year career before jumping to the upstart Mexican League in 1946.

"Jittery" Joe Berry, who hailed from Hunstville, Arkansas, was over the age limit for the wartime draft when he joined the Chicago Cubs in 1942 at the advanced age of 37. With Connie Mack's Philadelphia Athletics in 1944, the slender right-hander led the American League in saves and in games pitched in 1945. Every single one of his 133 appearances in the majors came out of the bullpen.

Covington, Kentucky's Joe Heving, mentioned earlier as fourth in saves with 63 for the period 1920–1945, started just 40 of the 430 games in which he appeared in the big leagues. During that period, the 6'1", 185-pound right-hander was first in games pitched in relief and second in relief wins.

When World War II ended in 1945, a glimpse at the 25 years intervening from 1920 on revealed that as far as pitching in the major leagues was concerned, the trend toward using relievers as a strategic weapon by managers in the game of baseball was well underway. While the downward dip in complete games continued in the period, it may not have been as dramatic a drop as the first 20 years of the 1900s, but route-going performances were definitely no longer considered the measure of success that they had once been.

♦ *Chapter 4* ♦

The Relief Specialist as a Profession (1946–1959)

The end of World War II brought the return of many former star players to major league baseball for whom the fans had long been yearning. However, it would soon become apparent to the "Lords of Baseball," as *New York Daily News* writer Dick Young had sarcastically branded the game's hierarchy, that these men were not the same people they were before going off to make the world safe for democracy again. These men would want and demand more not only in financial remuneration but in long-term security as well.

There were good reasons for this new-found perspective on the part of the players. The post-war economy was booming thanks in part to new home construction, the lifting of gas rationing and the wartime ban on automobile production, new jobs, better wages and overall increased spending by consumers. Along with this had come a perceived need to organize by workers, and ballplayers wanted their piece of the pie too.

Subsequently a committee of the more well-respected players in the game was put together and various stipulations were presented to ownership, among them the establishment of a pension fund, a new minimum salary ($5,000), a shorter spring training period and limited salary reductions. In the old days when the late Commissioner Kenesaw M. Landis had ruled the roost, these demands might have been sloughed off. But Landis was long gone and some players, even stars like Mickey Owen of the Brooklyn Dodgers and Vern Stephens of the St. Louis Browns, had gone off to the Mexican League where they were promised even more. The raids shook the very foundations of the game and there were fears that other players would also soon depart. So between the player raids and the formation of a players' union on the horizon, the owners began to capitulate.

On the field of play, changes were becoming apparent as well, particularly on the pitching front. The paucity of complete games in 1946 saw the National League dip below 40 percent for the first time in a decade and to less than 30 percent ten years later. It took the American League a little longer in dropping under 40 percent by 1948 and to under 30 percent by 1955.

Now relief "pitchers" were being converted into relief "specialists." Early in the period, most of the relievers were veterans who had been former starters. As time went on, though, any youngsters who were sent to the bullpen primarily to gain experience would usually stay there if they exhibited any sign of consistent success in that role. The remaining members of the staff either switched from starting to relieving or vice versa. Relieving itself was gaining respectability and the relief specialist was becoming an acceptable new profession in major league baseball.

No less a manager than Joe Cronin of the Boston Red Sox could see what was happening and how a relief specialist might possibly lead him and his team out of mediocrity. After the war, the Red Sox had acquired an aging right-hander named Bob Klinger in a waiver deal with the Pittsburgh Pirates. Klinger had toiled for seven seasons for the Bucs and compiled a rather nondescript record with a decidedly unsuccessful ball club. With time out for the war, he joined the Red Sox and in his first season in 1946 (he was only there for two years), the 38-year-old veteran appeared in 27 games as a reliever, leading the league in saves with nine and helping Cronin's Red Sox attain the first pennant for Boston since 1918.

It was fast becoming evident that the idea of relievers as failed starters was indeed now old hat. While starters had more appearances than relievers in 1946, ten of the 16 major league clubs recorded more appearances by relievers just a year later. And only five years after that, the number grew to 13 of the 16 clubs' staffs.

Other on-field changes coming to the fore included the use of platooning made popular by Casey Stengel, manager of the New York Yankees, beginning in 1949. Blessed with a plethora of talent, Stengel would make out his lineup based strictly upon whom the opposition was starting. If it was a left-hander, Hank Bauer would start instead of Gene Woodling in left field and vice versa. Both players detested it and hated the manager for it, but both agreed after their playing days ended that the "Old Man" had lengthened their careers.

Other managers aped Stengel and began to adopt platooning as a tactic also. Skippers like Al Lopez—the only American League manager other than Stengel to win pennants when Stengel didn't—won in both 1954 with Cleveland and in 1959 with the Chicago White Sox with several platoon players.

Naturally, platooning led other managers to juggle their pitchers accordingly. Late in the games fans would see southpaws entering the game to face lefty hitters and, to some degree, righties coming in to face right-handed batters. This practice continues today ad nauseam, as with Paul Assenmacher, Mike Stanton, *et al.* It all started with Leo Durocher and the Brooklyn Dodgers in the early '40s, reaching new heights in the late '40s and hasn't quit, nor will it in the foreseeable future in all probability.

Another change in the approach to the game during this period— which began due to the plethora of home runs that were beginning to plague managers and that were advanced by the use of lighter, more tapered bats—was the strikeout. Managers figured that if you had a potent bat or two in your lineup every day, so what if the guy either fanned or poked one into the seats. It might just win them the ball game. No matter if he did it two or three times a game if he had the capability of breaking up a game for the team. It didn't always work out that way but the fans loved it and they were paying the freight to see people like Mickey Mantle, Duke Snider, Larry Doby, Stan Musial, Hank Aaron, Willie Mays and Ted Williams, among others, deposit balls into the stands or beyond.

Of course, the pitchers were the ones who were being victimized by these outstanding power hitters of the day and they had to come up with something of their own to combat this growing threat to their livelihood. A new pitch called a "slider" came along around 1953 and hurlers were quick to add it to their arsenals. The pitch was thrown like a fastball with a stiff wrist, but a snap at the time it left the pitcher's hand caused the ball to break a few inches at the very last second. Since the ball was moving much more rapidly than a normal curve, it gave those who didn't have a particularly good curveball a neat addition to their high, hard one.

Hitters of the caliber of Ted Williams and Stan Musial were all unanimous in their hatred of the slider and said so loudly and often. But people like Rogers Hornsby pooh-poohed it, claiming it was nothing more than a "nickel curve" that would often find its way out of the ballpark. However, Hornsby didn't have to hit for a living anymore when he said that. Others, though, admitted grudgingly that the slider had the ability to make a lot of pitchers much healthier than they would have been without it. After his retirement, Sal "The Barber" Maglie, who went on to become a pitching coach, said at the time: "All pitchers today are lazy. They all look for the easiest way out, and the slider gives them that pitch." Like

Hornsby, Maglie no longer had to get the hitters out on a regular basis anymore when he made this observation.

A few rules changes also came along during the 1946–1959 period that affected game strategy. For example, one that has had a lasting impact on major league baseball until today was the narrowing of the strike zone in 1950. Another was the restoration of the sacrifice fly rule in 1954. Then, too, the reaction to the design of new ballparks in San Francisco, Los Angeles, Milwaukee, Kansas City and Baltimore led to the establishment of a rule in 1959 that all ballparks built after that year would have to conform to minimum distances of 325 feet from home plate to both the left and right field fences.

All in all these were not the best of years for pitchers, particularly starters. Managers began to assemble staffs that included what became known at the time as "short relievers." These relief specialists were called on to put out fires that may have been ignited in the later innings when the game was still in doubt. These specialists were becoming huge heroes to teammates and fans, and their contributions were being officially recorded as "saves." They were also being recognized with annual awards much like the Most Valuable Player and Cy Young awards. Theirs were called the "Fireman of the Year" awards (dispensed by *The Sporting News*) and a whole new generation of pitchers were becoming lionized for their exploits. Among the best known in this era were the Yankees' Joe Page, the Pirates' Elroy Face, the Phillies' Jim Konstanty and the Giants' (among other teams') Hoyt Wilhelm. The fact that Joe Page had such outstanding years for the World Champion Yankees in 1947 and 1949 definitely helped to speed up the recognition of the relief specialist as a force to be reckoned with in modern day baseball. A native of Cherry Hill, Pennsylvania, in the heart of coal mining country, Page had begun his career as many before him did—as a starter. However, he pitched with less than scintillating success from 1944 through 1946. Manager Joe McCarthy used Page sparingly because of his propensity for post-game frivolity. "Young man," McCarthy would say to Page, "you have the potential of being one of the great relief pitchers of our day. But you'll have to take yourself more seriously. You're going to have to bear down. You're going to have to forget this nightlife."

In 1947 under new Yankee manager Bucky Harris, Page had himself an ally but the skipper believed that the left-hander had lost his confidence. Harris enlisted the aid of Page's teammates, Joe DiMaggio (his roommate on the road), George "Snuffy" Stirnweiss and Tommy Henrich to rebuild his tattered psyche. The year began atrociously and he was literally one pitch away from being exiled to the Yankees' farm club in Newark, New

Jersey, when it suddenly all came together for him in a night game against the powerful Boston Red Sox at Yankee Stadium.

W.C. Heinz described the scene in his book, *Once They Heard the Cheers*: "It was May 26, 1947, and there were 74,000 in the stands that night, and all that Joe Page became and all that happened to him afterward stemmed from it. The Washington Senators had knocked him out in his first start that season, and several times he had failed in relief. In the third inning, with the Red Sox leading 3–1, two men on base and nobody out, Bucky Harris brought him in for a last try. He got Ted Williams to ground to George McQuinn, a great glove man, but McQuinn bobbled it. Now the bases were loaded, and he threw three balls to (Rudy) York and, as Yogi (Berra) walked to the mound, Bucky Harris had one foot up on the dugout steps, and Joe Page was one pitch away from the minors.

York took two strikes, and then he swung at that fast ball and missed. The count went to 3 and 0 on Bobby Doerr, and again Harris was at the steps and again the future of Joe Page hung on the next pitch. He threw three strikes past Doerr, and got Eddie Pellagrini to lift an easy fly ball up into that rising thunder of sound for the third out. The Yankees won, 9–3, and Joe Page was on his way."

The Yankees had been looking for a successor to "Fireman" Johnny Murphy, who had left the team to join ex–Yankee manager Joe McCarthy with the Boston Red Sox for the 1947 campaign, and in Page they found someone who may not have been as durable and even as talented as Murphy but who could work in more games. The southpaw went on to post a 14–8 won-lost record with 17 saves and a 2.48 ERA that year for the Yankees. Page saved the first game of the 1947 series against the Brooklyn Dodgers and, although he took the loss in Game Six, he bounced back to be victorious in the deciding seventh game when he held the "Flock" to just one hit in five innings of relief.

Page had an unremarkable 1948 season but came back in 1949 to have his best year of all. He set a new record for saves with 27 while compiling a 13–8 record and a 2.59 ERA. He was the winning pitcher against the Dodgers (who else?) in Game Three of the 1949 World Series and got the save in the clincher. His production tailed off in 1950 and he was just never the same pitcher again. He tried a comeback in 1954 with the Pittsburgh Pirates but it didn't take. However, for the 1947 and 1949 championship seasons, he was as good a relief pitcher as had ever lived.

When it was obvious to the Yankees that Joe Page's longevity with them had come to an end, they obtained a 6'2", 220-pound right-handed relief pitcher named Tom Ferrick from the Washington Senators in a multi-player deal in the middle of 1950. Ferrick had been nothing but a reliever since his career began in 1941 with the Philadelphia Athletics. He bounced around the AL serving time with the Indians, Browns (twice) and Senators before joining the Yankees. He was immediately successful and helped them capture the pennant by compiling eight wins and nine saves in only 30 appearances on his way to becoming the league's best reliever that year. He also was credited with the win in Game Three of the World Series sweep of the Phillies in but one inning of work. All told, he saved a total of 56 games in his abbreviated nine-year career.

A pitcher who didn't even get to the big leagues until he was 31 was Ellis "Old Folks" Kinder, who joined the St. Louis Browns in 1946 after eight years in the minor leagues and another in the military. He was a starting pitcher and a very good one for the Boston Red Sox following his two so-so years with the Browns. He didn't become a reliever until 1951 but he excelled there just as he had when he was a 20-game winner for the Red Sox. In his first year in the pen, he led the AL in saves with 14 and in wins with 10. Two years later at the age of 39, he made a then-record 69 appearances and again led the league in relief wins with 10 and saves with 27. He continued to pitch in the big leagues until he was 43, recording 102 saves, the most for any reliever in the period 1946–1959.

Unfortunately, a man that major league baseball fans never got to see at the peak of his greatness was the legendary Leroy "Satchel" Paige. The stories of his exploits both in the Negro Leagues and in barnstorming games against big league stars in the off-season convinced a good many observers that he may have been the greatest pitcher ever. Yet because of the segregation that existed in his peak years, Paige did not make his debut in the majors until 1948 when he was believed to be 42. But he could still "bring" it.

Over his more than 40 years in baseball, Paige had great control, even though he delivered the ball in a wild, windmill fashion. He used five different, unique pitches: a changeup that could really move, something described as a "two-hump blooper;" a medium fastball dubbed "Little Tom;" a hard fastball with the moniker "Long Tom;" and his tremendous "hesitation pitch" where he actually stopped halfway through his delivery and then finished.

The innovative Bill Veeck, who earlier had brought in Larry Doby from the Newark Eagles of the Negro League as the first black position player in the American League, signed Paige, a native of Mobile, Alabama, to a Cleveland Indian contract on July 7, 1948, to become the first black pitcher in the league. He was already past 40 and coming off a serious injury to his arm. Originally Manager Lou Boudreau used him only as a reliever but he later beat the Washington Senators in a starting role and also shut out the Chicago White Sox twice. He finished up at 6–1 with a glowing 2.41 ERA in helping the Indians win the pennant.

Paige appeared in 31 games in 1949 but was released after the season when Veeck sold the team. Veeck later purchased the St. Louis Browns and brought Paige back in 1951. He pitched for three more years and in 1952 at the age of 46, he was 12–10 with ten saves and a league-leading eight wins in relief.

After being released in 1954, he started to barnstorm once again and played another year for the Kansas City Monarchs of the Negro League. He spent another three years working for Bill Veeck, who then owned the International League's AAA Miami Marlins. He continued pitching in the 1960s and one day he concluded his magnificent career with a three-inning start for Charley Finley's Athletics on September 25, 1965, at age 59 or thereabouts.

Auburn, Illinois native Emil "Dutch" Leonard was a pitcher who also brought a new-found respectability to relief pitching late in his career. After spending 16 years working as a starter for some of the worst teams in both leagues, he and his famed knuckleball were traded by the Phillies to the Chicago Cubs following the 1948 season. A horrendous 1949 campaign at the age of 40 led him into the Cubs' bullpen, where he proceeded to become one of the best relievers in the National League.

Leonard, who started his major league career with the Brooklyn Dodgers back in 1934, developed a sore arm that year on his way to a good 14–11 record with a somewhat mediocre team. He was farmed out to Atlanta where he first came up with the knuckler. Two good seasons with the Southern Association club bought him a trip back to the big leagues with the sub-par Washington Senators. While he would use a fastball or slip pitch to keep opposing hitters guessing, his knuckleball was his ticket to staying around the majors for 20 years. A control pitcher, he averaged only 2.06 walks over nine innings.

He was 44 years old when he retired after the 1953 season and through it all still managed to win 191 games. He liked to tell about the time he was once called upon to relieve against the Brooklyn Dodgers in the ninth inning with the Cubs clinging to a one-run lead. With the bases loaded and none out, he retired future Hall of Famers Jackie Robinson, Gil Hodges and Roy Campanella in succession to preserve the victory.

To illustrate just how quickly relief specialists had become important, the Most Valuable Player Award in the National League in 1950 went to Jim Konstanty of the pennant-winning Philadelphia Phillies, the first time it had ever been given to a reliever since its creation 20 years earlier.

Jim Konstanty (right), shown here with his St. Louis Cardinals manager, Fred Hutchinson, was the first reliever to win his league's MVP award following his 1950 season with the Philadelphia Phillies. (Courtesy St. Louis Globe Democrat Archives at the St. Louis Mercantile Library, University of Missouri–St. Louis.)

A former star athlete at Syracuse University (baseball, basketball, soccer and boxing), Konstanty had virtually no success in earlier "cups of coffee" with either the Cincinnati Reds in 1944 and Boston Braves in 1946. However, he later perfected a pitch called a "palmball" and eventually caught on with the Phillies in 1949 at age 32.

It was Manager Eddie Sawyer's idea to have Konstanty called up from the club's Triple A team in Toronto in 1949. "But he's thirty-two years old," declared Stan Baumgartner, the team's beat writer with the *Philadelphia Inquirer*. "What are you going to do with him with these young pitchers around?" Sawyer replied: "Let me tell you about Konstanty. I managed him when I had the Toronto club. He's a strange character. He throws a lot of crazy, breaking stuff, and he knows how to pitch and how he wants to pitch. I may start him here or there, but we need a relief man who can hold a one- or two-run lead for a couple of innings. That's going to be his job. Just watch him."

In the next year with the so-called "Whiz Kids," Konstanty set a new record for appearances by a pitcher with 74, notching 16 wins and 22 saves, both of which also led the league. The Phillies' starters were very young that season and often could not complete what they had begun, hence Konstanty got the call in nearly half of the team's games. He was one of four Phillies players to make his league's All-Star team in 1950 and retired the American League in order in his one inning of work. Using a wicked slider, Konstanty struck out Jim Hegan and Hoot Evers and got Bobby Doerr on a roller to short.

"I didn't do anything different that season," he later recalled. "I had two pitches, a slider and a change-up. The usual slider was thrown like you'd throw a football to get a spiral pass and broke on a level plane. I held my ball off center and got it to break several inches down and out. My change-up had about a three-quarter inch tilt and broke opposite to my slider so I could go in or out to either type batter."

After having relieved in 133 consecutive games for the Phillies, Konstanty was called on to be a surprise starter against the Yankees in the first game of the 1950 World Series. He pitched remarkably well but lost 1–0 to Yankee ace Vic Raschi. New Yorks Manager Casey Stengel paid him the ultimate compliment: "Konstanty is one of the greatest I've ever seen in a clutch."

"That start was a matter of necessity," Konstanty said once. "Our ace, Robin Roberts, had pitched the last game of the season, Curt Simmons was in the Army and the other guys were dead tired. Just prior to game time Sawyer called me in and asked if I thought I could start. I had not pitched more than three innings all year and all in crucial games, yet I felt I could go nine."

Konstanty was sold to the Yankees late in 1954 and his 11 saves in the next season helped them win still another flag. His record-setting 1950 season remains a watershed year, which along with the feats of Hugh Casey, Joe Page and others of his era, helped to change the perception of the relief pitcher as it had been heretofore known.

A pitcher who packed a number of accomplishments into an all-too short career was Plainfield, New Jersey's Joe Black, a hard-throwing right-hander from the Negro Leagues who joined the Brooklyn Dodgers as a

28-year-old rookie in 1952. The son of a postal clerk, Black broke in with a bang by appearing in 56 games and compiling a 15–4 won-lost mark and a 2.15 ERA in 142 one third innings to garner the National League's Rookie of the Year award. He also finished a close third behind Hank Sauer and Robin Roberts in the league's Most Valuable Player voting and was a huge factor in getting his team into the World Series against the New York Yankees that year.

Black, who had only made two starts in the regular season, got the call to start Game One and beat the Yankees and Allie Reynolds, 4–2. The game itself was historic in that it marked the first time a black man had ever won a series game. Reynolds came back to shut out Black and the Dodgers 2–0 in Game Four, and in the seventh and deciding game, Black took the loss, again beaten by Reynolds, who had come in to relieve a game the Yankees eventually won, 4–2. Black never again had a year close to 1952, when they sang a parody on "Old Black Joe" called "Ol' Joe Black" at the Baseball Writers' dinner in New York. In fact, he was out of baseball after the 1957 season at the age of 33.

The year of 1952 represented a significant season in the evolution of relief pitching, as epitomized by the successes of Joe Black, Hoyt Wilhelm (more on him later) and two pitchers for the St. Louis Cardinals, left-hander Al Brazle of Loyal, Oklahoma, and rookie right-hander Eddie Yuhas from Youngstown, Ohio. Brazle, a sidearmer, labored for eight years in the minor leagues before being called up in 1943 at the age of 28. A starter for his first five years in the majors, he became a reliever exclusively in 1950 and led the National League in saves in 1952 with 16 to go along with a 12–5 won-lost record while Yuhas saved six and pitched to a 12–2 record. Together the pair made 110 appearances and, according to many historians, along with relievers like Joe Black and Hoyt Wilhelm, were establishing the role of the pure relief pitcher for years to come. While Brazle led the league in saves again in 1953 with 18, by 1954 Yuhas was out of the game after only two years in the majors.

Another relief specialist who was already 36 years of age when the call came was 6'3", 190-pound Marv Grissom, who had five excellent years with the New York Giants beginning in 1954. The Los Molinos, California–bred right-hander not only helped his team win the pennant and World Series that year by winning 10 games and saving 19 others, he also made the NL All-Star team. He got the win in the first game of the World Series at the Polo Grounds over the prohibitive favorites that year, the AL's Cleveland Indians, winners of a league record 111 games whom the Giants swept. In 1956, he turned in his best ERA year ever with a marvelous 1.56. During his five years with the Giants as a reliever, he finished in the top five of the NL three times. He later became the pitching coach for the Oakland A's.

Two of the reasons why the Cleveland Indians achieved their record-setting 111 victories in 1954 were because of the "Dynamic Duo" of Don Mossi and Ray Narleski, two fire-balling rookies who were well nigh unhittable in their combined 82 relief appearances that year. Mossi, a left-hander from Helena, California, possessed great control and worked to a stunning 1.94 ERA that season. Despite the Giants' sweep, they couldn't hit Mossi, who was unscored on in three relief appearance in the World Series.

The right-handed Narleski, a Camden, New Jersey, product, also had wonderful control along with a blazing fastball. He led the AL with 13 saves in his first year. He was even better in his sophomore season in 1955, leading the league in saves with 19 and in wins with eight during the course of his 60 appearances.

Both Narleski and Mossi were traded to Detroit for Billy Martin and Al Cicotte after the 1958 season and began to draw more starting assignments as their careers moved ahead. While Narleski finished his career with the Tigers in 1959 after a disappointing season, Mossi went back to being a reliever for the White Sox in 1964 and the Athletics in 1965, retiring with the best fielding average for a pitcher ever up to that time. For that one year though—1954—Don Mossi and Ray Narleski may have just been the best relief tandem the game has ever seen.

After spending five years in the minors and two years in the armed services, Clem Labine finally made it up to the Brooklyn Dodgers in 1950. A free spirit from Lincoln, Rhode Island, known for his durability, the right-handed Labine relied on a sinker for his out pitch. In the period 1946–1959, he is listed as third in relief appearances, first in relief wins and second in saves. He also led the National League in games pitched in 1955 and in saves in both 1956 and 1957 when he was also picked for the NL's All-Star team.

Labine pitched in four World Series for the Dodgers and in another one in 1960 for the series winners, the Pittsburgh Pirates. One of his proudest achievements was in the way he was able to handle Hall of Famer and Dodger nemesis Stan Musial. Remarkably, he once retired "The Man" 49 times in a row.

Like Jim Konstanty before him, Clem Labine was also called on to be a starter in a couple of big games. One was a 1–0 win over the Giants in Game Two of the 1951 National League playoff. The other was also a shutout, 1–0 in ten innings over the Yankees in the sixth game of the 1956 World Series. His other claim to fame was a real oddity: his only three

Clem Labine, who joined the Brooklyn Dodgers in 1950 after five years in the minors and two in the armed services, had the distinction of retiring Cardinal great Stan Musial 49 times in a row. (Courtesy St. Louis Globe Democrat Archives at the St. Louis Mercantile Library, University of Missouri–St. Louis.)

hits during the entire year of 1955 were home runs. After leaving the Dodgers, he pitched briefly for Detroit, Pittsburgh and the New York Mets, and even earned a world championship ring with the Pirates in 1960.

A record that may never be broken is the 18 wins in relief registered by Elroy Face of the Pittsburgh Pirates in 1959, of which seventeen were in succession (another record for a reliever). With his four consecutive victories at the end of 1958, he could claim an astonishing 22 straight wins from 1958 to 1959.

His 1959 18–1 record still represents the best winning percentage (.947) ever in the majors. There is a story that Face used to park his car at a gas station near Forbes Field for $1 a day that year. After he had won four or five games, it is said that the owner of the station told Face he could park there for free as long as he kept on winning. Consequently, he was able to park *gratis* well into September.

The Stephentown, New York, right-hander used a forkball he learned from Joe Page during the southpaw's brief tenure with the Pirates in their 1954 spring training camp. Face's confidence in the pitch grew to the point where he was not afraid to throw it no matter what the count was. Opposing pitchers called it a "freakball" because one had to have large hands in order to hold it. Wedged between the index and middle fingers, Face cushioned the ball into the palm of his hand. He would use it as an off-speed pitch that sank very quickly as it reached the batter and induced hitters to hit lots of grounders.

The Pittsburgh Pirates' Elroy Face holds a season's relief record that may never be broken—18 wins (17 consecutively) in 1959. (Courtesy Pittsburgh Pirates.)

Face also had one of the most uncanny pick off moves in history. One day in Cincinnati he came in to a situation with runners on first and second and none out. Before throwing a single pitch to the batter, he picked off the runner at second and then proceeded to pick-off the runner at first.

Small in stature—he was only 5'8", 155 pounds—the shy, gutsy Face ranks fifth all-time in wins for a reliever with 96 and sixth in saves with 193. He also holds the National League mark for most games finished with 574 and for the most games pitched for one team, 802 for Pittsburgh. He also led his league three times in saves and twice in appearances. And in the 1960 World Series best-of-seven victory for the Pirates over the Yankees, he saved three of the four wins.

Writer Edward Kiersh once wrote about Face: "Considered by many to be the best relief pitcher in history, [Face] confronted all types of jams in his career. Relying mainly on a forkball, he squelched so many rallies in 1959 ... that manager Danny Murtaugh tagged him Sam Spade."

What is particularly unique about Elroy Face's career when compared to today's closers is that he would be brought into games once a starter appeared to be faltering as early as the seventh inning and whether the Pirates were ahead or not. In his signature year of 1959, he came into games 13 times in the seventh inning, 19 times in the eighth, 21 times in the ninth and on four occasions in the tenth. Today's closers are more likely to come into a ballgame in the ninth inning, about 80 percent of the time.

"Blind Ryne" Duren, so-called because of his extremely poor eyesight, joined the New York Yankees at the age of 29 in 1958. The Cazenovia, Wisconsin, native, who was so nearsighted he carried five different types of eyeglasses, proceeded to have a few momentous years with the Yankees and his 95-mph fastball. The right-hander would enter a game and, squinting at home plate behind bottle-thick glasses, deliberately uncork a pitch that would sail to the top of the backstop, literally striking fear into the next hitter. It is said that he once hit a batter in the on-deck circle in the minor leagues.

Duren was a part of minor league folklore before arriving at the big league level. One scouting report at the time read: "Big guy. Throws like hell. Hitter can't see it. But he can't see you either. He's practically blind. Can't hit, field or run. Curve not much. Neither is sinker. Just throws fast one. Unpredictable where it'll go."

After being traded to the Yankees by the Kansas City Athletics in the Billy Martin deal, he spent most of the 1957 season with the team's farm club in Denver managed by Ralph Houk. He pitched well as a starter but Houk told Duren at year's end: "In my opinion you throw as hard as, or harder than Joe Page, and he was the fastest I ever saw in the majors. Your control is just as good, too. Page made money as a relief pitcher. You've shown me you can do it, too."

Although Duren bought into Houk's suggestion, Casey Stengel was unconvinced. However, the Yankee manager gave Duren a shot at relieving in spring training in 1958, liked what he saw and made him the club's stopper. Up until then, Stengel for the most part liked to bring in starters like Allie Reynolds and Whitey Ford to finish some of his team's close-call victories. That all changed when Ryne Duren arrived.

It also effectively ended the approach that most major league managers had been using since the beginning of the twentieth century and epitomized by pitchers like Chief Bender, "Three Finger" Brown and other combination starter-relievers.

Duren won six games and saved another 20 in 1958, topping off his season with both a win and a save in the World Series against the Milwaukee Braves. The following year, he saved another 14 games, including a streak of 18 games and 36 innings where he did not surrender a single run, compiling a 1.87 ERA, third best in the league. In 1958–1959, the fireballer gave up but 89 hits while striking out 183 batters in 151 innings. Duren was traded to the Los Angeles Angels on May 8, 1961, with Lee Thomas and Johnny James for Bob Cerv and Tex Clevenger. Ten days later he became one of only 17 big league pitchers credited with four strikeouts in a single inning. He was his own worst enemy, though, as he eventually drank himself out of baseball. However, he fought through his decline and despair, later turning his life completely around as he disclosed in his autobiography, *The Comeback*.

Little Bobby Shantz, at 5'6" and 139 pounds, spent the first eight years of his major league life primarily as a starter for some of the worst teams in American League history: the Philadelphia and later Kansas City Athletics. He was involved in one of the most unusual relief spells ever during the 1949 campaign. Sent into a game in the third inning against the Detroit Tigers, Shantz pitched nine consecutive no-hit, no-run innings before he gave up a couple of hits in the 13th to win, 5–4, although he never received credit for the "no-no."

He was forbidden to use his knuckleball by owner-manager Connie Mack, who also had a thing about smallish pitchers. But following Mack's retirement after the 1950 season, the new skipper, Jimmy Dykes, started to give Shantz more rest between starts and the southpaw began to come into his own. He was coveted by many teams, especially after winning 24 games and losing only seven for Dykes' 1952 Athletics, a club that finished sixth in an eight-team league and barely managed to win 70 games.

It was only after the 1956 season that the New York Yankees were able to pry the Pottstown, Pennsylvania, native away from Kansas City in a 12-player deal. After one season as a spot starter and reliever, Casey Stengel and pitching coach Jim Turner converted him into one of the AL's most dependable bullpen aces. In the Yankees' 1960 pennant-winning season, he saved 11 games, pitching to a 2.79 ERA in 42 games. He also picked up a save in one of the club's three wins against the Pittsburgh Pirates in the World Series that season. He had previously made three appearances in the 1957 World Series, which the Yankees also lost against the Milwaukee Braves. A tremendous fielder (he won the AL's Gold Glove award the first four times it was given out—1957–1960), Shantz combined a knuckleball with an outstanding curve (Ted Williams said it was the best in the league) and he was able to change speeds to get the hitters out as well.

Although his name rarely comes to mind when the top relief pitchers of all time are discussed, Bill Henry of Alice, Texas, ranks among the best 50 to ever inhabit the bullpen. In a 16-year career beginning in 1952 with the Boston Red Sox, the 6'2", 185-pound lefty got into 527 games (only 44 as a starter) and recorded 90 saves along the way. He came into his own as a key reliever in 1959, his second year in the National League with the Chicago Cubs, when he led the league in appearances with 65.

A teammate of Bill Henry's who is also not often given the recognition he deserves is Don Elston, a fireballing right-hander out of Campbellstown, Ohio. He broke in with the Chicago Cubs in 1957 and started 14 games for them with indifferent results. Switched to the team's bullpen the following year, he set a club record for appearances with 69, which led the National League, and also was selected for the All-Star team. All

Hoyt Wilhelm, who broke into the major leagues at 29, became the first true reliever to be elected into the Hall of Fame. (Courtesy St. Louis Globe Democrat Archives at the St. Louis Mercantile Library, University of Missouri–St. Louis.)

told, Elston saved 63 games for the Cubs in eight of his nine seasons in the big leagues. One time he said: "The most important asset of a reliever is his temperament. I wasn't too crazy about the term 'ice water in his veins,' but that is a good description."

Another member of the Rookie Class of 1956 who debuted as a starter for the Philadelphia Phillies and never started another game again for them in the next four years was Boston's Dick "Turk" Farrell. Possessor of a hard sinker, he led the National League in relief wins with 10 in 1957. Chosen for the National League All-Star team in 1958, Farrell fanned four of the seven batters he faced, including the legendary Ted Williams. He retired from baseball after the 1969 season after accumulating 83 saves in 456 relief appearances. While working in Great Britain on an offshore oil rig, Farrell was killed in an auto accident in Yarmouth, England, in 1977 at the age of 43.

When it comes to the question of who the top relief pitcher of the 1946–1959 period may have been, Hoyt Wilhelm could arguably be called the best. Up until recently, the knuckleballer who became the first true relief pitcher elected to the Hall of Fame, he had appeared in more games (1,070) than any other pitcher in history. Jesse Orosco supplanted him early in the 2000 season.

He was 29 when he came up to the New York Giants in 1952 following seven years in the minors and three in the military during World War II, which included receiving the Purple Heart for heroism in the Battle of the Bulge. He remained in the majors for 21 years, pitching for nine different teams. When his career finally came to a close in 1972, he had set records for the most relief wins with 123, the most games finished by a reliever with 651 and the most innings pitched in relief with 1,871. And he is among the leaders in saves with 227.

Wilhelm was a high school pitcher when he read about Dutch Leonard's knuckler and started to fool around with it. He worked on it during his first year in the minors but the war intervened and obviously delayed his progress. His rookie season with the New York Giants was sensational as he went 15–3 with 11 saves and led the league in both won-lost percentage (.833) and ERA with 2.43, the first rookie pitcher to ever accomplish this feat. Never a good hitter, he nonetheless holds the distinction of homering in his first time at bat in the majors and of getting the only triple of his career in his second at-bat.

Six years later after being acquired on waivers by the Orioles, he pitched a no-hitter against the pennant-winning Yankees. The following year he led the American League in ERA with 2.19 to become the only pitcher ever to win that crown in both leagues. The Huntersville, North

Carolina, native who pitched up until five days before his forty-ninth birthday, was elected to the Hall of Fame in 1985.

Among the more preeminent events that characterized the 1946–1959 period, the desegregation of the majors topped the list. Branch Rickey had brought Jackie Robinson into the big leagues in 1947 with the Dodgers, which gave him a leg up on other general managers in baseball with players from the Negro League and even Latin America. But that was only temporary. Dodger owner Walter O'Malley, who was being upstaged by the aging Rickey, forced him out in 1950. So Rickey went over to the Pittsburgh Pirates and began to do what he had always done—build a winner just as he had earlier with both the St. Louis Cardinals and Brooklyn Dodgers.

O'Malley, meanwhile, succeeded in convincing his intercity rival, Horace Stoneham of the New York Giants, to join him in moving their franchises to the West Coast after the 1957 season. Although O'Malley was still drawing more than a million customers a year in tiny Ebbetts Field, including a few contests a year in Jersey City's AAA Roosevelt Stadium, Stoneham's Giants were a losing proposition.

What these moves did, however, was to give Rickey the opportunity to propose the formation of a third major league, the Continental League. In an attempt to nip this idea in the bud, O'Malley persuaded his fellow owners to consider expansion, especially since fans in other cities were clamoring for either new franchises or ones to replace the lost New York teams. It worked and the Continental League was killed off before it could to get off the ground.

The teams that Rickey had built in Brooklyn won fairly consistently in the National League, seven pennants in all, and narrowly missed out in three others. And unlike the Yankees, who seemed to winning every single year in the American League, the NL could boast that the Braves won the flag on three occasions and a World Series, the Giants twice, including a World Series, and the Cardinals, Phillies, Pirates and Reds each won a pennant as well. So for sheer balance, the National League appeared to have it over the American League in this particular era.

◆ *Chapter 5* ◆

Relievers Begin Their Domination (1960–1969)

Major league baseball's response at the start of this decade to what had been a very real threat by the now-defunct Continental League was to expand as soon as possible. In 1960, the nation's population was more than 200 million with almost half of the populace located in 13 urban areas. Workers' wages were nearing a record annual average of $8,000 and spending on recreation, spurred on by the increasing popularity of televised sports, was now at a new peak of $18 billion a year.

Major league baseball worked out a plan whereby the American League would lead the way in 1961 with moves to Los Angeles (and a team to be called the "Angels") and a new franchise to be awarded to the city of Washington, D.C. The team already in the nation's capital and owned by Cal Griffith would move to Bloomington, Minnesota, and thereafter be called the "Minnesota Twins." The newer club would then be allowed to adopt the former occupant's name, "Senators." Everybody was happy — at least for the time being.

The National League, on the other hand, would add its new teams in the following year: the Houston Colt .45s and the New York Mets. After losing both the Giants and the Dodgers to the West Coast in 1958, NL fans in America's biggest city were champing at the bit for a new team. In addition to expanding each league by two teams, the playing schedule would be upped to 162 games, or eight more a season. Needless to say, this would wreak havoc on baseball's record-keeping as well as its scheduling, but these were the vicissitudes brought on by expansion that could not be avoided.

However, to say that the results of expansion were disappointing would be putting it mildly. Overall attendance didn't increase all that much mostly because the addition of four teams meant that players who would normally be in the minor leagues were now in the majors. Also, some players who were basically role players and others who were essentially over the hill continued to hold spots on big league rosters.

Then, too, major league baseball was being challenged mightily by professional football and its phenomenal growth due mainly to television. Also, there were growing complaints from owners, general managers and scouts alike that college and high school youngsters in increasing numbers were turning their sights to other sports like football and basketball for their futures.

Baseball's image wasn't being helped either by teams jumping from one city to another like Milwaukee taking its Braves to Atlanta after having moved them out of Boston earlier, and Charlie Finley moving the Athletics from Kansas City to Oakland. Many fans in the cities that were losing their teams were livid, not to mention that lawsuits were drawn up to try and prevent these moves which, at the very least, could affect possible future movements. All of these events did little to make the game look good.

Other situations that took place in the '60s that also contributed to the fragile state of the game and its perception by the general public included: the famous holdout by star Los Angeles Dodger pitchers Sandy Koufax and Don Drysdale prior to the 1966 season; the signing of tough labor negotiator Marvin Miller as executive director of the Major League Players Association; revealing books by pitchers Jim Bouton and Jim Brosnan with their less than flattering portraits of major leaguers; and the establishment of a union for umpires at the end of the decade.

On the field it was not the best of times for the hitters either. True, the Yankees' Roger Maris, who eventually broke Babe Ruth's home run record in 1961, and his teammate, Mickey Mantle, were hitting taters in bunches, but they were indeed the exception. Statistics clearly demonstrated that with almost half of the games now being played at night, this situation had a deleterious effect on batting averages. Then, too, hitters aiming for home runs instead of singles and doubles, the growing use of the slider, bigger and better fielding gloves, all helped to further reduce hitters' averages. Also the short porches in Sportsman's Park in St. Louis, the Polo Grounds in New York and Ebbets Field in Brooklyn were all gone, making way for new ballparks with their expanded foul lines that also contributed to reducing hitters' averages. But make no mistake about it, pitching, particularly the use of specialized relievers, was now dominating baseball.

In 1961, which was the first year of expansion since the NL and AL came together after the 1903 season, Whitey Ford's 25 victories—his first 20-game season—were helped substantially by Luis Arroyo's 29 saves. Earlier Lefty Gomez had his Johnny Murphy, now Whitey Ford had his Luis Arroyo.

The left-handed Arroyo had a so-so career up to that point in the National League during brief stints with the Cardinals, Pirates and Reds. However, his screwball proved to be a mystery to American League hitters beginning in 1960 when he joined the Yankees at the rather advanced age of 33. Hardly anyone noticed. In the very next year, though, in addition to the 29 saves he corralled, the rotund Arroyo, out of Penuelas, Puerto Rico, notched a league-high 15 wins, thereby contributing to 44 of the team's 109 wins. He also registered a win in the World Series over his former team, the Cincinnati Reds. It was a remarkable year for what had been a rather nondescript career.

Luis once characterized his workday as follows: "I sit around relaxing for the first five or six innings. Then I know it's time to go to work. I know it's my turn. I start watching carefully, studying the hitters. Then I warm up, slowly at first, gradually getting faster and faster and working on the screwball, my best pitch.

"When I get the call, I never rush. I'm in no hurry to get there. All the way to the mound I just keep reminding myself to keep the ball in the park and go with my best pitch.

"Naturally the hitter is expecting the screwball. They know that's my bread-and-butter pitch. He knows what's coming and I have to stop him, even so. But I have two speeds on the screwball—and once in a while I can throw a fastball past a hitter."

Arroyo's record-breaking season in 1961 is viewed by many baseball historians as the turning point toward the use of the bullpen as a strategic factor in the game of baseball. His career was cut short when he developed a sore arm the following spring. He never fully recovered from it and was forced to retire in 1963 at 36. "He was a handy man to have around," said Yankees Manager Ralph Houk. "And, boy, is that an understatement."

Both Hoyt Wilhelm and Elroy Face, who had starred in the '50s, were every bit as successful throughout the new decade. Wilhelm pitched mostly in the American League with the Chicago White Sox and Baltimore Orioles while Face stayed in Pittsburgh for virtually the entire ten-year period. Face, in fact, started off the period by saving three of the Pittsburgh Pirates' four victories in the 1960 World Series, his team's first championship in 35 years. That same year he led his league in games pitched and was on the NL All-Star squad. He was also picked for the team in the following year.

While Wilhelm ranked fourth in relief appearances, he finished first in both relief wins and saves in the decade. He also was selected to the AL All-Star team twice and in 1960 became the first pitcher to appear in relief in 400 games. Thereafter he surpassed the 500-game mark in 1962, the 600-game mark in 1964, the 700-game mark in 1965, the 800-game mark in 1967 and the 900-game mark in 1969.

Cincinnati, Ohio's Jim Brosnan, perhaps better known as an author than a relief pitcher, did have his moments coming out of the pen though. Starting out with the Chicago Cubs in 1954, he enjoyed his best years with his hometown's Reds from 1960 to 1963 before he was dealt to the Chicago White Sox early in 1963. Known as "The Professor," Brosnan had written a book, *The Long Season,* after the 1959 campaign, which recounted what some considered to be "tales out of school" about the comings and goings behind the scenes in major league baseball. It drew critical acclaim from the literary world and many players, but club owners as a whole thought it embarrassed the game.

Brosnan was credited with 41 saves and recorded 21 victories in 158 appearances for the Reds from 1960 to 1962. The 6'4", 197-pound right-hander helped to get his team into the 1961 World Series despite being a 100 to 1 shot in the spring to win the pennant. "We couldn't have won it without him," said his manager, the late Fred Hutchinson, at the end of the regular season. Relying heavily on a slider, he never lacked confidence. He once told *Los Angeles Times* columnist Jim Murray during a night on the town, "My slider can get those bums out," referring to the Dodgers.

A right-handed screwballer with flaming red hair, Jack Baldschun, who came from Greenville, Ohio, was the mainstay of the Phillies' bullpen for five years beginning in 1961. He saved 59 games and made at least 65 appearances a year for them during that span. He led the NL in relief wins with 12 in 1962, the same year he was credited with victories in both ends of a doubleheader on April 14. He had the distinction of being traded from the Baltimore Orioles (for whom he never pitched) with Milt Pappas and Dick Simpson for future Hall of Famer Frank Robinson, the only man to win the MVP award in both leagues. Baldschun later ended his career with the expansion Montreal Expos in their maiden season of 1969.

Originally a member of the Chicago Cubs, southpaw Ron Perranoski was traded to the Los Angeles Dodgers before the 1960 season in a deal that involved infielder Don Zimmer. Although he had begun his career as a starter, he was quickly converted into a reliever by the Dodgers with the express purpose of getting left-handed batters out, and that he did with alacrity. Born in Paterson, New Jersey (oddly enough, one day before Dick Radatz, with whom he later roomed, took the same courses and played

No one pitched in more games in the 1960s than Ron Perranoski, who was also second in relief wins and tied for third in saves in the decade. (Courtesy St. Louis Globe Democrat Archives at the St. Louis Mercantile Library, University of Missouri–St. Louis.)

on the baseball team at Michigan State), Perranoski quickly became the Dodgers' stopper and in 1962 led the big leagues in appearances with 70. He followed up that season in 1963 with a spectacular league-leading 16–3 won-lost mark and a 1.67 ERA. No one pitched in more games in the 1960s than Ron Perranoski, who was also second in relief wins and tied for third in saves in the decade.

Even before he got to the big leagues, Perranoski was noted for his poise. In fact as a child, his father, Pete, commented on his son's amazing composure: "He would come home after a game and you could never tell whether he won or lost. Sometimes I thought he was made of stone. If I met him at the front door after a game, I'd have to ask him how he made out. I could never tell." Poise, composure—call it what you will, it is a trait that most of the best relievers in history have possessed.

During his big league career, Perranoski mixed up his pitches well, alternating a fastball, curve and sinker that stood him in good stead year after year until the 1967 season with the Dodgers. He was subsequently traded to the Minnesota Twins prior to the 1968 campaign and, while it took him a bit of time to accustom himself to the American League, he wound up leading the AL in saves and received *The Sporting News'* "Fireman of the Year" awards in 1969 and 1970. All told, Perranoski recorded 179 saves in his 13-year career, which included three World Series championships with the Dodgers. He later served as Manager Tom Lasorda's pitching coach in Los Angeles.

One of the rare individuals to come directly into the big leagues with no minor league experience, Lindy McDaniel of Hollis, Oklahoma, was signed by the Cardinals as a starter in 1955. While successful initially (15–9 with a 3.49 ERA in 1957 as a 21-year-old), he ran into trouble in 1958 and found himself back in the minors in the American Association later that season. He returned as a reliever the following year and was an instant success, leading the National League in saves with 15 and recording 13 wins as well. He was the top reliever in the league in 1960 when he repeated as the saves leader with 26 and also was selected to the league's All-Star team.

A control pitcher without overpowering stuff, the long, lanky right-hander found himself in Chicago with the Cubs in 1963 and once again reigned as the NL's saves leader with 22. He moved from one windswept city to another when he was shipped to the San Francisco Giants in 1967 and was no longer being called on to close games. However, he received a new lease on life when he was traded to the New York Yankees in the middle of 1968 for Bill Monbouquette. He finished second in the American League in saves with 29 in 1970 and a career-best 2.01 ERA. By 1974 he was on the move for the last time when he was traded to the Kansas City Athletics for Lou Piniella and Ken Wright.

McDaniel ranked second in games pitched in relief in the '60s with 551, third in relief wins and sixth in saves. He retired from the game in 1975 after 21 seasons in the majors registering 172 saves, placing him fourth on the all-time list at the time and second only to Hoyt Wilhelm in appearances with 987.

After failing to make the grade as a big league outfielder, 6'6" Dick Hall was converted into a pitcher by the Pittsburgh Pirates. The former Swarthmore College "Little All American" end from St. Louis originally had little success with his new craft in the minors. However, after missing the 1958 season due to a bout with hepatitis, he enjoyed a very good year as a starter in the Pacific Coast League in 1959, leading the league in wins, winning percentage and ERA. Upon his return to the majors, he had a mediocre year with Kansas City in 1960 and was subsequently traded to Baltimore for the following season. It was with the Orioles that the right-hander with an unusual herky-jerky delivery had seven exceptionally good years there, primarily as a middle innings reliever. He had remarkable control—walking only 23 in the last 462 innings that he pitched in the majors. His 55 relief wins rank him fifth best for the decade.

Another outstanding reliever who began his career as a starter was the slender right-hander Stu Miller. Called up by the St. Louis Cardinals in the middle of 1952, Manager Eddie Stanky looked at the 165-pounder and asked the clubhouse man: "Who's that stenographer?" Like Dick Hall, Miller possessed a herky-jerky motion and served up a variety of curveballs, even shifting speeds on his excellent change-up that mystified batters in both leagues. It was said that he had three speeds: slow, slower and slowest and that he "threw a pitch that stopped." Miller was also grudgingly identified as a pitcher who "if you wait five minutes, the ball gets to you fairly fast."

Stu Miller recorded a league-best 2.47 ERA with the San Francisco Giants in 1958 and was selected as *The Sporting News'* "Fireman of the Year" in 1961 for the Giants when he led the league with 17 saves and 14 wins in relief. That same year the Northampton, Massachusetts, product became famous for being blown off the mound at Candlestick park during the All-Star game. However, he eventually got credit for the win and had the distinction of fanning Mickey Mantle, Roy Sievers and Elston Howard in succession as well.

In his first year after being traded to Baltimore (1963), Miller won his second "Fireman of the Year" award when he notched 27 saves and broke the league's record for appearances at the time with 71. That same season, he and starting pitcher Steve Barber combined to no-hit the Detroit Tigers, although the Orioles lost the game 2–1 due to walks, a wild pitch and an error. He was the best reliever in the AL in 1965 as well with 14 wins and 24 saves, and finished in the top five in two other seasons.

During the '60s, Stu Miller was seventh in relief appearances, fourth in relief wins and was tied for third in saves. At his retirement in 1968, he ranked third behind only Hoyt Wilhelm and Elroy Face in both career saves and wins.

In contrast to Stu Miller, the 6'6", 230-pound. Dick "The Monster" Radatz of the Boston Red Sox was probably the best reliever in the business in his first three years in the majors (1962–1964). He threw extremely hard and struck fear in the opposition every time he entered a game. In 444 innings pitched, he struck out a remarkable total of 487 batters in that brief stretch of time. Including 1965, the right-handed fireballer, originally from the Detroit suburb of Berkeley, saved 100 games and won 49 others in his four years in Boston. And for a one-pitch strikeout hurler, he had excellent control. In his rookie year, he copped *The Sporting News'* "Fireman of the Year" award by leading the American League with 62 appearances, nine wins in relief and 24 saves.

A former all-state end in high school, Radatz was a starting pitcher at Michigan State. His minor league manager at Seattle, Johnny Pesky, made him a reliever, which displeased him. However, when the Boston Red Sox came to Seattle for an exhibition game, Radatz relieved and struck out the likes of Frank Malzone, Carl Yastrzemski and Russ Nixon, among others. "I wanted to go over and kiss that Pesky," said Radatz. "He'd just made my fortune." "The Monster" was elevated to the big club the following spring.

Radatz had an even better year in 1963 than his rookie season, at one point winning ten games in a row on the way to a 15–6 won-lost mark, a 1.97 ERA and 25 saves. Yankee Manager Ralph Houk picked him for that year's AL All-Star team, calling him "the greatest relief pitcher I have ever seen." And Houk had caught Joe Page and managed Ryne Duren. In the game against the rival National League, Radatz struck out Willie Mays, Dick Groat, Duke Snider, Willie McCovey and Julian Javier in the final two innings. He copped another "Fireman of the Year" award in 1964 when he appeared in 79 games and led the AL with 29 saves, 16 wins and nine losses, all in relief. The Red Sox only won 72 games that year but Radatz had either a win or save in 45 of those victories, while striking out 181 batters in 157 innings of work.

Joe Adcock, at the time a member of the California Angels, said of Radatz: "He has three things going for him: his fast ball moves, he gets it over the plate, and he has a deceptive delivery." Hall of Famer Al Kaline observed: "He takes a very slow windup. Then all of a sudden the ball is on top of you. That windup fools me. I never expect the ball to get to the plate as quickly as it does."

Following what for him was an okay year in 1965 (22 saves and a 9–11 won-lost mark), Radatz was traded to Cleveland midway through the next season as it became increasingly evident that he was beginning to lose something off his fastball. He had a rough time adjusting to becoming another type of pitcher and drifted from the Indians to the Cubs, Tigers and Expos. In 381 appearances during his seven seasons in the big leagues, Dick Radatz finished his career with 122 saves.

Brooklyn–born Don McMahon, who pitched for seven different teams in both leagues in an 18-year career, relied on but two basic pitches: a fastball and a curve. Although he never saved more than 19 games in any year, the 6'2", 215-pound. right-hander was coveted by many teams because of his durability and dominance as a closer.

It was the great former Brooklyn Dodger hurler, Whitlow Wyatt, who was McMahon's manager in the minors and converted him into a reliever after a miserable season as a starter for Toledo in 1955. He joined the Milwaukee Braves two years later and in 1958 he was the man who was called out of the bullpen 32 times, registering a 1.54 ERA for the eventual world champions. The following year he led the National League in saves with 15.

Beginning in 1962, he was with six other teams in the next seven years, his last club being the San Francisco Giants, where he found a home for the last five and a half years of his career. In 1971 McMahon led the National League with nine wins in relief and a career-high 19 saves. At his retirement, he had pitched in 872 games out of the bullpen. During the 1960s he ranked third in relief appearances and ninth in relief wins.

Larry Sherry came up with his native Los Angeles Dodgers at the age of 24 in 1959 and had an unbelievable World Series, saving two and wining two in four appearances for the champions. The right-hander led the National League in saves with 13 in the following year. A power pitcher who could also throw a slider at varying speeds, he chalked up 82 saves in an 11-year career that included a career high of 20 with the Detroit Tigers in 1966.

Born with two club feet, Sherry had his malady corrected by surgery at the age of six. He returned to the Dodger organization as a minor league coach. His brother, Norm, was his teammate and batterymate with the Dodgers from 1959 to 1962.

After leading the National League in losses (18 in 1956 and 16 in 1958) as a starter for the Pittsburgh Pirates, Ron Kline of Callery, Pennsylvania, accumulated 108 saves after being converted into a reliever following his first eight years in the majors. The 6'3" right-hander made his way to the American League in 1961 and four years later led it in saves with 29 in 74 appearances, both single season club records for the Washington Senators.

Kline returned to Pittsburgh in 1968 where he was the National League leader in relief wins, including a string of ten in a row. He finished the '60s sixth in relief game appearances, eighth in relief wins and tied for eighth in saves. He was noted for the unusual ritual of touching his cap, belt and shirt before each and every pitch.

When Dubuque, Iowa's Joe Hoerner joined the expansion Houston Colt .45s in 1963, the 6'1", 200-pound. right-hander was immediately put in the bullpen and remained there for his entire 14-year career in the majors. One of the best short relievers in the game, this notorious clubhouse jokester became a sidearmer because the delivery placed less of a strain on his weak heart. From 1966 to 1971, his ERA was never above 2.89. His best year in the '60s came in 1969 when, as a member of the pennant-bound St. Louis Cardinals, he posted 17 saves and a 1.47 ERA, both career highs. On June 1 of that year he tied a National League mark for consecutive strikeouts by fanning six batters in a row.

Hoerner was part of the controversial trade to the Philadelphia Phillies in 1969 with Curt Flood, who refused to report and eventually helped to end the reserve clause due to his reluctance to be dealt away without his approval. Hoerner was to lead the National League in saves with nine in the following season. He appeared in two World Series for the Cardinals, notching a save and being pinned with a loss against the Detroit Tigers in 1968. He retired after the 1977 season with 99 saves on his record. His other claim to fame? The immortal Hank Aaron was unable to get a hit off of him in 22 at-bats.

Bill McCool, a hard-throwing left-hander out of Batesville, Indiana, came up to the Cincinnati Reds in 1964 at 19 years of age after just one, but extraordinary, season in the minors. Thrust in the midst of a four-team pennant race, the youngster relieved in 40 games, posted a 2.43 ERA and was voted the National League Rookie Pitcher of the Year. The following season at the still-tender age of 20, he appeared in 62 games and recorded 21 saves.

McCool's career only lasted seven years but in that time he recorded 58 saves, mostly with the Reds, and an ERA under four. He also fanned 471 batters in 529 innings but in his last three years in the majors (one each with the Reds, Padres and Cardinals), his pitching was plagued by wildness that eventually cut short his big league career at the age of 26.

Another reliever who may not be a household name among the all-time great relievers but nevertheless ranks among the Top 50 is Bob Locker, who came up with the Chicago White Sox in 1965. The 6'3", 200-pound Iowan with a wicked sinkerball gave the Chisox a formidable bullpen when added to the knuckleballing duo of Hoyt Wilhelm and Eddie Fisher. In 1966, the right-handed Locker came out of Manager Eddie Stanky's pen nine times in the first five weeks of the season and gave up nary a run. In the following year, he led all American League pitchers with 77 appearances and registered 20 saves. Combined with Wilhelm's 20 and Fisher's 24, the trio recorded a remarkable 64 saves of the 95 wins chalked up by Manager Al Lopez's second-place finishers. When asked the reason for his success, Locker, a geology major, attributed it to his consuming of honey, nature's essence. He spent ten seasons in the majors with five different clubs making 576 appearances, all in relief, and notched 95 saves and a very respectable 2.76 ERA.

Five seasons elapsed before Luis Arroyo's previously unmatched record of 29 saves was broken in 1965 by the Chicago Cubs' Ted Abernathy, who notched 31 to earn him that year's National League "Fireman of the Year" award. He won it again two years later with the Cincinnati Reds when he amassed 28 saves on his way to a career total of 148.

The trend toward calling in relievers more often than not to finish and, hopefully, either to save or win games, continued in 1966 when still a new record was set by right-hander Jack Aker of the Kansas City Athletics, who upped the mark to 32. It was becoming more and more evident that the bullpen was no longer the place where faltering starters were exiled but rather the domain of specialists who were now making an admirable profession out of relieving.

Complete games had now dropped into the 20 percent range with ERAs averaging 3.30. The latter figure even dipped down to 2.98 in 1968, the so-called "Year of the Pitcher," and batters were averaging a microscopic .237. The hitters had been griping for some time now about pitchers "loading up" the ball. As the use of chewing tobacco declined, the popular choices seemed to be petroleum jelly and other lubricants.

In 1967, it was rumored that the number of pitchers using a spitball was as high as 25 percent. It was also generally agreed that the number of illegal pitches being served up was the most since the end of the dead ball era. Batters also accused certain pitchers of scuffing up the baseball by any means available—a belt buckle, an emery board or a razor blade, all of which were usually close at hand.

One of the most successful pitchers of his era was Gaylord Perry, who was constantly being accused of throwing a spitter. He was often challenged by opposing managers, coaches and players but was never once shown the door during a game by the umpires. Hall of Famer Whitey Ford also was charged by some opposing teams of scuffing up the ball by using his wedding ring. After retiring from the game, Perry later admitted in his biography that he had hidden illegal stuff (mostly petroleum jelly) in the bill of his cap. Ford just smiles when asked if he ever doctored the ball while pitching.

Back in 1950, pitching staffs had averaged 597 strikeouts a season and by 1960 the number had ballooned up to 801. In 1968 pitching staffs were now averaging 937 whiffs a year. As far as shutouts were concerned, the staff averages were nine in 1950, ten in 1960 and up to 17 by 1968.

The consequence of all this was that the game had reverted back almost to an earlier time when base stealing, manufacturing runs one at a time, less overall run scoring, a shortage of the long ball and much stronger pitching were all prevalent. A perfect example of this was the 1965 World Champion Los Angeles Dodgers, who plated only 608 runners while their pitchers were keeping their opponents to a measly 2.81 earned runs per game. Yet they posted the best record in baseball at 97–65. Don Drysdale recorded 23 victories while his teammate, the venerable Sandy Koufax, compiled a 26–8 mark and registered 382 strikeouts to establish a new single season record.

A starting pitcher for the Detroit Tigers whose productivity fell off sharply in 1964 and 1965 and who was banished to the minors was Phil "The Vulture" Regan. The right-hander came back to the majors with a pitch called a "greaseball," which broke some 15 to 16 inches. The Los Angeles Dodgers, which had picked him up during the off-season, made him a relief pitcher. He was called "The Vulture" by none other than Sandy Koufax for his ability to win games in short relief. Regan was named both "Comeback Player of the Year" and *The Sporting News'* "Fireman of the Year" in 1966 with a 14–1 record, a 1.62 ERA and a league-high 21 saves.

Two years later the Otsego, Michigan–born Regan was traded to the Chicago Cubs and was again named "Fireman of the Year" by leading the league in relief wins with 12 and saves with 25. On July 7 of that year, he was credited with wins in both ends of a double-header.

Still another former starter who became a reliever after his first three full seasons in the majors, Allan "Red" Worthington from Birmingham, Alabama, spent six years with the Giants both in New York and in San Francisco. The right-hander had brief stays with the Boston Red Sox, Chicago White Sox and Cincinnati Reds before finally finding his niche with the Minnesota Twins. In 1965 when the Twins went to the World Series, Worthington won ten games and saved 21. He went on to lead the league in saves with 18 in 1968 and finished his career in the following year with a grand total of 110.

After a single season in the majors with the St. Louis Cardinals in 1968, Wayne Granger was swapped to the Cincinnati Reds along with outfielder and first baseman Bobby Tolan for outfielder Vada Pinson. It was a tremendous bargain for the Reds as the right-hander from Springfield, Massachusetts, promptly set a new record for appearances by a pitcher with 90 in 1969 to go along with a 9–6 won-lost mark, a 2.79 ERA and 27 saves. Also, Pinson only hit .255 for the Cards while Tolan batted .305.

Granger earned *The Sporting News'* "Fireman of the Year" award for his achievements that year and repeated as the winner in 1970 when he established still another new record at the time, this one for saves with 35. The 6'2", 165-pounder, who his teammates said could "shower in a shotgun barrel," led the National League in appearances once again in 1971 with 70. He was with the Minnesota Twins in 1972 and managed to save 19 games for them despite experiencing arm problems. He was never the same after that and drifted from the Twins back to the Cardinals and then on to the Yankees, White Sox, Astros and Montreal Expos during the next four years before retiring after the 1976 season.

Many observers blamed the dominance of pitching in the '60s and into the '70s for the falling attendance in major league baseball. While National League fans numbered a record 15 million in 1966, the league's attendance fell to an alarming 11.7 million in 1968—the "Year of the Pitcher." Bob Gibson of the St. Louis Cardinals posted an unbelievable ERA of 1.12 and struck out 35 Detroit Tigers in three games of that year's World Series. That same season Denny McLain won 31 games for the Tigers, the first pitcher to win over 30 in more than three decades (which no one has done since) and Don Drysdale of the Dodgers established a new record for consecutive shutout innings pitched with 58⅔. Finally, in the 1960s, 15 new pitchers were added to the top 20 all-time strikeout leaders.

The National League was doing far better at the turnstiles than the American League, as exhibited by the totals for the ten-year period (1960–1969) that had the NL besting its counterpart by 16 million more admissions. These figures were attributed mainly to the fact that seven of the ten new ballparks built at the time were in NL cities.

However, it was also strongly felt that something else had to be done, and it was. Apart from five teams bringing in their fences, the pitching mound was lowered from 15 to ten inches in 1969, which helped to make the curveball and the slider less potent weapons for pitchers. Umpires were also instructed to reduce the size of the strike zone. Heretofore the strike zone encompassed an area from the batter's knees to his armpits. Now a strike would be called only if the pitcher could get the ball between the hitter's knees and his belt.

And because relief pitching had now taken on a life of its own, the game's official statistics would include a "saves" category for the first time. Up until then, baseball as an institution had taken almost a grudging view of relievers' contributions to the game. After all, they reasoned, pitchers out of the bullpen could never win 20 games, nor could they accumulate the number of innings that starters produced. But now major league baseball knew it had to come up with something to finally acknowledge how much this game of theirs had really changed.

Consequently, the big leagues turned to Jerome Holtzman, a much respected writer for the *Chicago Sun-Times* at the time, to come up with a formula similar to the one he had been using for almost ten years for *The Sporting News* to evaluate the effectiveness of relief pitchers. It was a category called a "save" and would be an official statistic from then on. When it was first introduced in 1969, a reliever had to come into a game with either the tying or winning run on base or at bat and, of course, complete the game with the lead intact in order to qualify. Unfortunately, the rule was later modified to the point where all a reliever had to do to gain a save was finish a game regardless of what the score was.

This absurd way of evaluating a save was overturned in 1973 when a reliever had to work either at least three innings or enter a game with the tying or winning run on base in order to notch his save. The rule was once again eased in 1975 when it was determined that the tying run could be in the "on deck" circle.

No matter what one may think of the save statistic at any given point in time, it did at long last provide an appreciation for the craft of relief pitching and its overall importance to the game with the impending 70s.

Major league owners also agreed to add two new teams to each league that year: the Montreal Expos (the first ever to play outside of the United States) and the San Diego Padres in the National League and the Kansas City Royals and Seattle Pilots in the American League. Kansas City was awarded a franchise after Charley Finley's Athletics had been granted permission to move to Oakland, California, the year before.

The 162-game season was retained but the leagues were realigned to accommodate the now 24 members. Each league had an East and West division comprising eight teams and the winners of each would meet in a post-season best three of five format to determine which teams would represent their respective leagues in the World Series.

One of the objectives of expansion was to heighten interest in the game by finishing with four winners as opposed to two, and it seemed to work except in the case of Seattle, whose franchise went into bankruptcy after a single season. What it did allow was a move back to Milwaukee (as the Brewers) where baseball had always been popular and which had been abandoned by the Braves for Atlanta in 1966. The Padres were a little on the shaky side as well before Ray Kroc, the president and founder of McDonald's, came to the rescue and bought the team, thereby erasing any threat of a possible move from San Diego.

◆ *Chapter 6* ◆

The Steady Erosion of the Complete Game (1970–1979)

While the narrowing of the strike zone and the lowering of the mound in 1969 did not have an immediate effect in the National League in the 1970s, complete games in the "Senior Circuit" remained in the 22 to 28 percent range, while the American League dropped to an all-time low of 19.6 percent in 1970. However, the NL did take a sudden nose dive in 1977 when it experienced a sharp drop-off to 16.5 percent while the AL experienced an unexpected growth of 27.8 percent in 1971.

Eight years after its last expansion, the majors increased by two additional teams—both in the American League—with the addition of the Seattle Mariners and the Toronto Blue Jays in 1977. Naturally such a move would once again have an effect on the pitching profession, as at least 20 hurlers who probably should have either retired or plied their wares in the minor leagues were in the majors.

Unfortunately, the decade did not produce the type of competitive balance that the owners had anticipated. Despite the fact that the upstart New York Mets surprised the world by winning the NL flag and upsetting the heavily favored Baltimore Orioles in the 1969 World Series, the National League East was dominated by the Pittsburgh Pirates (four division titles) and the Philadelphia Phillies (four division titles), and the Mets only won once more in 1973. In the NL West it was the Cincinnati Reds leading the way with six division titles, the Los Angeles Dodgers with three and the Atlanta Braves, San Francisco Giants and Houston Astros. with one apiece.

Meanwhile in the American League, the Orioles (five division titles) and New York Yankees (three division titles) ruled in the East, while the Oakland A's (five division championships), Kansas City Royals (three division crowns) and Minnesota Twins (two division titles) dominated the West. By finishing second in three other seasons, Baltimore was the winningest club in all of baseball in the '70s.

What is strikingly similar to all of these teams is that not only did they possess outstanding starting pitching, but each was equally strong in the bullpen. Dave Giusti and Goose Gossage of the Pirates, Jim Brewer and Mike Marshall of the Dodgers, Clay Carroll and Pedro Borbon of the Reds, and Gene Garber of the Phillies contributed mightily to the success of their teams in the National League in the period. And Rollie Fingers and Darold Knowles of the A's, Sparky Lyle and Gossage of the Yankees, Paul Lindblad, Al Hrabosky and Tom Burgmeier of the Royals were vital links in the chain of their clubs' successes in the American League.

Ken Sanders, a St. Louis native, began his career in the majors with the Kansas City Athletics in 1964, one of eight different uniforms he was to wear until he left the game in 1976. The right-hander's seven victories and 31 saves in 1971 for the Milwaukee Brewers was good enough to earn him *The Sporting News'* "Fireman of the Year" award that season. The 5'11", 168-pound St. Louis native made 407 relief appearances during his ten years in the big leagues. He was credited with 86 saves and pitched to a very respectable 2.98 ERA.

In a 1972 interview Sanders made some cogent statements about relieving that bear repeating. "The most important thing for a relief pitcher is self-confidence," he stated then. "You have got to go out there feeling you can get any batter out. My best pitch is a sinker and even if I know the batter likes sinkers I am going to pit my strength against his. I also throw a slider, breaking pitch, and change of pace. I do not try to overwhelm the batters as relief men did in the past, the hitters today are too cagey to try that on ... the question I am asked most is would I rather be a starter or reliefer. Frankly, I like relief for I get into more ball games ... I find I do my best pitching when I am tired which is another reason I like to pitch a lot."

Selected by *The Sporting News* as one of major league baseball's 100 greatest players of the twentieth century, Rollie Fingers was neither fish nor fowl when he came to the Oakland A's in 1968. Two years later he had started 19 games and relieved in 26. In the next year there was little doubt what the right-hander from Steubenville, Ohio, would be—a relief specialist. How good the future Hall of Famer was actually to become no one could possibly have imagined. He spent 17 seasons in the big leagues with the A's, Padres and Brewers and there is little doubt that he redefined the role that late inning specialists were to play as the game grew.

Famed for his handlebar moustache that made him look like he just

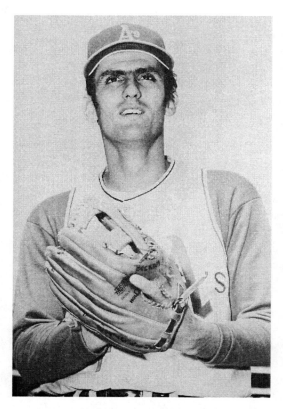

Rollie Fingers was one of only two relievers to be named to *The Sporting News'* "100 Greatest Players of the Twentieth Century" team. (Courtesy Oakland Athletics.)

stepped out of an old silent movie, the 6'4" Fingers depended upon a live fastball with a natural drop, a slider and a crushing forkball (now we call it a split-finger) to close out ballgames. It was during the Fingers era, so to speak, that other teams began developing the same type of put-'em-away killer instinct that he embodied. He always wanted the ball and he seemed to have a rubber arm because he never tired. He played a major role in Oakland's three consecutive World Series triumphs of 1972, 1973 and 1974 as he saved games for outstanding starters like Catfish Hunter, Vida Blue and Ken Holtzman, among others.

Fingers pitched in six of the seven games in the 1972 series and notched two saves and a victory. A year later against the Mets, he pitched 3⅓ hitless innings in the opening game and saved two others while giving up only one unearned run in 3⅓ innings in the series' last game. In 1974, he was credited with a victory in the first game, then saved the third and fourth games to earn the series MVP award.

The 1974 series represented the third straight world championship—all featuring Rollie Fingers—in which not a single complete game was recorded. It signified the role that relief pitching was to play forevermore in the strategy of major league baseball managers and their key to winning games.

The National League saw its pitchers finishing only 439 games that they started, or about one in four. The only reason the trend toward more and more relief pitching in the American League had slowed somewhat was the adoption of the designated hitter rule in 1973 as an attempt to get more offense into the game and broaden its appeal. The older NL opted not to use the DH and in interleague play, including the World Series, it is only used when the AL team is at home.

Fingers wound up in San Diego in 1977 following some contract disputes with A's owner Charley Finley. With the Padres, he led his new league in appearances with 78 and in saves with 35 to gain the NL's "Fireman of the Year" award. Though he eventually made it to the Hall of Fame, Rollie Fingers was 42 votes short in 1991, which prompted the distinguished columnist of *The New York Times,* Dave Anderson, to comment: "Shame on (you). Relief pitchers continue to be the most ignored of the Hall of Fame candidates."

Nobody—but nobody—worked more than Adrian, Michigan's Mike Marshall in the 1970s. Originally signed by the Philadelphia Phillies as a shortstop, he spent four years in the minors for them. Unfortunately, he couldn't play the position well as he led each of the leagues he was in for three years in errors and came up with a chronic back problem. All he knew was that he wanted play and on a regular basis so he switched over to pitching. All the 5'10", 180-pound right-hander accomplished was to wind up setting records for appearances in both the National and American leagues.

Marshall graduated from Michigan State University with three different degrees, including a Ph.D. in kinesiology, which led him to set up his own personal training programs, many of which were at odds with the regimens followed by most of the nine different teams he played for in the decade. For example, he believed that distance running was much better than

Mike Marshall's 106 appearances in relief for the Los Angeles Dodgers in 1974 constitute a record that still stands. (Courtesy St. Louis Globe Democrat Archives at the St. Louis Mercantile Library, University of Missouri–St. Louis.)

sprints for pitchers. He also preached that the right kind of training for certain muscles would enable a pitcher to throw every day. All these philosophical differences did was slow down his own progress.

It also didn't help that he was thoroughly disliked by many of his teammates because he had a habit of talking down to them. He was generally viewed by most everyone as an egomaniac who would give advice freely but would never take it himself. He possessed a wicked screwball but claimed that some of his managers and pitching coaches wouldn't let him throw it. Joe Schultz, his Seattle Pilots manager in the only year of the team's existence in that city—1969—complained about his pick-off move where he turned clockwise instead of vice versa. It was a good one but the controversy got him traded to Houston in 1970.

Not until he reached Montreal in the following year did Marshall start to become a terror out of the bullpen, mainly because his manager there, Gene Mauch, bought into Marshall's philosophies and let him be himself. That season he saved 23 games and followed that up in 1972 with a league-leading 14 wins in relief in 65 games. In 1973, he set a new big league record for appearances with 92 while leading the NL in saves with 31. Coupled with a 14–11 won-lost mark, he won the league's "Fireman of the Year" award.

The Expos felt they needed a center fielder and that perhaps Marshall's arm was about to fall off because of his extensive work, so they traded him to the Los Angeles Dodgers for Willie Davis in 1974. He helped the Dodgers win the NL flag that year and broke his own single season record by appearing in 106 games, an achievement that stills stands as the ultimate for relievers. He also established two new marks when he pitched in 208 relief innings and in 13 consecutive games. The latter record was "tied" by Dale Mohorcic of the Texas Rangers in 1987, although he did it by being brought in to face one batter in a game, the outcome of which was never in doubt. Although the Dodgers were beaten by the A's in five games, Marshall became the first pitcher ever to finish every game of a World Series. He was again voted the NL "Fireman of the Year" in 1974 and won the Cy Young Award as well.

Marshall's fortunes seemingly began to diminish in 1975 when he was afflicted with injuries for most of the year and lost what at the time was a new NL record for losses by a reliever—14. He was shipped out to Atlanta in 1976 but a dispute with another manager, Dave Bristol, got him traded to the Minnesota Twins early in 1978 and his old manager from Montreal, Gene Mauch. The "magic" returned and the following year he and Cleveland's Jim Kern were co-winners of the AL's "Fireman of the Year" award. Along the way, he worked in a new league record, 90 games. He also led the AL in saves with 32 but also lost 14 games in relief to tie the league record.

For the decade, Marshall set the pace in major league baseball in both total relief appearances and victories. He finished in third place in saves for the period and received selections to two NL All-Star teams. Whatever else one may wish to say about the man, his accomplishments speak for themselves and, as the song goes, he did it his way.

Dave Giusti, a 5'10", 175-pound right-hander from Seneca, New York, succeeded Elroy Face as the ace of the Pittsburgh Pirates' bullpen. Originally a starter with the Houston Astros, he was a 15-game winner and struck out 186 batters for them in 1966. After moving over to the Cardinals and following a mediocre season with that club in 1969, he was traded to the Pirates, who inserted him into their bullpen in the following year. He tied for second in the NL in saves in 1970 with nine. In 1971, he was named the NL "Fireman of the Year" when he picked up no fewer than 30 saves with the Buccos. In that season's League Championship Series against the San Francisco Giants, he became the first NL pitcher to appear in every game of a four-game LCS, saving all three of his team's victories. In the World Series against the Orioles that year, which the Pirates won in seven games, he did not surrender a single run and also picked up a save in 5⅓ innings of work.

All told, Giusti pitched in five NLCS for the Pirates throughout the decade. He also made the NL All-Star team in 1973 and had four other double-digit save seasons for Pittsburgh. In 1974 he established the National League record for saves up to that time with 110. He retired in 1977 with a total of 145.

Before Mike Marshall came along, Merced, California, native Jim Brewer was the man the Dodgers called out of the bullpen to save games for them in the early '70s. Thanks to a screwball the southpaw had learned from Warren Spahn in 1964, he averaged better than 19 saves a year for Los Angeles from 1968 to 1973, including a career-high 24 in 1970. Two years later his ERA was a dazzling 1.26 and he averaged but 4.69 hits per nine innings.

Along with Dave Giusti, Brewer was also a member of the 1973 NL All-Star team—another indication at that time of the growing recognition of the value of relievers—and he pitched one shutout inning. His manager, Walter Alston, once said of Brewer: "We've had a lot of great relief pitchers, but I've never seen one better than Brewer."

Brewer gained some unwanted notoriety as a rookie for the Chicago Cubs in 1960 when the volatile Billy Martin, then a player with the Cincinnati Reds, believed the mild-mannered lefty was throwing at him. Martin charged the mound and broke Brewer's jaw. Brewer passed away in 1987 at the age of 50 as a result of an automobile accident.

Someone who may not get the credit he deserves for his 16 seasons in the big leagues is left-hander Darold Knowles, who hailed from Brunswick, Missouri. A fast worker who collected 143 saves, he earned 13 of them as a rookie for the Philadelphia Phillies although, he had never spent a day in the bullpen in the minors. His manager at Philadelphia, Gene Mauch, said of him at the time: "He's got the courage of a daylight burglar." He posted one of the most unusual records in relief ever for the tail-end Washington Senators in 1970, when he lost a major league-record 14 games in relief but saved 27 other games to go along with a scintillating 2.04 ERA.

However, it wasn't until Knowles got to Oakland that he began to be

Sparky Lyle of the New York Yankees was the first American League reliever to ever win the league's coveted Cy Young Award in 1977. (Courtesy St. Louis Globe Democrat Archives at the St. Louis Mercantile Library, University of Missouri–St. Louis.)

noticed. In 1972 he made 54 appearances for the A's and his ERA was a minuscule 1.36. The following year in the World Series against the Mets, he became the only pitcher ever to appear in all seven games, saving two of his team's four wins and not giving up an earned run.

A lefty who pitched in the majors until he was 40 was Tom Burgmeier of St. Paul, Minnesota. Known for his smarts on the mound and slick fielding, he was originally signed by Houston but started his 17-season career in the big leagues with the then–California Angels. It wasn't until he was picked off the 1968 expansion draft by the soon-to-become Kansas City Royals that he achieved some renown. His role there at first was primarily as what would be called today a "middle reliever" or "setup man." When he did become a "closer" in 1971, though, he had a won-lost record of 9–7 with 17 saves and a 1.74 ERA, good enough for second place in the AL relief rankings.

If Rollie Fingers of the Oakland A's wasn't the best fireman of the 1970s, it surely had to be Albert "Sparky" Lyle of the New York Yankees. The left-hander certainly was the best there was in the American

League in 1972, 1974 and 1977. A rarity in that he never started a single game in his 16-year career, Lyle led the AL in saves in both 1972 and 1976 (a pennant-winning year) and became the first reliever in his league to ever win the coveted Cy Young Award in 1977, the same year that the Yankees beat the Dodgers in the World Series. Sparky is reputed to have once said: "Why pitch nine innings when you can get just as famous pitching two?"

A decidedly free spirit, Lyle relied on a hard slider that literally popped into his catcher's glove, but he also had a good fastball and a curve that he could use to give his repertoire some variety. Born in DuBois, Pennsylvania, he actually had some more than decent years with his original team, the Boston Red Sox, before being traded to the Yankees. As a rookie with the Sox in 1967, he pitched a little during the regular season but not at all in the World Series against the Cardinals. The next year he started to come into his own with a 6–1 won-lost record, 11 saves and a 2.74 ERA. He followed that up with 17 saves (good enough for third in the AL) in 1970 and another 16 in 1971, but he was traded to the Yankees just before the start of the 1972 season even-up for first baseman Danny Cater. Many consider it to be the second worst trade in the club's history after the Babe Ruth deal.

It didn't take Lyle long to establish himself as the best in the league, as he recorded 35 saves that year with a 1.91 ERA followed by 27 saves in 1973, a career-low 1.66 ERA in 1974 and a league-best 23 saves in 1976. The following season he won 13 games and saved 26 (second in the league) and won a World Series game over the Dodgers when the Yankees won it all. Selected for the AL All-Star team three times, he also recorded a combined 1.23 ERA in four World Series games in 1976 and 1977.

Following a feud with Yankees management in 1978 after they had signed relievers Goose Gossage and Rawley Eastwick in the off-season, Lyle was traded to the Texas Rangers in a ten-player deal that brought Dave Righetti to the Yankees in 1979. The year before he left the majors, Lyle led the NL in relief wins in 1981 as a member of the Phillies. When he retired, he had accumulated more saves—238—than any left-hander in AL history.

Across town in New York with the Mets, another flaky left-hander named Frank Edwin "Tug" McGraw came up with the battle cry "You Gotta Believe" during the latter stages of the 1973 season. The team actually struggled through the entire season and barely finished the year over .500 but somehow managed to best the Cincinnati Reds in a rugged five-game league championship that carried them into the World Series against the defending World Champion Oakland A's. Again, they nearly over-came all odds before bowing to the talented and more experienced A's in seven games. McGraw appeared in five games in the series, winning one and saving one with a 2.63 ERA.

McGraw came out of the Mets' bullpen 16 times in the final month of the regular season and literally carried the team on his back as he saved 11 of those games and won four others. Before that the club was 6½ games out of first place on August 30 and McGraw was in the middle of a hor-rible 0–6 season, blowing leads and getting pounded as well. Somehow he came to life in September and finished the season with 25 saves.

A barber school graduate, McGraw first showed up at the Mets' spring training base in St. Petersburg, Florida, in 1965 with a handlebar mustache and shoulder-length hair. A clubhouse prankster, he even grew tomatoes in the bullpen. When he was on the hill, though, he possessed a nasty screwball which is, in effect, a reverse curve that breaks in the opposite direction.

McGraw's best year with the Mets was actually 1972 when he had an 11–4 won-lost mark and 27 saves to go along with a nifty 1.70 ERA. He made the NL All-Star team that year and was given credit for his team's win, giving up but one hit and striking out four in two innings.

After being traded to the Philadelphia Phillies in 1975, he was again selected to the NL All-Star team. He helped the Phillies get to the World Series in 1980 against the Kansas City Royals and enjoyed some spectac-ular moments. One came in the fifth game when he struck out the dan-gerous Amos Otis with the bases loaded to preserve a 4–3 victory. In the sixth and deciding game, McGraw pitched himself out of bases-loaded jams in each of the final two innings, which brought the Phillies their first world championship ever. The save was McGraw's third of the series and his five league championship saves is a record.

The Martinez, California, native pitched in the majors for 19 years, making 824 appearances and notching 180 saves. Where did he get the nickname of Tug? His mother said she gave it to him because he used to tug at her when she breast-fed him.

Although not famed for their starting pitching, the Cincinnati Reds' "Big Red Machine" under Manager Sparky "Captain Hook" Anderson (so named because of his constant lifting of his pitchers), still managed to win 108 games in 1975 despite the staff's meager 22 complete games, the low-est in the majors. The team, which went on to win a memorable World Series over the Boston Red Sox that year, had a couple of top-notch reliev-ers on their staff, one of whom was right-hander Clay "Hawk" Carroll. The Clanton, Alabama, native had come up originally through the Braves' chain and had led the National League in appearances with 73 back in 1966. He came to the Reds in the middle of 1968 and never had a losing season. Although his fastball was his "out" pitch, he could also throw a variety of breaking balls effectively. He led the NL in relief wins in 1970 with nine, in both games pitched and saves in 1972 and also repeated as an All-Star that year after having been selected for the team in 1971 as well.

During his eight years in Cincinnati, the durable Carroll pitched in more than 50 games every single season. His Hall of Fame catcher Johnny Bench said of him: "Clay tells you he can do the job and then he goes out and does it." Although the Reds lost the World Series in five games to the Orioles in 1970, he had the team's only victory and appeared in four games without allowing a run. In the now-historic 1975 World Series against the Red Sox, Carroll was the winning pitcher in the seventh and deciding game. Altogether he appeared in 14 games in three World Series for the Reds, picking up two wins, a save and a very respectable 1.33 ERA.

Another capable reliever for the Reds in the '70s was another right-hander, Pedro Borbon out of the Dominican Republic. After spending one season with the California Angels, he was traded to the Reds in the off-season and spent more than nine years of his 12-year career there beginning in 1970. He was credited with 66 saves in the decade, good enough for sixth place during the period. While with the Reds, he appeared in ten games in four National League Championship Series years and picked up a couple of saves, and was called on in another ten games in three different World Series.

Borbon had an ability to warm up and be ready to pitch on a moment's notice. A cockfighting enthusiast, he could also throw a ball farther than most and would delight in throwing strikes to home plate from the outer reaches of center field during batting practice. His best years were in 1973 when he recorded 14 saves and in 1977 when he picked up another 18 to go with a 10–5 won-lost mark.

During his 14 seasons in the American League, Paul Lindblad of Chanute, Kansas, was as competent a left-hander out of the bullpen as anyone in the game. Called upon primarily as a "middle reliever" or "setup man," his best year recordwise was probably 1975 when he won nine games and saved another seven for the AL Western Division champion Oakland A's. The nine victories were the most he ever won in a single season, but he did rack up 64 career saves all told to go along with 68 victories, 61 of which came in relief.

In the A's crucial 11-inning, third game win over the Mets in the 1973 World Series, the left-handed Lindblad pitched two scoreless innings to get the victory. One of the best fielding pitchers in the game during his time, he set a record by not making an error in 385 consecutive appearances on the hill from 1966 to 1974.

John Hiller, who spent his entire 15-year career in the big leagues with the Detroit Tigers, was another very productive left-hander out of the bullpen in the 1970s. Born in Toronto, Ontario, Canada, he came up as a starting pitcher in 1965 but before long was converted into a reliever. A free spirit who paid little attention to the niceties of clean living, he came close to dying in 1971 due to a massive stroke and sat out the entire season. In fact, most thought he would never return to the game, including his general manager, Jim Campbell, who believed Hiller would be posing a danger to himself. But return he did the following year, beginning as a batting practice pitcher in June. Eventually he made it back to the bullpen that season and not only got into 24 games to help his team reach the playoffs but also picked up a win in the ALCS. At the time of his near-miraculous return, the Tigers were scuffling while trying to maintain some air of respectability. Hiller led them back.

One of the most colorful relief pitchers ever was Al "The Mad Hungarian" Hrabosky, whose 13 years in the majors were spent with the St. Louis Cardinals, Kansas City Royals and Atlanta Braves. Famed for his Fu Manchu mustache, long tresses and mean expression, the 5'11", 185-pound lefty would stomp angrily around the back of the mound before delivering the ball. *The Sporting News* chose the Oakland, California, native as their National League "Fireman of the Year" in 1975 off his 13–3, 1.67 ERA, league leading 22-save campaign for the Cardinals. The year before when he was left off the NL All-Star team, Cardinal fans honored him with a "We Hlove Hrabosky Hbanner Hday."

Hrabosky was traded to the Royals in the winter of 1977 and he made three appearances in the American League Championship Series against the Yankees in 1978. He was signed as a free agent by the Braves in 1979 but only seven of his 13-year career 97 saves were made for them.

Colorado Springs, Colorado's Richard "Goose" Gossage had outstanding performances in both the 1970s and 1980s. The hard-throwing right-hander, who grew up in rural areas, would spend hours flinging whatever he could find to throw, usually rocks. Then he would wander on to a nearby park and throw baseballs at anyone daring enough to try and catch them.

He started out in 1972 with the Chicago White Sox, where he teamed with another flamethrower, Terry Forster, to form one of the most feared relieving tandems in baseball history. His first three seasons in Chicago were only so-so but in 1975 he firmly established himself by winning nine and saving a league-high 26 games, finishing second to Rollie Fingers for top relief honors that year. For some reason, the White Sox elected to

make him a starter in 1976, but his 9–17 season ended the year-long experiment and he never started another game.

Gossage was traded along with his bullpen buddy, Terry Forster, to
the Pittsburgh Pirates in 1977 in exchange for Richie Zisk. He had enjoyed
an 11–9, 1.62 ERA and league leading 26-save season there that brought
him the top relief honor in the National League that year. However, Gossage opted to sign on as a free agent with the New York Yankees in the
off-season. He had a phenomenal season there, going 10–11 with 27 saves
in 134 innings, which was the fourth highest on the club's pitching staff.
He helped get the Yankees into the American League Championship Series
by getting Carl Yastrzemski to pop out to end a one-game playoff against
the Red Sox. He was also on the mound for the final outs of both the ALCS
against the Royals and the World Series victory over the Los Angeles
Dodgers. In his three appearances in the 1978 World Series, he won one,
saved another and did not give up an earned run. He was selected to the
All-Star game four times in the decade.

Gossage would scowl at batters but once he went into his windup he
would never look at home plate. The result was that batters were afraid
to dig in against him. All they would see were arms and legs twisted like
a pretzel with his back to the plate and hiding the ball until it came roaring into his catcher's glove at almost a hundred miles an hour. George
Brett described Gossage thus: "There is no one else who can come in and
get out of a bases loaded jam with strikeouts like Gossage can."

Gene Garber called Lancaster, Pennsylvania, his home town. The
5'10", 175-pound right-hander pitched for four different teams during his
19-year career that began with the Pittsburgh Pirates in 1969. A cagey
pitcher who relied on a marvelous changeup to get hitters out, he went
on to become one of the game's all-time leaders in saves, appearances and
relief wins. Famous for an unusual corkscrew delivery, he pitched in 249
games for the Philadelphia Phillies, including a league-leading 71 games
in 1975, where he and Tug McGraw formed an awesome righty-lefty combination. He pitched in five games for the Phillies in the 1976 and 1977
National League Championship Series, picking up a victory in the latter
against the Dodgers.

Garber was traded to the Atlanta Braves in the middle of 1978 for Dick
Ruthven and set team records there with 558 relief appearances and 141
saves. He also established club records for finishing 56 games and recording 30 saves in 1982 to help the Braves get to the National League playoffs.
His contribution also led to his bullpen's winning of that season's outstanding relief staff award from Rolaids.

Garber was on the hill that year when Pete Rose, in his final time at bat, was attempting to extend his 44-game hitting streak. But the sidearmer ended it by striking him out. Garber's display of enthusiasm after getting Rose out drew the wrath of the Cincinnati legend, who said the pitcher acted "like he'd just won the World Series." Like so many other fine relievers both before and after him, Garber lost his consistency and, until he finally left the game in 1988, he was only able to turn in outstanding seasons that year and in 1982 and 1986 after that.

Jim "Emu" Kern, a 6'5" right-hander who got his nickname because some thought he looked and acted like a big bird, came to the major leagues with Cleveland Indians in 1974. After a couple of mediocre years, the offbeat but brilliant short reliever from Gladwyn County, Michigan, could throw hard and was very intimidating to American League batsmen. His breakthrough year was 1977 when he was selected to the league's All-Star team and repeated the honor in both 1978 and 1979.

In August of 1980, the fun-loving Kern was hit in the mouth with a throw from his catcher while gazing up at a foul ball. He fell backwards off the mound as a result of a concussion. Some say the incident, which led to the "temporary amnesia" he said he had, may have been brought on by never missing a chance to inject some humor into a situation.

Averaging 8.6 strikeouts per nine innings, Kern won 41 games and saved 75 through 1979. Though he had lost a league-leading ten games in relief in 1977, by 1979 when he had been traded to the Texas Rangers for Bobby Bonds and Len Barker, he was 13–5 with 29 saves and a 1.57 ERA that won him "Fireman of the Year" co-honors with Mike Marshall. In Texas, he joined another newcomer, Sparky Lyle, who had been dealt over the winter from the Yankees, to form "Craziness, Inc." and the pair of pranksters were infamous for their locker room antics as well as their off-field mishaps.

After spending seven-and-a-half long seasons in the minor leagues, southpaw Gary Lavelle finally received a call to come up the big leagues with the San Francisco Giants in the middle of the 1974 season. The 6'2", 190-pounder from Scranton, Pennsylvania, would go on to spend 11 years in the Bay Area and become the club's all-time leader in games pitched, surpassing Hall of Famer Christy Mathewson. He established single season team records in 1977 for both appearances (73) and saves (20). Seven years later he was the club's all-time leader in both categories. Lavelle led all National League relief pitchers with 13 wins in 1978 and, when he retired in 1987, he ranked third among left-handed relievers in total saves with 136.

Dave LaRoche, like Goose Gossage, was another exceptionally good reliever from Colorado Springs, Colorado. The 6'2", 200-pound left-hander was used almost exclusively out of the bullpen during his 14 seasons in major league baseball. In fact, he lost all six of the decisions in the 15 games he started. As a reliever, though, he made 632 appearances and recorded 126 lifetime saves. He had his best year with the California Angels in 1978 when he saved 25 games and posted a 10–9 record and 2.81 ERA.

LaRoche, who was chosen for his league's All-Star team in 1975, had five other seasons in which he had double-digit saves, including 21 with the Cleveland Indians in 1976. He was famed for a blooper pitch he threw known as "LaLob." Every time he entered a game, the fans would call for him to throw it, much to the chagrin of opposing hitters.

A basketball star at Notre Dame and with two years under his belt as a member of the NBA's Detroit Pistons, Ron Reed was forced to give up the game if the Atlanta Braves were to sign him to a contract. The 6'6", 215-pound right-hander from LaPorte, Indiana, did just that and joined the Braves in 1966 as a starter. He helped the Braves reach the first-ever division playoffs in 1969, albeit a losing one to the New York Mets, and he was the winning pitcher in Hank Aaron's home run record–breaking game on April 8, 1974. But after a season with the St. Louis Cardinals, it wasn't until he was dealt to the Philadelphia Phillies in 1976 that he found his true niche—relief pitching.

After starting more than 200 games in the previous ten years, Manager Danny Ozark put Reed in the bullpen with Tug McGraw and together the pair combined to give the Phillies eight incomparable seasons as a dynamic righty-lefty duo. He had his best year in 1978 when he saved 17 games and posted a 2.23 ERA, including saving the club's division-clinching game. He topped the major leagues in relief victories with 13 in 1979. He retired from baseball at the age of 42 after 19 seasons and at the time ranked 15th on the all-time list for games pitched, with 751. He also recorded 103 career saves.

Today's most popular pitch, the split-fingered fastball, was given its greatest acclaim by Bruce Sutter, who actually came up with it because arm surgery had nearly ended his career even before it began. In 1976 he joined the Chicago Cubs and aided by the team's pitching coach, Mike Roarke, he began using a pitch that literally fell off like a rock just before it reached home plate. Actually, it represented a revival of Elroy Face's forkball with a slight nuance, and is today the most widely used pitch in baseball.

The batters detest the split-fingered fastball for obvious reasons—it's hard to catch up with. Sutter began throwing the former junkball with a snap of his wrist in the same motion as he would deliver a fastball. He developed the knack of making it break off like a curve or a screwball.

Bruce Sutter will always be remembered for introducing the split-fingered fastball, now the game's most popular pitch. (Courtesy St. Louis Globe Democrat Archives at the St. Louis Mercantile Library, University of Missouri–St. Louis.)

Sutter, who like Gene Garber hailed from Lancaster, Pennsylvania, really blossomed in 1977 as he saved 31 games and was almost unhittable while posting a 1.35 ERA thanks to his new-found pitch. That same year on September 8, he achieved a milestone shared by very few pitchers in the history of the game, and that is getting the side out in one inning with nine pitches—all strikes. Fellow relievers Rob Dibble of the Cincinnati Reds and Ugueth Urbina of the Montreal Expos later accomplished the same feat.

In 1979 when he registered 37 saves, Sutter attained the ultimate reward, especially for a reliever, when he was voted the National League's Cy Young Award winner. A member of the National League All-Star teams in 1977, 1978 and 1979, he pitched in the last two and won both without surrendering an earned run. When he retired, he held the NL record for career saves with 300 and had been voted his league's "Fireman of the Year" on four occasions. As his career was drawing to a close, Sutter would throw his now-famed split-fingered fastball nine out of ten times.

Up until his retirement in 1989, Kent Tekulve, who relieved in 1,050 games, held the all-time record for games pitched. Like Sparky Lyle, he never started a single game in the majors. Coming up to the Pittsburgh Pirates in 1974, the right-hander was used largely as a setup man for Goose Gossage and as such attained a 10–1 won-lost mark in 1977. He became the club's closer after Gossage signed with the Yankees that winter.

Tekulve went on to become one of the most successful relievers in baseball history. The bespectacled 6'4" sidearmer, who called Cincinnati, Ohio, his hometown, set a team record for saves in his first year as its closer with 31. Equally mystifying to both left-handed and right-handed batters, he led the National League in appearances in 1978 and 1979. And in the '79 World Series against the Baltimore Orioles, he set a new record for saves with three and struck out ten in 9⅓ innings.

When Mike "Moose" Morgan came into major league baseball with the Oakland A's in 1978 at the tender age of 19 right out of high school, he was heralded as a "phenom" who could possibly be the "second coming" among big league pitchers. Perhaps the Tulare, California (same home town as Olympic champion Bob Mathias), native's career didn't turn out the way a lot of the so-called experts thought it would, but the 6'2", 220-pound right-hander is a survivor and pitched in his fourth decade in the big leagues at the age of 40 in the year 2000.

The A's gave up on Morgan quickly after two sputtering years in the Bay Area and he was shunted to the minors, where he spent the next two years before the New York Yankees took a chance on him in 1982. Pitching for a team that suffered a losing season under three different managers, Morgan had the same kind of year the other starters did—mediocre—winning seven and losing 11 and recording a 4.37 ERA. Traded to Toronto for the 1983 season, he slipped into the third of the 12 different uniforms he would don in his major league career, later on to include the Mariners, Orioles, Dodgers, Cubs, Cardinals, Reds, Twins, Rangers and Diamondbacks.

Morgan's "tour" of both the American and National leagues during the past 20 seasons has always seen him used as a starter who could give his teams lots of innings when healthy. But it wasn't until he reached the twilight of his career after the 1999 season that Manager Buck Showalter of the Arizona Diamondbacks felt that he could use the crafty veteran out of the bullpen as both a long reliever and a closer in certain situations.

One of the best managers in the '70s or, for that matter, of any era, was Earl Weaver of the Baltimore Orioles. A man who could never be accused of trying to win a popularity contest among either his players or the opposition, Weaver was a master strategist. "I hate to let a starting pitcher, from the seventh inning on, throw to the winning run," he once said. "This, of course, doesn't apply to one-run games, where, if a man singled or walked, the next man up would be the winning run. But if we're in the seventh two runs up and our pitcher has worked hard and two men get on, then I won't let him work to the winning run at the plate.

"I remember once we were playing the Yankees in the Stadium. It was the first game of a double-header. [Jim] Palmer was pitching. We were ahead 4–2 in the ninth. They got a man on, then Jim retired two, but then they got another man on. Everything was ripe for me to take Jim out. Not only was he obviously tiring, but Jake Gibbs was the batter, a left-handed pull-hitter in a stadium with the shortest right field fence down the line. But for some crazy reason, I decided to let Jim continue. Conscious of the home-run situation, he worked too cautiously and walked Gibbs.

"Then I made the move, obviously too late. Pete Richert got the job of pitching to Roy White, who probably hasn't made the last out of any ball game he's ever played in. White singled for two runs, Richert struck out the next man, Bobby Murcer, on three pitches, but we lost the game in the fourteenth. After the game, Palmer kidded me, 'What's the matter ... get polio?' That shook me up so much that Ralph Houk and I ended up using twenty-one pitchers during both games of the double-header."

Weaver believed in going with his starters for as long as possible while he waited for the three-run homer or the big inning to erupt. An example of his reluctance to remove his starters can be seen in the 1979 season when he used only 167 relievers in 159 games, by far the fewest of any team in baseball. Other American League teams were averaging 219 relievers over the course of the season.

The 1970s could easily be characterized as a breakthrough year for relief pitchers. Managers had no hesitation about calling down to the pen anytime the club was in trouble to avert a possible impending disaster. This decade, more than any other up to now, established relievers as important cogs in the wheel of a team's success. Many of them hopped over the fence now and ran in to a musical theme that identified them from other players, as Sparky Lyle did to "Pomp and Circumstance." The business of relief pitching had truly come of age.

♦ *Chapter 7* ♦

Middle Relievers, Setup Men and Closers (1980–1989)

By the time the 1980s arrived, the business side of the game had begun to occupy center stage, much to the displeasure of the fans. Salaries hastened by the now-booming free agent market had catapulted to a point where the owners felt they had to draw a line in the sand, arguing that they would no longer allow players to depart teams unless they were compensated. Although a last-minute strike was averted on the eve of the 1980 season, there was no such luck in the middle of June of the following year and the players walked out in the midst of what was a record year in attendance and interest.

Thereafter the longest strike in the history of professional sport took 50 days to settle and on July 31, 1981, a compromise of sorts was reached and major league baseball resumed. Ownership accepted a modified compensation plan and agreed to let players not yet eligible for free agency in an upcoming season file for arbitration and have an independent arbitrator decide what their salaries should be.

When all was said and done, though, the image of the game had been tarnished and a great many fans decided to boycott the remainder of the season. The tensions between the owners and the players' union would not disappear, however. These storm warnings did not bode well for either the short- or long-term future of major league baseball, and everybody knew it.

On the field of play, the decade of the '80s saw the number of complete games almost vanish, particularly in the National League, where it fell to 9.7 percent by 1987. Although the exclusive use of the designated hitter by the American League kept its complete game percentage above

20 percent early in the period, it, too, dropped down to 11.7 percent by 1989.

The AL was now perceived as the "offensive" league while the NL was thought to be the "pitching" league and each had the records to prove it. For example, every year since 1973 when the DH was created, the AL's ERA and batting average figures exceeded the NL's. Two years—1988 and 1985—saw dramatic evidence of this. In 1988, AL hitters averaged .259 versus the NL's .248, and in 1985 the ERA in the NL was 3.59 while the AL's was 4.15.

The long ball was now more prominent than ever and the AL led the way, averaging some 2,000 a year from 1980–1987. In the last three years of that span—1985–1987—the league broke its own record each year by slamming 2,178 in 1985, 2,240 in 1986 and 2,634 in 1987. The NL, while breaking its own record, which had been established in 1970, chimed in with 1,824 blasts in 1987. Twenty-eight players hit more than 30 homers that season, 20 of them in the AL. Rookie Mark McGwire of the Oakland A's was the league leader with 49, to set still another record for a first-year player.

In the year that followed, a timely rule change redefined the strike zone and helped to squelch the home run explosion. By 1990 a record number of no-hitters—nine—were hurled in the big leagues, a figure that matched a total produced in some earlier decades. Nolan Ryan was adding to his massive strikeout aggregates by fanning another 232 batters and Bobby Thigpen of the White Sox set the all-time saves record by registering an unheard of 57, a mark that still holds sway and may not be in danger of falling anytime soon. The self-styled "Nasty Boys"—Rob Dibble, Norm Charlton and Randy Myers of the Cincinnati Reds—spearheaded a bullpen crew under the direction of first-year skipper Lou Piniella that notched 42 saves and went on to win the World Series over the defending champion Oakland A's.

The arguments over the use of the designated hitter raged on throughout the 1980s and focused upon whether or not a big leaguer could be considered a complete player if he didn't hit, and also that the rule virtually took the strategy of the game out of the hands of the manager. Baseball purists were—and still are—of the opinion that a manager should have to wrestle with a decision on when or not to remove a pitcher, and the designated hitter rule suppresses his ability to strategize at a key point in a ballgame.

Yet no less an authority than Bill James in his *Baseball Historical Abstract* claims that by taking such incompetent hitters as pitchers usually are out of the lineup, managers are not forced into a bunch of obvious moves that really don't amount to options for them at all. In James' view, a DH gives the manager many more choices by allowing him to decide whether or not to bunt, or to give a "steal," "swing away" or "hit-and-run" sign.

So with offense as big a factor in the majors as it was in the '80s, managers set up their pitching staffs to counteract the trend thus: typically five starters, two middle relievers, two setup men and a closer more often than not formed most of the staffs. It was becoming more and more apparent that one of the primary methods available to managers to achieve some balance between pitching and hitting was going to be found in the bullpen.

Managers lamented the fact that they were being forced to use pitchers who just weren't equipped to achieve success in the big leagues. Pitchers on the other hand complained that the rules were now tipped in favor of the hitters. In order to help their cause, some pitchers were being accused more frequently of using illegal pitches like spitters and scuffed-up baseballs.

Meanwhile, Goose Gossage, Bruce Sutter, Rollie Fingers and Kent Tekulve continued to effectively put out fires through most of the '80s while new stars like Dan Quisenberry, Jeff Reardon, Lee Smith and Dennis Eckersley began to arrive on the scene.

Gossage came back from a long stretch on the disabled list in 1979, which resulted from a fight in the shower with Yankees' teammate Cliff Johnson, to save a career-high 33 games in 1980. In the strike-shortened 1981 season, he was equally impressive as he gave up only 22 hits in 47 innings and struck out 48 while picking up 20 saves. In the playoffs that year, he saved all three wins against the Milwaukee Brewers in the ALCS and both Yankee victories over the Dodgers in the World Series.

After two more years in New York, where he compiled 30 additional saves in 1982 and a 13–5 won-lost mark to go along with 22 saves in 1983, he joined the San Diego Padres as a free agent in 1984. All he did was help his new team reach its first World Series ever that year and rack up 72 more saves for them in his first three years there. He was selected for the All-Star game five times during the '80s.

Bruce Sutter remained a dominant pitcher after he was traded to the St. Louis Cardinals from the Chicago Cubs for the 1981 season. In his first two years in the "Mound City," he led the NL in saves with 36 and 35 respectively. He worked in four games of the 1982 World Series against the Milwaukee Brewers, winning one and saving a pair for the eventual world champions.

Sutter's save total fell off to 21 the following year but he achieved a career-high 45 in 1984. He signed a gargantuan contract with the Atlanta

Braves that winter and had a good year with them (23 saves) in 1985, but was plagued by a shoulder injury that caused him to miss most of the 1986 season and all of 1987. He came back in 1988 as his team's closer and attained his three hundredth and final career save until shoulder problems and a battle with Bell's palsy forced him into retirement. He was chosen for the league's All-Star team three times during the period: 1980, 1981 and 1984.

The irrepressible Rollie Fingers left the San Diego Padres after the 1980 season to return to the American League with the Milwaukee Brewers. In strike-shortened 1981, he was the first reliever to ever win both the Cy Young and MVP awards in the same year, as he registered 28 saves along with a minuscule 1.04 ERA. On the strength of that season, and although now 35 years of age, he won his fourth "Fireman of the Year" award as well.

While he saved another 29 games in the following year, he was forced to miss the World Series and the entire 1983 season due to tendonitis. He came back the following year and recorded 23 saves by the month of July but a herniated disk ended not only his season but his career. He was elected to the Hall of Fame in 1992.

Kent Tekulve led all pitchers in appearances during the 1980s with 687. He took the top spot in appearances in 1982 with 85 and in relief wins with 12 for the Pittsburgh Pirates. By the time he was traded to the Philadelphia Phillies in 1985, he had become the all-time saves leader for the Pirates with 158 and was second on the club only to Elroy Face in games pitched with 722. He ultimately broke Face's NL record of games pitched (846) on September 16, 1986.

After moving on to Philadelphia he was made the setup man for the Phillies for the new kid on the block, Steve Bedrosian, and became the first pitcher in his league to record three 90-appearance seasons by getting into 90 in 1987. He had appeared in 91 games in 1978 and 94 games in 1979 while a member of the Pirates. Also at the age of 40 in 1987, he earned the distinction of being the oldest pitcher to ever lead the NL in appearances. He went on to break Sparky Lyle's major league record for career games pitched without ever having started a game at 943. He was very instrumental in helping the team's new closer—Bedrosian—achieve the Cy Young award. Following his release from the Phillies after the 1988 season, he joined the Cincinnati Reds and promptly broke Hoyt Wilhelm's record for relief appearances. With no significant role in sight for a losing team, he decided to retire in the middle of the season rather than try to hang on and exceed Wilhelm's record for total appearances.

From the time he joined the Kansas City Royals in 1979, Dan Quisenberry's role was never considered to be anything but coming out of the bullpen. A master of control to go along with a whip-like submarine delivery, the right-hander kept opposing batters off stride by employing a sharp-breaking slider. Amazingly, he never gave up more than 15 passes a year despite the fact that he pitched in more than 125 innings a season five times.

As he wound up, "Quis" would twist and bend down so that the ball would come within five or six inches of the ground before he would let it go. He was not considered a hard thrower as his primary submarine delivery would come in at about 80 mph. In addition to his sinker, he would also throw a lot of junk *à la* Eddie Lopat of years past. Always the joker, Quisenberry once said of his pitching: "I found a delivery in my flaw." He also is reputed to have stated: "I have seen the future. It is much like the present, only longer."

It was evident from the start of his career that Quisenberry would become one of the best relievers in the game when in his first full year— 1980—he would win 12 games while compiling 33 saves (tying for the AL lead) in 75 games. He was to lead the AL in saves five times, including a record-breaking 45 in 1983, following up with 44 more in the next year. He was named his league's "Fireman of the Year" by *The Sporting News* in five different years.

For the decade, Quisenberry ranked second in saves and appearances and sixth in wins among all relief pitchers. Three times he led the AL in appearances—1980, 1983 and 1985. After winning the Rolaids Relief Award in 1982, he quipped: "I want to thank all the pitchers who couldn't go nine innings and Manager Dick Howser who wouldn't let them." He was selected for the league's All-Star team three times and pitched in two World Series, winning two and saving another. The much beloved Quisenberry passed away in 1999 from cancer at the much-too-young age of 46.

No one had more saves in the 1980s than Pittsfield, Massachusetts, product Jeff "The Terminator" Reardon, who pitched for the New York Mets, Montreal Expos and Minnesota Twins. After a good year with the Mets in 1980, he was traded to the Expos in late May of the following year for outfielder Ellis Valentine. From 1982 to 1988, the hard-throwing right-hander was the only pitcher to record 20 or more saves for his teams in each of those years. The University of Massachusetts graduate led all relief pitchers in the big leagues in saves in 1985 with 41 for the Expos.

Early in 1987, Montreal traded Reardon to Minnesota, a team with a bunch of good position players but no stopper in the bullpen. He paid immediate dividends for the Twins by becoming their MVP and leading them to a world championship over the Atlanta Braves in Tom Kelly's rookie year as manager. To get to the World Series, he had saved two games and won another in the ALCS against the Detroit Tigers. During the regular season, his fastball helped him strike out more batters than innings pitched.

Picked for three All-Star teams, Reardon rarely if ever pitched more than one inning as his team's closer. From 1986 to 1988, he registered more than 30 saves each year, winding up with 367, good enough for fourth on the all-time list.

Reardon loved pitching in critical situations. If the game was on the line, so much the better. Like a lot of relief pitchers, he had some unorthodox habits. One of them was carrying around a lead ball about the size of a softball so that when he entered a game the baseball would feel that much lighter. Although his teammates would kid him about this by calling the object his "pet," Reardon would pay them no heed and just go out and get the job done on a consistent basis.

There was nobody who could appear more menacing on the mound than the 6'6", 245-pound Lee Smith, who debuted with the Chicago Cubs in 1980. Possessor of a 95-mph fastball, the Shreveport, Louisiana, native chalked up 29 saves to lead the National League in 1983. Up until 1988, the right-hander saved at least 30 games a year for the Cubs to join both Dan Quisenberry and Jeff Reardon as the only relievers in that select group.

In 1987—his final season in Chicago—Smith was the winning pitcher in the All-Star game after pitching three shutout innings for the NL. His 180 saves for the Cubs remain the club's tops in that category. Rumors that his bulk was affecting his knees led to a trade to the Boston Red Sox for the 1988 season. After a rocky start, he proceeded to record 29 saves, a 2.80 ERA (his best since 1983) and 96 strikeouts in 83⅔ innings. During the 1980s, he was third in saves and fifth in relief appearances among all relievers.

After spending the first 12 seasons of his career as a starting pitcher, it wasn't until he returned to his home town of Oakland, California, that Dennis Eckersley became a relief pitcher. And he wasn't exactly enamored with the prospect either. After all, he had pitched a no-hitter for the Cleveland Indians in 1977, won 20 games for the Boston Red Sox in 1978 and recorded more than 150 victories as a starter overall, and now Manager Tony LaRussa was asking him to pitch out of the bullpen. Yet for all his success as a starter, his pitching had started a downward trend in 1980 due in part to a series of nagging injuries. His ERA ballooned up to 4.28 that season and by 1984 it had escalated to 5.01. He was finally traded to the Chicago Cubs and, after a poor 1986 season there, he found himself in Oakland in 1987.

The wild-maned Eckersley had a cockiness and swagger about him that LaRussa felt would make him the ideal closer for the A's. Plus he always had great control and, with the ability to enter a game with the outcome on the line and throw strikes, the possibilities intrigued both LaRussa and pitching coach Dave Duncan. The latter had this to say about him: "'Eck' always throws strikes and he has the heart of a giant. His natural response is to challenge a crisis head-on. That's what makes him such a great reliever." After he bought into the idea, Eckersley, who earlier had conquered alcoholism and numerous confrontations with his opponents because of his flamboyance on the mound, went on to become one of the greatest relievers of them all.

After winning more than 150 games as a starter, Dennis Eckersley reluctantly became one of baseball's greatest relievers ever, thanks to the urging of his Oakland manager, Tony LaRussa. (Courtesy Oakland Athletics.)

The A's won three division championships and a World Series from 1988 to 1990 with Eckersley's better-than-average fastball and slippery slider showing the way. He gained *The Sporting News* selection as AL "Fireman of the Year" in 1988 but the year merely served as a steppingstone to what lay ahead for the 6'2", 190-pounder in the '90s.

One of Eckersley's prime setup men was a former University of Tennessee All-American first baseman, Rick Honeycutt, who began his long major league career in 1977 with the Seattle Mariners as a starting pitcher. After four uneventful seasons in the northwest, the left-hander was part of a multi-player deal that brought him to the Texas Rangers in 1981. He had a good year there in his first full season and then fell off in 1982. However, he won the AL's "Comeback of the Year" award in 1983 and was leading the league in ERA when he was dealt to the Los Angeles Dodgers just before the trading deadline.

A control pitcher, Honeycutt continued his role in the starting rotation for the Dodgers until 1987 when he was struggling through a 2–12 season and was shipped out to Oakland in an even-up trade for Tim Belcher. He found his niche for the A's under Manager Tony LaRussa and the watchful eye of the pitching coach, Dave Duncan. He came in to his own as the setup man for Dennis Eckersley and in 1988 he was credited with the win in the first game of the ALCS and picked up yet another one in the second game of the World Series.

Another starting pitcher who achieved below average results until being sent to the bullpen was still another native Californian, Mark Davis. He joined the Philadelphia Phillies in 1980 after an outstanding year with their AAA farm club in the Eastern League. The southpaw was traded to the San Francisco Giants before the 1983 season where he remained a starter. He actually was the Giants' opening day pitcher in 1984, but after he went on to post a 5–17 season, he spent most of 1985 and 1986 in the club's bullpen. He struck out an average of more than one hitter an inning there but only saved 11 games. It's reported that in a game against the New York Mets in 1985 he threw a curveball 23 times in a row.

The Giants put Davis back in their starting rotation at the beginning of the 1987 season and he was 4–5 before moving on to the San Diego Padres in July as part of a seven-player exchange. The trade jump-started his entire career as the club immediately made him their closer and he was virtually unhittable in his new role. He was his team's only All-Star selection that year, finishing with 28 saves, a sparkling 2.01 ERA—his best ever—and 102 strikeouts in 98⅓ innings.

A reliever with an effective sinker is worth his weight in gold for a bullpen and such a pitcher was right-hander Greg Minton of the San Francisco Giants. From 1980 to 1984, the Lubbock, Texas native, was one of the NL's premier relievers, saving at least 19 games a year for the occupants of windblown Candlestick Park. Drafted first by the Kansas City Royals, he made his way to the Bay Area via a trade for catcher Fran Healy while still in the minors. His first full season with the Giants was in 1979 and he made a name for himself by attaining a 1.80 ERA in 46 appearances.

As the club's new "go-to" guy in 1980, Minton saved 19 games. In the next two years, he finished second in the NL in saves to Bruce Sutter with 21, in the strike-shortened 1981 season, and 30 in 1982. He also pitched for the NL All-Star team in the latter season. In the following year, he teamed with Gary Lavelle to become the first NL relief tandem ever to notch 20 saves each in a single year. After losing his closer's job in 1985 and having elbow surgery two years later, the Giants let him go and he signed on with California Angels at the age of 35. He saved 10 games for his new team in 1987 and stayed with the Angels through the remainder of the decade and pitched well for them.

One of the hardest-throwing relievers in the 1980s was right-hander Jay Howell, a 6'3", 200-pounder from Miami, Florida. Howell came up with Cincinnati in 1980 and moved on to the Chicago Cubs, not exactly setting the world on fire in either city. He joined the New York Yankees in 1982 and by 1984 he was leading the American League in average strikeouts per inning. He was part of a seven-player deal with the Oakland A's that brought Rickey Henderson to the Yankees in 1985. It was in the Bay Area that Howell began to hit his stride and by 1989 he enjoyed his best season yet by registering a 5–3 won-lost mark, a 1.58 ERA and 28 saves.

Like a number of relievers who had enjoyed success during their careers, Howell suffered from inconsistency as well. In 1983 and 1987, he was hammered pretty well from time to time and his ERA climbed above 5.00 in each of those years. He was even tagged with the loss in the 1987 All-Star game. He was also a member of the AL All-Star team representing the A's in 1985 as well as the NL All-Star team for the Los Angeles Dodgers in 1989.

After spending 7½ years in the minor leagues, Steve "Bedrock" Bedrosian was easily one of the top relievers of the 1980s, working his way up from being named *The Sporting News'* "Rookie Pitcher of the Year" in 1982 to achieving the National League Cy Young Award in 1987. Strangely enough, while in the minors, the right-hander only appeared once as a relief pitcher. The Methuen, Massachusetts, native arrived in the majors with the Atlanta Braves in 1981 with a hard slider and an excellent changeup to go along with a 96-mph high, hard one. He was urged to throw as hard as he could for as long as he could and was used in middle relief at first. As a rookie, he led all league relievers with 123 strikeouts, a 2.42 ERA and 11 saves.

Bedrosian's early success continued in the next two seasons but the Braves decided he should go back to his roots and become a starter in 1985. Unfortunately, he never completed a single one of his 37 starts on the way to a disappointing 7–15 season, earning him a ticket out of town to Philadelphia the following year. The Phillies quickly made him their ace out of the bullpen and he responded by securing 29 saves for them in 1986 and a major league high of 40 saves in 1987 to win the Cy Young Award. He was also selected to the NL All-Star team that year. At one point in the season, Bedrosian registered a record-setting 13 saves in succession.

After missing the first month of the season in 1988 due to a bout with walking pneumonia, Bedrosian still came on to save 28 of the Phillies' 65 wins that year. The Giants wanted him for their pennant drive in 1989 and sent three youngsters to Philadelphia for him. He did assist the Giants in reaching the World Series and pitched for them in the earthquake-delayed loss to their Bay Area rival Oakland A's.

Bedrosian went to the Minnesota Twins in 1991 and became a free agent in 1992 but was not signed. When it looked like his career was just about over, he rejoined the Atlanta Braves and became the team's middle inning reliever on its way to the NL's Western Division championship.

Now pitching in his fourth decade is left-hander Jesse Orosco, who first came up to the big leagues with the New York Mets back in 1979. Currently the all-time record holder in games pitched (1,090 at the start of the 2000 season), his three wins and four shutout appearances in the 1986 NLCS for the Mets in their victory over the Houston Astros in six games is probably the highlight of his remarkable career. He will always be remembered for striking out Kevin Bass in the 16th inning with the tying and winning runs on base in one of the most memorable playoff games ever contested.

Orosco first became the Mets' closer in 1983 when Jerry Koosman wanted to go back to his home state of Minnesota to pitch for the Twins. Combining a fastball that really moved with a so-called "backdoor" slider, he saved 13 games and won an equal number while recording a 1.47 ERA and making the All-Star team. He reached a career-high total of 31 saves the following year and made the All-Star team again. The southpaw was forced to share time as the team's closer in 1985 when right-handed sinker-baller Roger McDowell was brought in by Manager Davey Johnson to try and get groundouts on grass. Orosco, basically a flyball pitcher, was used mostly on artificial surfaces within more spacious NL ballparks.

After being rumored to have a tender elbow and suffering through a 3–9, 4.44 ERA season in 1987, Orosco was traded to the Los Angeles Dodgers. His nine saves that year helped the Dodgers get into the playoffs. He wasn't particularly effective against his old team, the Mets, in the NLCS and wasn't used at all in the series. The following year he signed on with the Cleveland Indians and became an efficient setup man for closer Doug Jones in 1989.

The aforementioned Jones did not get to the major leagues until he was 30 years of age. After he languished in the Milwaukee Brewers system for some seven years, the Cleveland Indians took a chance on the right-hander in 1985 and placed him in AA ball. While recuperating from some shoulder miseries, he came up with a new pitch called a "circle change" that acts much the same as a screwball.

Brought up to the big club in 1987, he was used sparingly as a middle reliever and setup man at first. The following year, he made his presence felt throughout baseball by reeling off 15 consecutive saves and breaking the Tribe record for saves in a single season. Jones continued to pitch effectively into the new millennium for the Oakland A's at the age of 43.

Another big—6'5"—left-handed reliever who continues to toil out of the bullpen today, as he has his entire career, is Gary, Indiana's Dan Plesac. The North Carolina State University product was thrown into the breach almost immediately in his rookie year and responded by picking up 14 saves out of 17 chances with a 2.97 ERA in 51 games. Between 1987 and 1989, he saved 86 games and his ERA for those years was 2.61, 2.41 and 2.35 respectively.

During his 15 years in the big leagues, Plesac has also worked for the Chicago Cubs, Pittsburgh Pirates, Toronto Blue Jays and Arizona Diamondbacks. He has not been used as a closer since 1996 when he saved 11 games for the Pirates, but the man who has appeared in as many as 78 games (in 1998 with the Blue Jays) and never less than 44 has always given his teams innings as either a middle reliever or setup man.

Like Dennis Eckersley, San Jose, California's Dave "Rags" Righetti was another starting pitcher who railed against going to the bullpen when the idea first surfaced in 1984. Like Eckersley, he, too, had pitched a no-hitter—a Fourth of July game against the Boston Red Sox in Yankee Stadium in 1983. The left-hander had been acquired from the Texas Rangers (for whom he never pitched) in the Sparky Lyle deal following the 1978 season.

Righetti started three games for the big club in 1979 but was sent back to the minors and did not make it back to the majors until 1981. He promptly won the AL's "Rookie of the Year" honors that season. He also pitched well in the post-season, winning a pair of games against the Milwaukee Brewers and another over the Oakland A's. But despite his success, the Yankees needed someone to replace Goose Gossage as their closer and Manager Yogi Berra selected the reluctant Righetti for the job. All Righetti did was to go out and prove Berra right by saving 31 games that year and another 29 in 1985 to go along with 12 victories.

And if that wasn't enough, he set a new single season record for saves in the major leagues with 46 in 1986. That year he converted on 29 of his final 30 save opportunities, which included both ends of a season-ending double-header against the Red Sox. The new mark eclipsed the old record of 45 saves held by both Dan Quisenberry and Bruce Sutter. Now the all-time saves leader in Yankees history, Righetti ranks second in games pitched and 12th in strikeouts for the Bronx Bombers. During the 1980s, he also pitched in two All-Star games for the American League. As the current pitching coach for the San Francisco Giants, he is credited with turning the fortunes of that team's staff completely around.

Up until 1984, the mustachioed Willie Hernandez had been considered both a reliable reliever and spot starter for the Chicago Cubs and Philadelphia Phillies. Prior to being traded to the Detroit Tigers in the spring of that year, he had attained a modest 23 saves in seven big league seasons. But under the tutelage of new manager Sparky "Captain Hook" Anderson, the Puerto Rican–born left-hander became the premier closer in the American League as the Tigers went on to win the world championship.

Few could have imagined the kind of year that Hernandez and his deadly screwball would go on to have in Detroit: a 9–3 won-lost mark, a 1.92 ERA, 32 saves in 33 opportunities, 80 appearances and 112 strikeouts in 140 innings. It was the stuff that dreams are made of, as Hernandez was rewarded with both the MVP and Cy Young honors in the American League. The post-season was equally compelling. He saved three games in three appearances, including two in the World Series.

The following year, Hernandez came back to become the first Tiger reliever in the team's long and storied history to achieve successive 30-save seasons. However, the three-time AL All-Star lost ten games in 1985 and his insistence on now wanting to be called "Guillermo" did not sit well with the home town fans. Eventually, his role as the team's closer was usurped in 1987 and 1988 by Mike Henneman.

Henneman, a rookie in 1987, picked right up where Hernandez left off as the Tiger, closer going 11–3 and notching seven saves. He was also instrumental in Detroit's successful chase of the front-running Toronto Blue Jays for the AL's Eastern Division title that year. His two wins plus a save helped the Tigers pass Toronto to capture the flag. For his role, he received the AL's "Rookie Pitcher of the Year" designation by *The Sporting News*.

In 1988, he saved ten games in the first month but experienced arm problems that forced the Tigers to place him on the disabled list. He still finished up the season with a 9–6 won-lost record, a 1.87 ERA and 22 saves. The following year he was 11–4 with a 3.70 ERA and only eight saves, but his best years still lay ahead of him.

Now pitching in his third decade, Brooklyn's John Franco became the all-time left-handed saves leader (416) in the big leagues in 1999. Drafted by the Los Angeles Dodgers (for whom he never pitched), he was in the minor leagues when he was traded to the Cincinnati Reds in 1982. He made it to the majors in 1984 and registered an impressive 2.64 ERA in 54 appearances.

In 1985, he became the setup man for closer Ted Power and led the NL in relief wins with 12 while saving 12 other games. In 1986 Franco was anointed the Reds' closer himself and went to save 29 games that year and followed up with 32 more in 1987 and 39 in 1988. He was a three-time All-Star in the National League during the '80s, having been named to the 1986, 1987 and 1989 teams.

Dave Smith, a durable right-hander from Richmond, California, pitched for the Houston Astros throughout the '80s. From 1985 to 1989, he never saved fewer than 24 games. His career-high year came in 1986 when he picked up 33 as his team vied with the New York Mets for the NL pennant. He was also selected for his league's All-Star team that year. In between he sandwiched in two other fine years—1985, when he placed third among all NL relievers and 1987, when he finished second.

Before John Franco was to join the New York Mets in 1990, southpaw Randy Myers from the state of Washington was their closer. Myers pitched sparingly in 1985 and in the world championship season of 1986 but came on to record six saves in six opportunities in 1987. From then on he was the one Manager Davey Johnson called on to stifle the opposition late in the game. In 1988 he saved 26 of 28 games and posted a glittering 1.72 ERA. The following season he was almost as good, registering 24 saves out of 26 chances and recording a 2.35 ERA. With John Franco on the way home to New York from Cincinnati, Myers went in the opposite direction to join the Redlegs' "Nasty Boys."

Following two part-time and one full-time season for the Texas Rangers, right-hander Tom "The Terminator" Henke was claimed as compensation by the Toronto Blue Jays who had lost Cliff Johnson via a free agency signing. Once he had arrived north of the border in 1985, the 95-mph fireballer was sent to his new team's AAA farm club in Syracuse and eventually brought up at mid-year. In his first month, he picked up eight saves, which was only three fewer than any Toronto reliever had recorded before 1985. He went on to save 13 altogether out of 15 chances that year in only half a season.

In 1986, Henke, who also had a wicked forkball to go along with an awesome fastball, set a new club record for saves with 27, which he broke the following year when he led all American League relievers with 34. That season the Kansas City, Missouri, native permitted fewer hits (5.9) and registered more strikeouts (12.3) per nine innings than any other pitcher in the league. A member of the AL All-Star team in 1987, he pitched in a total of six games in both the 1985 and 1989 ALCS, winning two of them. He stands at Number 7 on the all-time saves list with 311, one ahead of Goose Gossage.

Arcadia, California's Todd Worrell was the first round draft pick of the St. Louis Cardinals after attaining All-American status in college. However, the 6'5" right-hander who fired a 93 to 95 mph fastball accompanied by a hard slider had been somewhat of a dud in the minors as a starter. Consequently, the team moved him into their bullpen during his first season in the majors late in 1985 and he succeeded almost immediately by posting three relief wins and five saves in just 17 games. He also tied a World Series record that year by striking out six consecutive Kansas City Royals batters in the fifth game.

Worrell came close to becoming a unanimous choice the following season for "Rookie of the Year" by saving 36 games, a National League record for a first-year pitcher. In 1988, he became the only pitcher in history to save 30 or more games in his first three seasons. At the same time he was the only Cardinal pitcher ever to record three 30-save years.

A pitcher with a tremendous fastball who didn't always know where it was going was the left-hander Mitch "Wild Thing" Williams. Originally with the Texas Rangers, Williams pitched with a lunging follow-through that would leave him almost on the ground and unable to field his position. Nevertheless, he always was ready to take the ball and registered 80 appearances for the Rangers in 1986. He also appeared in another 85 games for Texas the following year but was only able to save 14 games over those two seasons. He achieved better success for the Rangers in 1988 by improving his control and notching 18 saves. His three years in Texas left him with 220 walks in 275 innings and the Rangers finally decided to give up on him.

It wasn't until after he was traded to the Chicago Cubs in the off-season as part of an eight-player deal that Williams broke through and had his best season ever in 1989, when he saved 36 games. He was extremely popular with Cub fans, who would serenade him with their version of the rock standard "Wild Thing" every time he entered a game.

Auburn University's Gregg Olson was not only the fourth draft pick overall in 1988 by the Baltimore Orioles but obtained a $200,000 bonus in the bargain. He was pressed into service with them immediately. The following year the Scribner, Nebraska, native had a scintillating season out of the pen, saving 27 of 29 games with a microscopic 1.69 ERA in 64 games. He followed that up with another year in which he appeared in 64 games, slamming the door shut on the opposition in 37 of 42 game-saving opportunities.

During his 13-year career, the 6'4" right-hander has also spent time with the Atlanta Braves, Cleveland Indians, Kansas City Royals, Detroit Tigers, Houston Astros and Minnesota Twins. With the expansion Arizona

Diamondbacks since 1998, Manager Buck Showalter used Olson in a variety of ways including closing, as a setup man and in middle relief.

What distinguished the business of baseball in the 1980s were the changes in ownership. Fourteen new owners took over in this decade alone and all of them had made their fortunes outside of the game. It appeared that most of them looked on their franchises primarily as a hobby and virtually as a public relations vehicle that would make them better known to the general public.

Since most of these new owners felt it was incumbent upon them to build winning teams instantaneously, they went out on the free agent market and spent their money readily but not always wisely. Some were disposed to trading some of their younger players for proven veterans without considering if the chemistry would mesh. So if the trades and free agent signings would not work for whatever reason, heads would roll. General managers and field managers in the '80s passed each other like ships in the night.

It was also apparent that a new type of game was emerging, one that highlighted more power, speed and, of course, specialized pitching. It was reflected in the ballplayers who were now coming onto the scene in greater numbers such as African-Americans and Latinos. And all of them were bigger, faster and indeed stronger than their predecessors had ever been. In the 1950s only a handful of major leaguers on each team were in the 200-pound weight class. Keep in mind that the average player in 1908 was about 5'10" tall and yet 80 or so years later a baseball player averaged 6'3", or five inches taller. Not only were the players in better shape than their predecessors, they also were into dieting, weight lifting and other methods of staying in tip-top condition the 'year round.

But more than anything else, the greatest innovation of all was represented by the new and growing use of relievers. As slow as major league managers were as a group were to adapt to this significant change in strategy and not beholden to the sacredness of the complete game as they had been, they now moved to close the gap by concentrating heavily on developing a specialized group of relievers.

These relief specialists, aided considerably by new pitches like the split-fingered fastball and slider, as well as an improved defense, were now being employed to combat a smaller strike zone and the unbelievable strength of the hitters now in the game. As Mike Schmidt put it so succinctly: "It usually takes a hitter two or three at bats to gauge a pitcher. Now you probably get no more than two looks at a starter. The next at bat you get another guy, usually with one outstanding pitch. And for the final at bat, you get the closer with one *great* pitch."

♦ Chapter 8 ♦

Expansion, Realignment and a "Wild Card" Accentuate the 1990s

With a new millennium on the horizon, the decade of the 1990s would bring continued change not only in the makeup of the major leagues but in the relationship between the players and the owners of big league baseball teams. From 1977 until 1992, the American League comprised of 14 teams while the older National League made do with 12. That situation would be altered in 1993 as the NL brought in two new teams—the Colorado Rockies and the Florida Marlins—to equalize the complement of clubs and bring on realignment.

Both the Players' Union and ownership agreed to form three divisions in each league—Eastern, Central and Western. The NL East was included of the New York Mets, Montreal Expos, Atlanta Braves, Philadelphia Phillies and Florida Marlins; the NL Central had the St. Louis Cardinals, Chicago Cubs, Pittsburgh Pirates, Cincinnati Reds and Houston Astros; and the NL West included the Los Angeles Dodgers, San Francisco Giants, San Diego Padres and Colorado Rockies.

The AL East had the New York Yankees, Toronto Blue Jays, Detroit Tigers, Baltimore Orioles and Boston Red Sox; the AL Central consisted of the Kansas City Royals, Cleveland Indians, Chicago White Sox, Minnesota Twins and Milwaukee Brewers; and the AL West included the Seattle Mariners, Texas Rangers, California Angels and Oakland A's.

The owners were also attempting to align teams geographically more than ever before and to a certain extent they were successful. Unfortunately, in their attempts to bring about a more competitive balance, the scheduling of games, which now had each team meeting a like number of times—ten or 11—diluted some of the old rivalries like Dodgers-Giants, Yankees-Red Sox and Cardinals-Cubs, which did not sit well with anyone, especially the fans.

The regular season winners of each division would now meet in a best-of-five opening round playoff series that would also include a "wild card" team (the runner-up in each league with the best record) just as professional football had been doing successfully for years. The winners of that round would then clash in a best-of-seven League Championship Series that led to the World Series.

The immediate effect of expansion in the 1993 season, along with its accompanying dilution of talent, was to bring on even more offense than ever in both leagues. The numbers exceeded the previous highs of 1987 and some old-timers thought it even conjured up memories of the 1930 and 1893 flare ups. Pitching ERAs jumped to higher than 4.00 in both the NL and AL and, collectively, shutouts dropped by more than 100 games. Batting averages in the majors zoomed to .266 or ten points more than the previous year. Sixteen AL players banged out more than 30 homers apiece while five others hit over 40 dingers. All told the league home run total was 2,074 (about 300 more than in 1992) compared to the NL's 1,956 or some 700 better than the previous season, thanks in no small measure to the thin air of Denver's Mile High Stadium, where the Rockies played while awaiting their new stadium, Coors Field. And close to 30 hitters in the "Junior Circuit" drove in more than 100 runs, which had not happened since 1930.

Complete games continued to take a hit now that another 20 or so pitchers who should have either been retired or left in the minor leagues were throwing to big league batters. A new low was established in both leagues as 7.1 percent of the pitchers in the National League finished what they started in 1993, while the figure for the AL and its continued use of the designated hitter dropped to 9.2 percent. In fact, the New York Yankees set a new record with only three complete games that season.

Over in the NL, both the expansion Florida Marlins and San Francisco Giants hit rock bottom with only four complete games per squad. It all added up to much more work for the relief staff as the old days of carrying eight or nine relievers were upped to ten, 11 and even 12 on some teams.

But as attendance was reaching all-time highs in most big league markets, there was continued unrest between the players and ownership and it finally erupted on August 12, 1994, when still another strike occurred. This one was the most crippling of all as the unthinkable happened—the playoffs and the World Series were canceled, the first time such a thing had happened had since back in 1904. It was unthinkable in the minds of many but nevertheless a fact.

The majors resumed again the following year with a 144-game schedule and with much public relations work to be done. Many fans were turned off and some even refused to set foot in a big league ballpark ever again. The results were there for all to see as attendance dipped and TV ratings in 1995 suffered as well. It didn't matter to the fan who was right or wrong, just that they had been deprived of baseball through no fault of theirs. Much remained to be done by players and management alike to get the game back on track.

Relievers like Dennis Eckersley and Lee Smith picked up right where they left off in the '80s and continued to be as effective as ever in the period, as did Rick Aguilera, Doug Jones, John Franco, Dan Plesac, Gregg Olson and Jesse Orosco, each of whom has continued to pitch even into the new millennium. Others who pitched well for a few years in the early '80s and eventually called it quits in the period included Tom Henke, Mitch Williams, Mike Henneman, Randy Myers and Duane Ward. Meanwhile, the era began to produce new stars who are still making their mark today, such as John Wetteland, Rod Beck, Billy Wagner, Roberto Hernandez and Mariano Rivera.

Eckersley displayed the same flamboyance and panache he always had since debuting as a starter with Cleveland in 1975 right up until his final year in the majors in 1998. In 1990 (48 saves and a career-best 0.61 ERA) and 1992 (51 saves, a 1.91 ERA and the Cy Young Award), he was still the top reliever in the game and the Cy Young runner-up in 1991 with a not-too-shabby 43 saves and 2.96 ERA. He continued to irritate batters, not only because he could get them out regularly, but because when he did he would dance around the mound, pump his fist in the air and taunt them with stares and trash talk. It was his excellent control, better than average fastball and crafty slider that would do them in though and, more often than not, he was their conqueror.

"Eck" pitched in the 1990 and 1991 All-Star games for the American League and earned saves in both games. He also pitched in both the 1992 All-Star game (his sixth) and the 1990 World Series for the Oakland A's, where he spent most of his career (nine seasons). He moved on to the St. Louis Cardinals in 1996 to rejoin his former manager in Oakland, Tony LaRussa, and stayed for a couple of eventful seasons (30 and 36 saves respectively) before moving back to another former team, the Boston Red Sox. After a less than spectacular season there in 1998 and nearing the age of 44, he finally packed it in after 24 years in the big leagues, finishing second on the all-time saves list (since surpassed by John Franco) with 390. Always a hard worker and in superb condition, Eckersley is almost a sure bet to be selected the Hall of Fame once he becomes eligible.

After being traded back to the National League from the Boston Red Sox early in 1990, Lee Smith went on to tie for second among all NL relievers while recording 27 saves and a 2.10 ERA for the St. Louis Cardinals. He followed up that season with a career-high 47 saves (tops in the league) and 2.34 ERA, which earned him second place in the league all by himself. Once clocked at 101 mph, he notched 43 more saves in each of the next two years for the Cardinals before being dealt to the New York Yankees late in 1993.

Smith moved on to Baltimore in the following season and had a fine year there, picking up 33 saves to go along with a respectable 3.29 ERA. He spent 1995 and part of 1996 with the California Angels and recorded 37 saves there in his first year. He was dealt to Cincinnati, where he was no longer relied on as the primary a closer and could only muster two saves in 43 appearances during the 1996 campaign. He finished up his career with Montreal (his eighth team) in 1997 and after 18 seasons was by far the all-time saves leader in the major leagues with a remarkable total of 478.

The decade began with a bang for the profession of relief pitching when a young man who was destined to have an all-too-brief career, one Bobby Thigpen of the Chicago White Sox, saved an astonishing record number of games — 57 to be exact — which may or may not stand for a long, long time. The right-hander from Tallahassee, Florida, came up to the Sox in 1986 and saved 7, 16, 34 and 34 games respectively in his first four years in the majors, making a total of 77 appearances and finishing 73 of them. In his next two years, his numbers began to diminish as he saved 30 and 22 games respectively in the 1991 and 1992 seasons.

As his saves decreased so did Thigpen's value to the team and by 1993 he was a forgotten man and eventually dealt to the Philadelphia Phillies. He no longer closed games and his one save for the White Sox early that season was his last one. He found himself in Seattle in 1994 and, in a strike-shortened season, he ended a nine-year stint in the big leagues at the still-tender age of 31. But for one bright, shining season back in 1990, there never was a more effective closing reliever than Bobby Thigpen.

Rick Aguilera of San Gabriel, California, entered his sixteenth season in the big leagues in 2000 and showed no signs of slowing down at the age of 38. Born on New Year's Eve, the 6'5", 210-pound Brigham Young University graduate was the Minnesota Twins closer for most of his ten-plus years with them in the '80s. In his first full year as a reliever in 1990, when he replaced Jeff Reardon, who had signed on with Boston in the off-season, the big right-hander saved 32 games and pitched to a 2.76 ERA. In the following season, Manager Tom Kelly's first as the Twins' skipper, he saved 42 more games to tie Reardon's old team record and lowered his ERA to 2.35, thereby helping lead the team to the world championship. He won one game and saved two others in the World Series victory over the Atlanta Braves that year. A fairly good hitter, he became the first pitcher since Don Drysdale in 1965 to be used as a pinch-hitter in the 1991 World Series.

In the years that followed, Aguilera saved 41, 34, 23 and 32 games from 1992 to 1995. The 41 saves in 1992 allowed him to pass Ron Davis as the Twins' all-time saves leader. Earlier as a starting pitcher for the New York Mets, Aguilera always had great control and relied heavily upon an odious slider, particularly when he was up against left-handed batters. When he switched to relieving, he used an effective sinker to go along with a pretty good split-fingered fastball to get hitters out. Over the next five years, he averaged 35 saves and fewer than 18 bases on balls per season.

Aguilera pitched briefly for the Boston Red Sox in 1995 and returned as a free agent in 1996 to the Twins where he went back to his old role as a starter and won eight and lost six in 19 starts, accompanied by a rather lofty 5.42 ERA. It was back to the bullpen for Aguilera in 1997 and he saved 26 games that year and 38 more in 1998. He was dealt by Minnesota to the Chicago Cubs late in 1999 in a move to cut payroll and to continue in the club's youth movement mode.

Doug Jones started off the '90s right where he left off with the Cleveland Indians when he pitched more than adequately for a team that was not winning a whole lot of games at the time. "Mild Thing," as he was called because of his even temperament (as opposed to Mitch "Wild Thing" Williams), Jones saved 43 of 51 games for the Indians in 1990 but his output fell off dramatically in 1991 and he was traded to the Houston Astros the following year.

Jones resurrected his career there by becoming the Number One reliever in the National League. As his club's stopper, he posted an 11–8 won-lost mark, saved 36 games in 42 opportunities and appeared in 80 games while pitching to a marvelous 1.85 ERA. His numbers and overall record went down in 1993 and he found himself in Philadelphia by 1994. In that strike-shortened season he saved 27 games in 29 opportunities and compiled a nifty 1.17 ERA.

Jones bounced around the American League for the next five years, hurling for the Baltimore Orioles, Chicago White Sox, Milwaukee Brewers, Cleveland Indians (for the second time) and the Oakland A's, for whom he still toils. He never appeared in fewer than 52 games in that stretch and got into as many as 75 in 1997, his best year in the bunch when he saved 36 in 38 opportunities and worked to a very smart 2.02 ERA for the Brewers. Today at the age of 43 and with 16 seasons of big league ball behind him, he's still called on by the Oakland A's either as a setup man or an occasional closer.

Following six productive seasons (148 saves) for the Cincinnati Reds, John Franco, a Brooklyn boy, went home to New York and the Mets in 1990. Now in his twelfth season with them and, though he has pitched for some rather mediocre teams during most of his tenure there, he had still managed to register 268 saves for the club through the 1999 season for an average of 24 a year. While he is no longer the team's closer (he lost that job to Armando Benitez after being injured toward the end of 1999), the 40-year-old St. John's University product ranks as the major league leader in saves for a left-handed pitcher with 416 prior to the 2000 season, which ranks him second on the all-time saves list to only behind Lee Smith.

Big Dan Plesac, who had spent most of his time in the '80s as the closer for the Milwaukee Brewers, took his bag of tricks with him to the Chicago White Sox in 1993 and began a second career there as a setup man for a couple of seasons. From the "Windy City" he moved on to Pittsburgh, where Manager Jim Leyland, who seemed to have a fondness for veteran players, had him close games on occasion (11 of 17 chances in 1996) although he was used principally for an inning or even just to get one or two batters out. He hit the road once again in 1997 and landed in Toronto pitching for the Blue Jays up until the middle of 1999, when he was traded to the Arizona Diamondbacks. Former Manager Buck Showalter, who like Jim Leyland appreciated veterans like the reliable, experienced Plesac, continued to use the Gary, Indiana, native on occasion to get the last out or two of an inning or a game.

Another veteran right-hander who entered his third decade in the majors in 2000, Gregg Olson had been the closer for the Baltimore Orioles for five consecutive seasons beginning in 1989. The 6'4" Nebraskan reeled off 27, 37, 31, 36 and 29 saves consecutively in those years. His best year in the ERA department in the '80s coincided with his final year in Baltimore—1993—when he recorded a very sharp 1.60. He was shunted from one team to another in the next four years—Atlanta, Cleveland, Kansas City, Detroit, Houston, Minnesota and back to K.C. again before winding up in Arizona in 1998. Buck Showalter called on Olson to be his closer then and he responded with 30 saves in 34 opportunities that year and kicked in with another 14 in 1999. He continued in that role until the club traded for the younger Matt Mantei from the Florida Marlins. Olson began the 2000 season, his thirteenth in the big leagues, in Los Angeles where he pitched to a batter or two for then–Manager Davey Johnson.

Jesse Orosco, who began the 2000 season back with the major league team he broke in with—the New York Mets—was dealt away to the St. Louis Cardinals in spring training suffered an injury that severely limited his usefulness to Manager Tony LaRussa for most of the year. The 21-season veteran had spent the previous 11 seasons in the American League with the Cleveland Indians, Milwaukee Brewers and Baltimore Orioles, where his specialty was to get left-handed hitters out in crucial parts of a ball game. A notorious clubhouse jokester, the southpaw experienced his best season in the AL in 1997 when, at the age of 40, he had a 2.32 ERA. During the period, he averaged better than a strikeout an inning and, overall, his strikeout-to-walk ratio was better than two-to-one.

Tom Henke finished third among American League relievers in 1990 and 1991 as he saved 32 games in each season for the Toronto Blue Jays and recorded ERAs of 2.17 and 2.32 respectively. In the following year, he was even better as he helped to get the Jays into the playoffs and the World Series with 34 saves and a 2.26 ERA. In the series, which Toronto won over the Braves in six games, he relieved in three of the games and saved two of the club's four championship victories.

After eight seasons north of the border, Henke went back to his original team, the Texas Rangers, in 1993 and enjoyed his best saves year ever with 40 while pitching to another excellent ERA, 2.91. Following a less than heroic 1994 season—only 15 saves and a relatively high 3.79 ERA in the strike-shortened year—he moved on to the St. Louis Cardinals where, at the age of 37, he closed out his 14-year major league career with 36 saves and his best-ever ERA of 1.82.

Mitch Williams started the '80s with the Chicago Cubs and had an indifferent year there with only 16 saves and a 3.93 ERA. However, he was "the man" again in Philadelphia during the next three years, saving 30, 29 and 43 games respectively for the Phillies. He was the best reliever in the National League in 1991 when he won 12 games alongside 30 saves and a 2.34 ERA. The erratic left-hander with the volcanic but, at times, unmanageable fastball got the Phils into the playoffs and the World Series in 1993, winning two and saving two others in the NLCS, but fared less well in the World Series against the Blue Jays, gaining only one save.

Unfortunately, Williams will forever be remembered for being tagged for a walk-off home run by Joe Carter in the final inning of the seventh game of the 1993 World Series to give the Toronto Blue Jays the championship. He tried to come back in 1994 with the Houston Astros and in 1995 with the California Angels but to no avail. Nonetheless, "Wild Thing" had a fine career, compiling 192 saves during his ten years in the majors.

Mike Henneman, who had taken over as the Detroit Tigers closer from Guillermo Hernandez in 1987, continued to do his thing from 1990 to 1993. The 6'4" St. Charles, Missouri, native was very consistent in those years as he saved 22, 21, 24 and 24 games respectively to hold down second place among all American League relievers in that span. He tailed off somewhat in the strike-shortened 1994 season when he only notched eight saves and his ERA skyrocketed to 5.19.

Henneman came back a bit in 1995 when he picked up 18 saves for the Tigers and his ERA came back down to earth where it usually had been at 1.53. His club, which was going nowhere that year, traded him to the Houston Astros at mid-season and he finished the season there with eight more saves and a 3.00 ERA. His final year in the big leagues was spent with the Texas Rangers and he had an excellent season with them in the saves department with 31, but pitched to his worst ERA ever, 5.79. He retired at the end of 1996 with 193 saves during his ten years in the majors.

After five years with the New York Mets, Randy Myers was dealt to the Cincinnati Reds for the 1990 season, where he saved 31 games in 37 opportunities combined with a neat 2.08 ERA in 66 appearances. His role changed somewhat in the following year as he was in a "bullpen by committee" called the "Nasty Boys," which also featured Rob Dibble and Norm Charlton, and all three took turns in closing out games. He moved on to the San Diego Padres in 1992 and had a marvelous year with them, picking up 38 saves in 46 chances during his 66 appearances.

Myers had his best seasons ever in the next three years for the Chicago Cubs with 53 saves in 59 opportunities in 1993, 21 saves in 26 chances in the strike-shortened 1994 campaign and 38 saves of 44 possibilities in the 144-game 1995 season. Moving on to Baltimore in 1996, he had another fine year for the Orioles, saving 31 games out of 38 opportunities in 62 appearances. But his best year lay ahead of him—1997—when he notched an incredible 45 saves in 45 chances and a career-best 1.51 ERA. Just think of it—Myers never blew a single save opportunity in that entire season. He split 1998—his last one in the big leagues—with the Toronto Blue Jays and San Diego Padres, recording a combined 28 saves to complete his 14-year career with 347 saves, good enough for fifth place on the all-time list.

Duane Ward is a reliever whose career is easy to overlook because he doesn't appear on any of the all-time record lists, but during his all-too-brief stint in the major leagues, he was very productive for the Toronto Blue Jays. Originally signed by the Atlanta Braves as their first-round draft choice in 1982, the 6'2" right-hander out of Park View, New Mexico, was traded to the Blue Jays in 1986 as part of the Doyle Alexander deal. He compiled a 9–3 won-lost mark as a middle reliever for Toronto in 1988 and also helped ace stopper, Tom Henke, with part of the closer's load. A hard thrower who could sometimes be wild, he really came into his own in 1993 when he was the best reliever in the American League, leading all closers with 45 saves. He was also very effective in both the 1992 and 1993 World Series, winning three games and saving two overall. He was also selected for and pitched in the All-Star game in 1993.

If ever a player epitomized the "situational" reliever it was Paul Assenmacher, who retired from the game after the 1999 season. Originally signed by the Atlanta Braves from a tryout camp the team conducted in 1983, the southpaw came up to the big club in 1986, appearing in 61 games mostly as a setup man for closer Gene Garber. The 6'3", 195-pound native of Detroit tied for the National League in appearances with 54 in 1988, posting an 8–7 record and five saves.

The Chicago Cubs acquired him for their stretch drive in 1989 and he later pitched briefly for the New York Yankees and for several years with the Cleveland Indians. It was with those clubs that he became known for an almost uncanny ability to put away left-handed batters, usually one at a time, in critical circumstances.

Before there was a Mariano Rivera—considered by many to be the top reliever in the business today—there was a John Wetteland. When he came into the big leagues with the Los Angeles Dodgers in 1989 at 22 years of age, the club was undecided about what to do with him. Was he a starter or a reliever? After three unspectacular years in L.A., he was sent packing to Montreal, which definitely knew what to do with him. Pitching on a young team where everyone got a chance to show what they could do best, the San Mateo, California, native was immediately inserted as the team's closer and he responded by saving 37 games in 46 chances in his first year there—1992. The following years were no exceptions as he successfully closed out 43 more games in 1993 accompanied by a career-low 1.37 ERA while fanning 113 batters in only 85⅓ innings. He picked up another 25 saves in the strike-shortened 1994 season.

Since money has always seemed to be a problem in small-market Montreal, Wetteland was dealt to the New York Yankees before the 1995 season and closed out 31 of 37 games to help them reach the playoffs for the first time in some 14 years. Unfortunately for him, then–Manager Buck Showalter lost confidence in the hard-throwing right-hander toward the end of the season and into the best-of-five playoffs, where the manager used him sparingly against Seattle. The Mariners got to the ALCS by winning the final three games of the first round in Seattle after the Yankees had won the first two at home.

Enter Joe Torre. The New York Yankees manager gave the ball to Wetteland as second-year man Mariano Rivera set up for the loose-goosey fireballer. Wetteland not only picked up 42 saves in 47 chances in 1996 but also went on to have an unbelievable World Series in which he was named the Most Valuable Player. After not being signed by the Yankees, the "Rolaids Reliever of the Decade" moved on to Texas in 1997 where he has saved 31, 42, 43 and 34 games respectively through 2000.

Rod "Shooter" Beck, who came to the San Francisco Giants in 1991, had some tremendous years for the Bay Area denizens from 1992 through 1997. Born in Burbank, California, the 6'1", 235-pound right-hander saved 17 of 23 games pitching to what has turned out to be his lowest ERA ever—1.76—in 1992. His best saves year for the Giants came in the following season when he notched 48 in 52 chances and recorded another fine ERA of 2.16. In the strike-shortened 1994 season, he was credited with a save in every game in which he had an opportunity—28.

Although his ERA numbers were on the increase in 1995, 1996 and 1997, he still managed to save 33, 35 and 37 games respectively. Beck's best saves year was ahead of him, though, when he pitched for the Chicago Cubs in 1998 and picked up 51 in 58 opportunities to help get his team into the playoffs for the first time in 15 seasons. His productivity decreased in 1999 and he was eventually dealt away to the Boston Red Sox. Before the start of the year 2000, Beck stood at Number 14 on the all-time major leagues saves list with 260 in 307 opportunities. He was on his way to a fine year (2.23 ERA in 25 games) as a setup man for the Red Sox in 2000 when he was disabled during the middle of the season and was only to appear in nine more games.

Santurce, Puerto Rico, native Roberto Hernandez made his major league debut as a sometime starter for the Chicago White Sox beginning on September 2, 1991. The following year the Chisox put him into the bullpen and he never started another game again. Following a 12-of-18 save vs. save opportunity year in 1992 coupled with a 1.65 ERA, the 6'4", 235-pounder corralled 38 saves in 44 chances during 70 appearances while striking out 71 batters in 78⅓ innings. In strike-shortened 1994, he was limited to 14 saves in 20 opportunities but he followed that up with 32 more saves in 1995. He picked up another 31 saves when he split time with the White Sox and San Francisco Giants, where he was traded in one of the strangest deals in history.

Picked up in the expansion draft by the Tampa Bay Devil Rays in 1998, he saved 26 games for a team that did not enjoy many victories or save opportunities for an experienced closer like Hernandez. In 1999, he had a sensational year for a rather mediocre club but it didn't faze him, as he saved 43 games in 47 attempts while making 73 appearances. His saves dropped down to 32 in 2000 in 68 games while pitching to a 3.19 ERA.

Tannersville, Virginia's Billy Wagner came up to Houston Astros. late in 1995 and the southpaw has made his presence felt there ever since. At 5'11", 180 pounds, he is far from the biggest or strongest reliever in the game but he throws extremely hard and opposing batters find it very difficult to make contact with his deliveries; witness his 394 strikeouts in but 243 innings of work through 1999. Surprisingly, he has good control, and his strikeout-to-walk ratio is better than four-to-one.

In his first four full seasons with the Astros, Wagner saved 101 games in 119 opportunities, a remarkable number for a young man who appeared to have his best years ahead of him at the age of 30 before a season-ending injury midway through 2000 untracked him. Prior to that, his ERA had never been above 2.85 and in 1999 he checked in at 1.57 for the season. To illustrate the kind of dominance this young man possesses, witness the 124 batters he struck out in 1999 in only 74⅔ innings (an average of 14.9 per nine innings) and permitting the opposition to hit a measly .135 while he was on the mound.

When all is said and done, though, the man whom almost any manager would choose to close out a game in the new millennium is the Panamanian Mariano Rivera of the New York Yankees. What distinguishes him from others is his delivery, which is graceful yet comes at hitters in an explosive manner. The right-hander came up to the big club from the minors early in 1995, almost like John Wetteland broke in, as a starting pitcher. Recordwise, he didn't do badly, winning five and losing three in ten starts, including an 11-strikeout, two-hit shutout over the Chicago White Sox on July 4, but his 5.51 ERA did not convince anyone that his career lay in the starting rotation. He also blew the one and only save opportunity he had that season, but the Yankees and chief scout Gene Michael felt they knew the raw talent lying within the 6'2", 170-pounder.

Arguably the best closer in the game today, the New York Yankees' Mariano Rivera established a new record for post-season shutout innings in the year 2000. (Courtesy New York Yankees.)

Sent to the bullpen in 1996, he emerged as the perfect setup man for Wetteland by usually pitching the seventh and eighth innings before the veteran righty moved in for the kill. He even saved five games himself in eight chances. When the Yankees reached the first round of the playoffs, Manager Buck Showalter, who had become disenchanted with Wetteland, turned to Rivera to go up against a team, the Seattle Mariners, that possessed one of the most potent lineups in the majors. Rivera, apparently buoyed by the manager's faith in him, responded by pitching 5⅓ innings in three games without surrendering a single run and striking out eight.

Following Wetteland's departure and Joe Torre's arrival in 1996, Rivera was installed as the Yankee closer and through 1999 he had recorded 129 saves in 151 opportunities. Combining his 95-mph rising fastball with an occasional slider and change-up, he came up with a devastating cut fastball in 1999 that enabled him to save 45 games in 49 opportunities, including his last 22 chances in a row. His 2000 regular season figure saves numbered 36 but it was in the post-season that he reached new heights. He broke Whitey Ford's all-time consecutive shutout innings record at 34 and set a new mark for saves in the post-season with seven.

"No one has a cut fastball like him," says Mike Stanley of the Oakland A's, who used to catch Rivera when he was with the Yankees in 1995. "You sit there in amazement. You're thinking it's a slider, then you see it hit 96–97 mph on the screen and you're like 'Geez, no wonder this guy is so good.'

"He's so smooth with his motion," continues Stanley, "you try to recognize the pitch out of his hand, and by the time you figure out what it might be, it's by you. Sometimes the ball will look good out of his hand, then it rises up. Sometimes it will look like a pitch on the outer half of the plate, then it cuts out of the zone. You have no chance. Your only hope is to foul it off."

Rivera won his third world championship ring in the 1999 World Series as the Yankees swept the Braves and he capped off a tremendous season by registering two saves and a win to earn the coveted Most Valuable Player Award. During the Yankees' playoff run, he pitched twelve scoreless innings adding to his record-breaking 0.38 ERA in the post-season, the lowest in the history of the game.

There was little surprise after the 1999 World Series that the Yankees with their 25 championships would have been declared the "Team of the Century" for the twentieth century. What may have disappointed some followers of the game was that in the poll Major League Baseball conducted among its fans to select the 100 members of the "All Century Team," only two relievers, Rollie Fingers and Dennis Eckersley, made the cut. Actually each barely got on the list—Fingers was No. 96 and Eckersley No. 98. Perhaps relievers selected for the "All Century Team" in the 21st century will fare a whole lot better.

Chapter 9

The New Millennium Brings a Mixture of the Old and the New

A group of current middle or long relievers and setup men whose major league baseball careers began back in the late '80s deserve recognition for their ability to continue get men out in the new millennium. One is Fort Worth, Texas, native Greg Swindell, who broke in with the Cleveland Indians as a starting pitcher for them in 1986. After six seasons with the Tribe, including one year—1988—when the lefty won 18 games, he moved on to Cincinnati, Houston, back to Cleveland, Minnesota and Boston during the next seven years. All in all as a starter, he recorded 100 victories.

It was under Tom Kelly and the Twins where Swindell began to be employed as a competent middle reliever and setup man, appearing in 65 games in 1997 and another 81 in the following season, splitting his time between Minnesota and Boston. At the age of 35, he began his second year in 2000 with Arizona, for which he appeared in no fewer than 64 games and pitched to a very respectable 3.20 ERA while striking out 64 and walking only 20 in 76 innings.

Another left-hander now with his eighth team since 1988 is another Texan, Dennis Cook. As a reliever and spot starter for the San Francisco Giants, Philadelphia Phillies, Los Angeles Dodgers and Cleveland Indians during his first six years in the big leagues, it wasn't until he got to the Chicago White Sox in 1994 that he carved out a role for himself in the bullpen. From there he moved on to the Texas Rangers, Florida Marlins and New York Mets, where his appearances numbered 60, 59, 73 and 71 respectively from 1996 through 1999.

Cook was able to pick up a World Series championship ring along the way with the Marlins in 1997 as Florida defeated the Cleveland Indians that year. He contributed mightily to the Mets in 1999 as the club made a valiant attempt to overtake the Atlanta Braves in the NLCS but fell a bit short. In 2000, he helped get his club into the NLCS series once again as well as the World Series after making 68 appearances during the regular season

Stan Belinda's major league career started back in 1989 with the Pittsburgh Pirates. He was a particular favorite of Manager Jim Leyland, who used him in a variety of ways out of the bullpen. In his first full season— 1990—he appeared in 55 games saving eight in 13 chances. In 1991, the right-hander had 18 saves out of 24 possibilities in 60 games. The Huntingdon, Pennsylvania–bred Belinda followed that with 19 saves in 23 opportunities in 63 games in which he divided his time between Pittsburgh and Kansas City. During the next six seasons—two in Boston, three in Cincinnati, and beginning in 2000 with Colorado, Belinda had been used primarily as a setup man or middle reliever. His 1997 season in Cincinnati was one of his best when he appeared in 84 games and struck out 114 batters in only 99⅓ innings of work. In 2000, he found himself in Atlanta, where he helped get the Braves into a division series after appearing in some 56 games during the regular season, striking out 51 batters and walking but 22.

Some might say that Mike Stanton has had two careers during his 12 seasons in the big leagues. Coming up initially with the Atlanta Braves in 1989 at the age of 22, the 6'1", 215-pound lefty was brought along gradually until 1993, when he became the club's bullpen ace and received credit for 27 saves in 33 opportunities in 63 games. Control problems got the best of the Houston, Texas, native in the next couple of years and the Braves eventually moved him on to Boston in 1995. He also pitched for the Texas Rangers in part of a forgettable 1996 season.

Stanton then signed with the Yankees, where he has enjoyed his most consistent success as a setup man ever since, specializing in getting left-handed hitters out. Always ready to pitch, he has notched 64, 67, 73 and 69 appearances for New York in his four years with them. He was virtually unhittable in the 2000 post-season, particularly in the World Series, where he pitched in 4⅓ innings, striking out seven, walking no one and not even giving up a single hit while being credited with two of his team's four victories.

Mike Stanton's Yankee teammate and fellow Texan Jason Grimsley began his major league career as a starter for the Philadelphia Phillies in 1989 but had difficulty finding home plate with any degree of consistency. After three mediocre seasons in the "City of Brotherly Love," he moved on to Cleveland and the American League in 1993 where his walks-to-strikeouts ratio continued to mount. After three less-than-scintillating seasons with the Indians, he spent 1996 with the California Angels which released him at the end of the year at the age of 29.

To his credit, Grimsley went to the minor leagues and after two years in exile was given a tryout by the Yankees in their 1999 spring training camp. The 6'3", 180 pound right-hander responded by having a good camp and proceeded to make the team as a middle and long reliever. He appeared in 55 games for New York and got himself a world championship ring in the process. He filled an important role for the team by giving them innings and often keeping the club in games when their starters faltered early. Grimsley was even used as a spot starter, further increasing his value to the club. In 2000, he chalked up 96⅓ innings of work in 63 appearances while picking up a second world championship ring.

Mike Fetters, a burly right-hander out of Van Nuys, California, also made his major league debut in 1989. He was employed somewhat sparingly by the California Angels in his first three years in the big leagues and it was not until he reached the Milwaukee Brewers in 1992 that he found a niche for himself. In 1994, he began to assume the closer's role and saved 17 games in 20 attempts. He followed up with 22 saves out of 27 chances in 1995. His best year ever as a closer was in 1996 when he saved 32 of 38 games in a career-high 61 appearances.

After an off-year in 1997, Milwaukee shunted him to the Oakland A's in 1998, and he also spent part of that season back with his original team, the Angels. Now a role-player, Fetters has been used as a setup man for the club's closer, Troy Percival. In 1999, he performed in that capacity with the Baltimore Orioles and continued to act in that capacity in the year 2000 with the Los Angeles Dodgers, for whom he appeared in 51 games and pitched to a fine 3.24 ERA.

Right-handed fireballer Jose Mesa was one of the most awesome closers in the game when he toiled for the Cleveland Indians in the mid–1990s. But personal problems and changes in scenery altered the Dominican's role to that of a setup man for the Seattle Mariners, which didn't always sit too well with the 6'3", 225-pounder. Originally signed by Baltimore as a starter, Mesa debuted in 1987 and pitched with indifferent success for the Orioles until he wound up with Cleveland in 1992. It wasn't until the hard-throwing Mesa was sent to the bullpen in 1994 that he found his true calling in the major leagues.

In 1995, he was credited with 46 saves in 48 opportunities and pitched to a 1.13 ERA. He followed that up with a 39-of-44 saves year in 1996 but fell off in 1997 and was ultimately shipped out to the San Francisco Giants the following season.

Signed by the Seattle Mariners in 1999, Manager Lou Piniella, constantly on the lookout for relievers ever since he arrived in the northwest, anointed Mesa as his closer and he responded with 33 saves in 38 chances, although his ERA and walks-to-strikeouts ratio could have stood improvement. Early in 2000, Piniella relied on a stateside rookie but veteran Japanese League pitcher, Kazahiro Sasaki, as his closer, converting Mesa into a setup man. He finished up the regular season by making 66 appearances and in 80⅔ innings he struck out 84 batters to help get his team into the American League Championship Series as a "wild card." Mesa, hoping to earn a role as a closer once again, signed on to pitch for the Philadelphia Phillies in 2001.

One of the tallest major league pitchers in the game today at 6'8", Jeff Nelson put in four creditable seasons out of the Seattle Mariners bullpen from 1992 to 1995. The Baltimore native who conquered early control problems to become one of the best setup men around today does occasionally make it to the disabled list, but when healthy, the big right-hander can get hitters out with a better than average degree of regularity.

Nelson was part of a big trade for Tino Martinez after the 1995 season and played a major role in assisting the New York Yankees achieve four world championships since 1996. He averaged better than a strikeout an inning while being used as a middle reliever before Mariano Rivera began setting up for John Wetteland. Since 1997 when Wetteland left for Texas, Nelson joined with Mike Stanton to become the setup men for Rivera and earn three more World Series rings in 1998, 1999 and 2000. He had his best season ever in 2000, posting a won-lost mark of 8–4 with a 2.45 ERA in 73 games and striking out 71 batters in 69⅔ innings. At season's end, Nelson signed a free agent contract to return to his original team, the Seattle Mariners, for the 2001 season.

Former New York Yankee Graeme Lloyd, another skyscraper at 6'7", was used by the club as a specialist primarily to get left-handed batters out. More often than not, the Australian southpaw would face no more than one batter per game while helping his team win the World Series in 1996 and 1998.

Brought to the major leagues by the Milwaukee Brewers in 1993, his role there was essentially as a setup man who could pitch for an inning or a little more for a pitching-short team. Lloyd was inserted into the David Wells trade to Toronto along with infielder Homer Bush for Roger

Clemens spring training 1999. Although he had a decent year, he found himself in Montreal with another Canadian team, the Expos, just prior to the 2000 campaign. His wife's illness forced him to the sidelines for practically the entire season.

Turk Wendell made his major league debut for the Chicago Cubs on June 17, 1993, and was used as a sometime starter and reliever in his first two years in the National League. The right-handed New York Met setup man, along with the left-handed Dennis Cook, has been a reliever there almost exclusively and a most productive one at that. When he was with the Cubs he was even used as a closer at times; witness his 18 saves in 21 chances during 70 appearances and his 2.84 ERA in 1996. The following year he was sent to the Mets at midyear and was called into a total of 65 games for both clubs. He teamed with Cook in 1998 as the setup men for the then-closer John Franco, and chalked up 66 appearances with a 2.93 ERA. In the unsuccessful but exciting chase in 1999 to overtake the Braves for the pennant, Wendell, who always wants the ball, turned in a career-high 80 appearances. He was in 77 games in 2000, pitching to a 3.59 ERA in 82⅔ innings while striking out 73 batters. At the age of 33, the rubber-armed Pittsfield, Massachusetts–born Wendell looks like he can go on for many more years.

Formerly an ace closer out of the Philadelphia Phillies bullpen, Ricky Bottalico now operates as both a setup man and part-time closer for Manager Tony Muser's Kansas City Royals. The New Britain, Connecticut, right-hander saved 34 games in 38 attempts in 1996, averaging more than strikeout an inning in 61 appearances. In the following season, he saved another 34 games in 41 opportunities while striking out 89 batters in just 74 innings. After a sub-par 1998, he was dealt to the St. Louis Cardinals, where he made a bit of a comeback with 20 saves in 28 opportunities but had some control problems. The Central Connecticut State University product moved on to the American League with the Royals at the start of the year 2000, where he was working to find an adequate role for a team that had started to show signs of becoming a contender in the AL's Central Division. On a team that recorded a major league low total of only 19 saves, Bottalico had 16 of them in 62 games. For 2001, he signed a contract to return to the Phillies and try to again become their closer.

The most glamorous role in today's bullpen, of course, is that of the closer. It's also the position on a ball club that will spell either the rise or fall of a team's success. Consequently, whoever accedes to being the stopper on a given major league team is under the microscope constantly. His numbers—total saves in save opportunities, strikeouts-to-walks ratio, ERA, double-play groundouts to snuff out rallies—all become part and parcel of his stock and trade. Most every team either has such an individual or is on the prowl to find one throughout the season in a "Bullpen by Committee" approach.

Earlier this chapter focused on a few relievers like Mariano Rivera, John Wetteland, Roberto Hernandez and Billy Wagner, who are considered by many as blue-chip closers, but there are a number of others who also carry on this heady distinction. Let's take a look at them beginning with the National League's Eastern Division:

Now in his twelfth year in the big leagues, Florence, Alabama's Jeff Brantley actually began his career in the bullpen with the San Francisco Giants in 1988 and remained with them for six years. In 1990, he got credit for 19 saves in 24 attempts and pitched to a 1.56 ERA in 55 appearances. The following year he saved 15 in 19 chances and recorded a 2.45 ERA in 67 games. After a couple of not-so-spectacular years in which he was also used occasionally as a starter, he went to Cincinnati, where he really sparkled as the Reds' closer. In strike-shortened 1994, he appeared in 53 games, saving 15 in 21 opportunities and fashioning a 2.48 ERA. He followed up in 1995 with 28 saves in 32 chances and a 2.82 ERA in 56 games.

The year of 1996 was a career season for Brantley as the right-handed Mississippi State product was credited with 44 saves out of 49 chances in 66 games along with a stylish 2.41 ERA. His 1997 numbers were limited to only 13 appearances and he found himself in St. Louis in the following season. Under Tony LaRussa, he resumed his role as a closer for the Cardinals with 14 saves in 22 opportunities during 48 games. He moved on to Philadelphia in 2000 where he had to help assume the closer's role with Wayne Gomes as Mike Jackson, who had signed on as a free agent from Cleveland to become the Phillies closer, was injured and lost for the entire season. Brantley was credited with 23 saves for a club that chalked up a total of only 34.

The aforementioned Gomes, while not as experienced as Brantley, demonstrated in 1999 that he, too, was capable of closing out games when he recorded 19 saves in 24 attempts. The 6'2", 227-pound Hampton, Virginia, native joined the Phillies in 1997 and throughout the following season was employed mostly as a long reliever and setup man. A hard thrower, the right-hander has also been plagued by control problems during his brief career, but appears to be a capable counterpart to Jeff Brantley in the Philadelphia pen. Gomes slipped to seven saves in his 65 appearances in 2000.

Mike Jackson, whom Brantley and Gomes replaced, actually started out his big league career with the Phillies back in 1986 but management gave up on the Houston, Texas, native and he made his way to Seattle in

1988. Manager Lou Piniella used the hard-throwing right-hander as both a setup man and part-time closer for the next four seasons. He returned to the National League with the San Francisco Giants in 1992 and continued his role as a setup man, putting in a career-high 81 appearances there in 1993. He moved on to Cincinnati for the 1995 season and then once more back to Seattle in 1996 before landing in Cleveland to enjoy his greatest success in the majors for the next three years. He began to assume Jose Mesa's closer role in the Tribe's pennant-winning year of 1997 when he picked up 15 saves in 17 opportunities. He followed up that stint with his best ERA ever—1.55—in 1998 while saving 40 games in 45 chances. His final season in Cleveland—1999—saw Jackson pick up 39 saves in 43 attempts before signing with the Phillies for the year 2000. The Houston Astros signed him to a free agent contract for the 2001 season.

Caracas, Venezuela's Ugueth "Ugie" Urbina has been the Montreal Expos' go-to guy since 1997. He has also been that rarity of rarities these days in that he has only played for one club since coming to the big leagues as a starting pitcher at the age of 21 in 1995. Although the fireballing right-hander enjoyed some success as both a starter (10–5, 3.71 ERA) and reliever in 1996, Manager Felipe Alou, who desperately needed a closer, converted him into the club's stopper to replace the departed John Wetteland in 1997. Combining better than a strikeout an inning average with excellent control, Urbina proceeded to increase his number of saves from 27 to 34 to 41 in 1997, 1998 and 1999 respectively. In an injury-plagued 2000 season, he only got into 13 games, saving eight of them.

When the 6'5", 235-pound Antonio Alfonseca joined the Florida Marlins in 1997, Matt Mantei was the club's closer. The Dominican right-hander's job in 1998 was essentially to be a setup man for Mantei as well as a sometime long reliever and occasional closer when Mantei was not available. When the team suddenly and surprisingly traded Mantei to Arizona in the middle of 1999, the position was awarded to Alfonseca and he was credited with 21 saves in 25 opportunities. All he did in 2000 was to lead the majors in saves with 45 in 68 appearances.

The Atlanta Braves have had an embarrassment of riches in their starting pitching rotation for years. However, their bullpen has not always been equal to the starters they possess but, then again, whose could be? When Mark Wohlers was no longer able to find home plate in 1998 and 1999, and Kerry Ligtenberg was disabled for all of 1999, the club turned to 24-year-old John Rocker in 1999. The 6'4", 225-pound southpaw responded by turning in 38 saves in 45 opportunities, a 2.49 ERA, 104 strikeouts in only 72⅓ innings and a puny .180 batting average by Braves' opponents. However, when Rocker shot his mouth off in an extremely controversial interview that appeared in *Sports Illustrated* over the winter, for which he drew a fine and an early season suspension from Major League Baseball, the team was forced to turn to right-hander Ligtenberg and lefty Mike Remlinger to share the stopper's role until Rocker's return.

Ligtenberg, a native of South Dakota, had been the team's closer in 1998 and did a fine job that year with 30 saves in 34 chances, a 2.71 ERA and 79 strikeouts in 73 innings. However, he suffered a career-threatening injury that disabled him for all of the following season. He came back to the bullpen along with Remlinger, whose early career had seen him on both coasts—in San Francisco and in New York with the Mets, who traded him to Cincinnati in the middle of 1995.

The Dartmouth College product has always been more of a long reliever and spot starter, but his blazing fastball, which was good enough to fan 448 batters in 496 innings, made him a leading candidate for a closer's role. Remlinger and Ligtenberg had 12 saves each in 2000 as Manager Bobby Cox shuffled them and Rocker about in his search for a Number One closer. Cox and pitching coach Leo Mazzone ultimately found the man they were looking for once again in Rocker, who wound up with 24 saves in 59 games and a 2.89 ERA. Rocker is still young and, if he is able to put aside his contentious nature, he could continue to be a stopper for years to come.

If Armando Benitez is not the hardest thrower in baseball today, he is certainly up there among the leaders. The fireballing Dominican came up to the Baltimore Orioles as a raw right-hander at the age of 21 in the strike-shortened 1994 campaign and saw action in only three games. For the next four seasons, he was utilized in all capacities—long reliever, setup man and closer. After an injury-plagued 1996 season, he appeared in 71 games in both 1997 and 1998. In 1997, he pitched to a 2.45 ERA, saved nine games in ten chances and struck out 106 batters in only 73 innings. He saved 22 games in 26 chances in 1998 but his ERA and strikeouts-to-walks ratio elevated somewhat and he joined the New York Mets in 1999, starting out as the club's setup man, usually following appearances by Dennis Cook and Turk Wendell.

Benitez eventually replaced John Franco as the team's closer when the veteran left-hander went down with an injury toward the end of the year. He had a superb season as the team chased and nearly caught the Braves, finishing with 22 saves in 28 chances, a 1.85 ERA and a career-high 128 strikeouts in just 78 innings (a remarkable 14.8 average per nine innings). It also marked the second year in a row that the opposition batted under .200 against Benitez.

As the 2000 season unfolded, Franco was now the setup man for the

27-year-old Dominican who continued his brilliant work as the Mets' closer, helping them not only reach and win the NLCS, but also to get his club into its first World Series since 1986. In the regular season, Benitez picked up 41 saves in 76 appearances while pitching to a 2.61 ERA and striking out 106 batters in just 76 innings.

Apart from Rick Aguilera of the Cubs and Billy Wagner of the Astros who were profiled earlier, here is a thumbnail sketch of the other principal closers in the National League's Central Division:

Green Bay, Wisconsin's Bob Wickman came back to his home state in the middle of the New York Yankees' world championship year of 1996 as a member of the Milwaukee Brewers . The 6'1", 227-pounder began his big league career with the Yankees in 1992 primarily as a starting pitcher and enjoyed some success in that capacity with a 6–1 won-lost mark in eight starts in his rookie year. In 1993, the right-hander was a spot starter and reliever and had a fine year recordwise at 14–4, although he pitched to a rather high 4.63 ERA. From 1994 on, he was employed exclusively out of the bullpen by the Yankees, primarily as a long reliever and setup man, before being traded away in 1996.

Wickman was used as a long man and setup man for the Brewers in 1997 before being called on by Manager Phil Garner to take over as the club's closer in 1998. He performed well in that role in 1998 by garnering 25 saves in 32 opportunities while striking out 71 batters in 82⅓ innings. He had an even better year in 1999, picking up 37 saves in 45 chances and recording a strikeouts-to-walks ratio of 60-to-38 in 74⅓ innings. At the 2000 trading deadline, the veteran was acquired by Cleveland and finished the season with 14 saves in 26 opportunities as the Indians failed to make the post-season for the first time in many years.

Virginia Tech product Mike Williams, like Bob Wickman, made his major league debut in 1992 as a member of the Philadelphia Phillies and, like Wickman, as a starting pitcher. He remained with the Phillies for five rather unproductive seasons as the club used him as a sometime starter and reliever. After a horrendous 6–14, 5.44 season as a starter in 1996, he moved on to Kansas City for a year and only appeared in ten games out of the pen. It wasn't until he reached Pittsburgh in 1998 that Williams showed he could really pitch in the big leagues. That first season the hard-throwing right-hander appeared in 37 games as a long reliever, registering a 1.94 ERA and fanning 59 batters in only 51 innings. He assumed the closer's role in 1999 and, while his ERA soared to 5.09, he still managed to save 23 games in 28 opportunities and strike out 76 batters in just 58⅓ innings. In the year 2000, the-now permanent Pirate closer reduced his ERA to 3.50 and his strikeouts were nearly one an inning as he fanned 71 in 72 innings.

Now pitching for his fourth team in seven years in the majors, Dave Veres of the St. Louis Cardinals is another pitcher who took a while to find himself. Starting out with the Houston Astros in 1994, the Montgomery, Alabama, native has always thrown extremely hard as evidenced by his 395 strikeouts in 437 innings pitched prior to the year 2000. With Houston, the 6'2", 220-pounder was primarily a long reliever during his two years with the Astros. He continued in that capacity with Montreal in 1996 and 1997 and it wasn't until his second year in Colorado—1999— that he was converted into a closer. Throwing to batters in Denver's thin air has always been a challenge to pitchers, but Veres managed to save 31 games in 39 attempts in 1999, the first time that he had been consistently used in that capacity. He carried on that role effectively with the Cardinals in the new millennium by helping his team get into the NLCS. During 2000, he was called into 71 games, pitched to a 2.85 ERA in 75⅔ innings and fanned 67 while walking only 25.

Born in Saigon, Vietnam, Cincinnati's Danny Graves first came into the big leagues with Cleveland in 1996 and has always pitched out of the bullpen. A product of one of the finest college baseball programs in the nation, Miami (Florida) University, the 5'11", 185-pound right-hander was always considered to be a long reliever by the Tribe and even by the Reds when they traded for him in the middle of 1997. He responded well to the closer's role when Cincinnati's "Bullpen by Committee" in 1998 gave him a chance to save games eight times and he proceeded to save all eight. Manager Jack McKeon took notice and gave him the job full-time in 1999 and he helped the club surprise everyone in baseball by coming one game short of making the playoffs. Graves copped 27 saves in 36 tries while appearing in 75 games, pitching to a 3.08 ERA in 111 innings. Troubled at times by control problems, Graves was only 26 at the start of the 2000 season and showed signs of being considered among the top closers in the game by completing the year with 30 saves in 66 games and a nifty 2.56 ERA.

Over in the National League West, the closers in that division are among the most competent in the game, including Jeff Shaw of the Los Angeles Dodgers, who was among the many who began their big league careers as starters for the Cleveland Indians. The Ohio native was placed in the bullpen by the Tribe during his second year there in 1991 after an inconclusive season in the starting rotation. He has remained there almost exclusively throughout his 11 years in the majors. The 6'2", 200-pounder moved on to the Montreal Expos in 1993 and after a couple of indifferent seasons he was traded to the Chicago White Sox and finished up the year with them in 1995.

Shaw's career really took off after one season with his new team, the Cincinnati Reds, who gave him their closer's role in 1997 and for whom he saved 42 games in 49 opportunities, pitching to a 2.38 ERA in 78 appearances. At mid-season in 1998 with the Reds seemingly going nowhere, the baseball world was stunned when Shaw was dealt off to the Los Angeles Dodgers. His combined record that season was a healthy 48 saves in 57 chances and a career-best 2.12 ERA in 73 games.

Shaw continued his closer role with the Dodgers, saving 34 games in 39 opportunities in 1999 while pitching to a 2.78 ERA. He appears to have conquered the control problems he encountered early in his career, which remains one of the strongest points of his makeup, so important for any closer who usually is called in with men on base. While his strikeout rate is relatively low for a closer (only 39 in 57⅓ innings during 2000), he still manages to get batters out and save games (27 in 60 appearances) which, after all, is all that counts.

Colorado's Jose Jiminez came to the Rockies from St. Louis, where he had been used as a starter for the two seasons that he was with the Cardinals. The Dominican, who was born in the fabled San Pedro de Macoris, which has produced so many prominent major leaguers, had a poor season with the Cardinals (5–14, 5.85 ERA and a ton of walks) and found himself exiled to the Mile High City of Denver before the 2000 campaign. Early on he established himself as the club's closer by reeling off ten saves in his first 11 chances. He completed the season with a total of 24 in 72 games and also reduced both his ERA (3.18) and his walks-to-strikeouts ratio in 70⅔ innings of work.

The Arizona Diamondbacks felt that Matt "Ice Man" Mantei would help get them into the playoffs in 1999, which was the reason they traded for him that year. He did not let them down as he recorded a combined 32 saves in 37 opportunities and a 2.76 ERA for them and the Florida Marlins from whence he came. The hard thrower also blew away 99 batters in only 65⅓ innings in his 65 appearances. Although the D-Backs failed to get out of the first round, the Tampa, Florida–born right-hander was being counted on to carry the load for them in 2000, but he was injured and spent most of the early part of the season on the disabled list. Fortunately, Manager Buck Showalter had the veteran Mike Morgan to step into the breach as well as the 21-year-old Byung-Hyun Kim. The 5'11", 176-pounder with a blazing fastball, with only a part of one season behind him, joined with Morgan to form a dynamic duo. Kim chipped in with 14 saves while fanning 111 in only 70⅔ innings to lead all National League relievers.

In addition to the premier closer in the business, Mariano Rivera of the Yankees, and Roberto Hernandez of Tampa Bay, the American League's Eastern Division boasts the following stoppers:

Derek Lowe of the Boston Red Sox, although not designated as the team's closer, acceded to the position when Tom "Flash" Gordon went down with an injury early in 1999 and was lost for the entire 2000 season. Lowe, who came over to the Sox from Seattle in 1997, was nothing to write home about as both a spot starter and long reliever throughout 1998. However, with Gordon incapacitated early in the 1999 campaign, the 6'6" Dearborn, Michigan, right-hander gave the Sox more than they could ever have anticipated. In 74 appearances he pitched to a very creditable 2.63 ERA and saved 15 games in 20 opportunities. His walks-to-strikeouts ratio was a fine 25-to-80 and he only gave up four homers in 109⅓ innings of work. His work in 2000, as the Sox battled the Yankees for first place in their division for much of the year, helped keep his team in contention almost until the end of the season. He finished up with 42 saves in 74 appearances, a smart 2.56 ERA and 79 strikeouts and only 22 walks in 91⅓ innings.

Replacing Tom Gordon was no easy task, as the former starting pitcher for the Kansas City Royals as well as the Red Sox left some mighty big shoes to fill. Gordon spent eight years in Kansas City and was a key member of their starting rotation when he joined the pitching-short Red Sox. The 5'9", 190-pounder out of the racing town of Sebring, Florida, was a hard thrower who in his years as a starter for the Royals and the Red Sox had recorded more than 1,100 strikeouts during his first ten seasons, including 175 in 1990 with the Royals and 171 in 1996, his first year in Boston. But the Red Sox needed a stopper and when Gordon, who was used in that role toward the end of 1997 and saved 11 games in 13 tries was their man for 1998. He enjoyed a great year for them, saving 46 in 47 opportunities during 73 appearances, fanning 78 in 79⅓ innings and surrendering only two home runs. He started off well in 1999, saving 11 in 13 attempts, but his injury then and in 2000 has threatened his career altogether at the age of 36. However, the Chicago Cubs signed him to a two-year deal during the 2000 winter meetings, hoping that he could become the club's closer in 2001.

Many believe that 25-year-old Billy "Captain Chaos" Koch of the Toronto Blue Jays throws at least as hard if not harder than any reliever in baseball today. The 6'3", 205-pounder out of Rockville Centre, New York, stepped right into the closer's role as a rookie, saving 31 games in 35 opportunities while striking out 57 batters in just 63⅔ innings in 1999. In 2000, the Clemson University product picked up where he left off in the previous season by saving 33 games in 68 appearances while striking out 60 and walking only 18 in 78⅔ innings. His work helped keep the Jays in the pennant chase until the final week of the season, although none of the so-called experts expected the club to be in contention.

The American League's Central Division is led by the following closers:

The Detroit Tigers' Todd Jones, a right-hander out of Marietta, Georgia, began his time in the major leagues in 1993 with the Houston Astros. The 6'3", 230-pounder who pitched for Jacksonville State in college has never been anywhere but in the bullpen during his eight years in the big leagues. Jones was both a long reliever and closer before 1995 when Billy Wagner joined the team. In 1996, when he and Wagner shared the load, the fireballing Jones saved 17 games out of 23 opportunities.

Considered expendable with Wagner on the scene, he went to Detroit in 1997 and had an excellent maiden year there by saving 31 games in 36 chances while fanning 70 batters in 70 innings. He followed that up with 28 saves in 32 opportunities in 1998 and 30 more in 35 tries in 1999. In the 2000 season with a team that underachieved for much of the year, Jones recorded 42 saves in 67 appearances while chalking up 67 strikeouts and a meager 25 walks in 64 innings.

Former Oakland A's starting pitcher Steve Karsay for a time was "Numero Uno" as the closer in Cleveland until the acquisition of Bob Wickman. The 6'3", 205-pound Flushing, New York, native had three frustrating years in the Bay Area with a poor ball club. The Indians and Manager Mike Hargrove knew from the start that the right-hander's future lay in the bullpen and that is where he was assigned primarily as a long or middle reliever. He took over the closer's role almost by default at the beginning of the 2000 season under new manager Charley Manuel. His first 12 save chances resulted in ten saves as he struck out 24 hitters and walked only three in 25 innings while giving up only one homer and pitching to a 2.52 ERA. He finished up the year with 20 saves, as Wickman assumed the closer's spot following the trade with Milwaukee.

Perhaps the surprise team of major league baseball in the year 2000 was the Chicago White Sox and one of those helping to lead the way was closer Keith Foulke out of San Diego, California. He came over to the Sox from San Francisco in a blockbuster trade that confounded many at the time, but all of the minor leaguers Chicago received have panned out tremendously, including Foulke. Used as both a spot starter and reliever in his first two seasons in the majors, the 27-year-old Foulke began to assume the closer's role in 1999 when he saved nine games in 14 opportunities. An extremely hard thrower, he also struck out 123 batters in 105⅓ innings and only walked 21 while pitching to a 2.22 ERA. In 2000, Foulke had a tremendous start along with his team by saving 13 games in his first 14 opportunities, fanning 42 and walking only eight in 38⅔ innings while pitching to a remarkably low 1.16 ERA. His work contributed mightily toward getting his team into the division series against the more experienced Seattle Mariners and in which the younger Sox club was swept in three games. That did not diminish Foulke's year. He recorded a total of 34 saves in 72 games, a 2.97 ERA and 91 strikeouts and only 22 walks in 88 innings on the hill.

In addition to Texas' John Wetteland, the other clubs in the American League West have their share of fine closers, such as:

Troy Percival of the Anaheim Angels has been an outstanding stopper for them since 1996, his second year in the big leagues. The 6'3", 236-pound right-hander from Fontana, California, is only 30 years old but has saved 154 games in 181 opportunities during his five-plus years in the big time. Percival, who pitched in college for the University of California at Riverside, is another fireballer who can put hitters away at opportune times. In 344⅔ innings, he has struck out 429 while only walking 151, an outstanding strikeouts-to-walks ratio. After his first year in Anaheim, when he was used primarily as a middle reliever and occasional closer, he saved 36, 27, 42 and 31 games for the sometimes struggling Angels. He started off very well in 2000, saving 15 in 18 attempts and striking out 18 in 21 innings while giving up only one home run. He finished up what started out as a promising year for his club with 32 saves in 54 games while striking out 49 and walking 30 in but 50 innings of work.

Right-hander Jason Isringhausen was considered one of the brightest prospects on the short list of future starters for the New York Mets along with Paul Wilson and Bill Pulsipher, but for a variety of reasons, including injuries, it just didn't happen for the trio. After parts of four seasons in New York and back in the minor leagues, the Mets discarded the 6'3", 210-pound Illinois native to the Oakland A's, who decided to make a closer out of him. While making great strides to curb his early wildness, Isringhausen saved nine games in nine opportunities and struck out 51 batters in 64⅔ innings in 1999. He started off the first third of the 2000 season in fine style as his team was wrapped up in a four-way battle for first place in its division and which the club eventually won on the last day of the regular season. At the outset, he saved 11 games in his first 14 chances, struck out 23 batters in 23⅓ innings and walked but eight batters while only giving up one homer. Isringhausen's final numbers showed 33 saves in 66 appearances and a 3.78 ERA.

Lou Piniella, who has been tinkering with his relief staff along with an assortment of pitching coaches ever since he got to Seattle, believes he may have found the team's closer in flamethrower Kazahiro Sasaki. The 6'4", 209-pound right-handed veteran of Japanese baseball was a 32-year-old rookie in the major leagues when the 2000 season began. He let his presence and previous experience be known from Day One. He saved seven games in his first eight opportunities while striking out 26 and walking only nine in 18 innings. He played a major role in getting the Mariners into the ALCS against the world champion Yankees by virtue of 37 saves in 63 games, a 3.16 ERA and 78 strikeouts and 31 walks in 62⅔ innings.

In today's game and beyond, one thing is for sure—no bullpen remains intact from one season to the next. What it boils down to is that a manager and his pitching coach are rebuilding their relief corps almost every year. Dominating closers appear to be transient. For instance, of the 30 men who have won the Rolaids Relief Man award since it was begun in 1976 through 1999, only eight have won it more than once. The National League has had eight different winners in the last eight years and posted 15 different leaders in the past 17 seasons. In that time, the closer's role has shifted to virtually a "ninth-inning only" situation that results in the setup men having a profound effect on the outcomes of games.

While a team's closer may be in place for a few years (barring burnout, of course), it's the long or middle relievers and setup men who are usually on the move for one reason or another. That's where the role of a club's scouts are so important. These people are out there and everywhere constantly scouring the countryside looking for pitchers who can fit in with their team's relief staff. But it's not an exact science so there is never a guarantee that as good a collection of arms as can be assembled can put it all together in the same year. One can only hope.

◆ *Chapter 10* ◆

The Great World
Series Performances

Center stage each fall is in one arena, and that's wherever the World Series is being played. Even non-baseball fans get caught up in it. It is without a doubt riveting theater.

True, it has been canceled twice. The first time was in 1904, a year after it began, when John McGraw felt it beneath his dignity to let his New York Giants go up against the fledgling American League's representative for the title of "kings" of the baseball world. Then again we can all recall, indeed with great sorrow, 1994, when a prolonged labor dispute between players and ownership forced the second—and, hopefully, last—cancellation in the game's storied history.

Over the years during each autumn, baseball fans have thrilled to the exploits of Lefty Grove, Joe DiMaggio, Willie Mays, Mickey Mantle, Sandy Koufax, Bob Gibson and other Hall of Famers, not to mention unlikely heroes like Dusty Rhodes, Cookie Lavagetto and Don Larsen. Most of the action has been focused upon game-winning home runs, complete game shutouts and unbelievable fielding plays, but a number of World Series have turned on the performances of role players like relief pitchers who either have won, saved or contributed to the saving of one or more games, ultimately leading to victory.

This chapter presents a sampling of 17 of the most outstanding achievements attained by relief pitchers in the 96 years that the World Series has been played.

1926 World Series: St. Louis Cardinals vs. New York Yankees

It was Game Seven at Yankee Stadium and the series was tied at three games apiece. With two out in the bottom half of the seventh inning, the Yankees loaded the bases against Cardinals starter Jesse Haines. Haines, who had shut out the home club in Game Two, had begun to develop a blister on one of his fingers and was trying to protect a slim 3–2 lead. So what was player-manager Rogers Hornsby to do?

In the bullpen warming up was 39-year-old Grover Cleveland "Ol' Pete" Alexander, who had started and pitched his team to a complete game victory just the day before. However, Hornsby had told the then-future Hall of Famer to go easy on the celebrating because he might need him to come out of the pen the following day. The Cubs' castoff, whom the Cardinals had obtained on waivers in June, was being called in to get the sensational 22-year-old rookie Yankee second baseman, Tony Lazzeri, to end the inning.

As Earl Combs led off third base, Bob Meusel held second and Lou Gehrig occupied first, Alexander's first pitch to Lazzeri was a ball and his second a called strike. With the count at 1–1, Lazzeri hit a screaming liner just foul down the third base line. Pitch number four was swung on and missed for strike three as Alexander had done the impossible, or some thought, but he wasn't done yet.

Hornsby put his complete faith in the veteran right-hander and kept him in there to try and preserve the one-run lead and win the series. The Cardinals threatened but failed to get an insurance run in the top of the eighth. Alexander went out and got the Yankees in one-two-three fashion in the bottom half of the inning. Once again the Cardinals were unable to pad their puny lead and it all rested on Alexander's shoulders once again.

Combs led off the bottom of the ninth by grounding out, as did Mark Koenig. One out to go. Who was coming up to the plate but none other than the "Bambino," Babe Ruth. The slugger worked Alexander for a full count before proceeding to get a walk and thus become the tying run. Meusel, the Yankees' cleanup hitter, stepped in and represented the winning run.

Ruth, however, who had stolen second the day before, inexplicably attempted to steal it again to try and put himself in scoring position. But he guessed wrong as catcher Bob O'Farrell made a perfect throw to Hornsby, who tagged Ruth out to give the championship to the Cardinals. Alexander had saved the day.

1929 World Series: Chicago Cubs vs. Philadelphia Athletics

Although on paper this series might have looked like a cakewalk for Connie Mack's Athletics (they won it in five games), it was far from that. In fact, it took two consecutive remarkable late inning comebacks by Mr. Mack's team to cop the championship.

After dividing the first two contests at Wrigley Field (Game One went to the Athletics, 3–1 and Game Two was won easily by the Cubs, 9–3), the teams were now scheduled to play the next three games in Philadelphia's Shibe Park. The Cubs took a 2–1 series lead behind Guy Bush, who despite giving up nine hits in a route-going performance, bested George Earnshaw, 3–1. Earnshaw had started the previous game in Chicago and, consequently, had only a day's rest. In Game Four, which would have given the Chicagoans a commanding 3–1 series lead, the Athletics fell behind 8–0 going into the bottom of the seventh inning. Charley Root, the Cubs' ace, was virtually unhittable for the first six innings. What happened next was extraordinary.

After Al Simmons led off the bottom of the inning with a home run, Jimmy Foxx, Bing Miller and Jimmy Dykes singled, which plated the second run, and Joe Boley scored Miller with still another one-base hit. But when George Burns popped out to Woody English, the home club thought Manager Mack's plan to play the youngsters after taking out his veterans in the top of the eighth was sure to happen. However, Max Bishop singled home a fourth run and Cubs Manager Joe McCarthy removed Root in favor of southpaw Art Nehf, who was supposed to get the left-hand hitting Mule Haas out. Someone forgot to tell Haas, though, as he hit a rocket over second base that got away from Hack Wilson. By the time Kiki Cuyler tracked down the ball and fired it back into the infield, another three runs had scored and it was now just a one-run lead, 8–7.

Nehf then walked Mickey Cochrane and was replaced by "Sheriff" Fred Blake, who was promptly greeted by still another single from Simmons. Foxx thereupon drove in Cochrane with the tying run as McCarthy brought in Pat Malone to try and stop the bleeding. Malone proceeded to hit Miller with a pitch to load the bases and Dykes smashed a double to left that scored both Simmons and Foxx. Although Malone struck out the next two batters, the damage had been done and the entire complexion of the series had changed abruptly in favor of the Athletics.

Mr. Mack's top reliever now was future Hall of Famer Lefty Grove, who was then called upon to still the Cubs' bats in the eighth and ninth innings to preserve the bizarre turn of events. That is exactly what Grove did as he set down all six batters that he faced consecutively, including fanning four of them. The Athletics had won it, 10–8, and now led the series, three games to one, with another game to go at Shibe Park.

The Cubs were determined to bring the series back to the friendly confines of Wrigley Field and led the fifth game, 2–0, behind Pat Malone, heading into the bottom of the ninth inning. Malone had limited the Athletics to three hits over the first eight innings and seemed invincible. Howard Ehmke had started the game for Connie Mack but was relieved by Rube Walberg in the Cubs' two-run fourth inning. Walberg shut down the visitors for the next 5⅓ innings to keep his team within striking distance.

After Mule Haas delivered a two-run homer in the ninth to tie the game, Simmons and Miller doubled with two out to give the Athletics the world championship. Although the hitters had set the table, it was the relievers, Lefty Grove and Rube Walberg, who had applied the finishing touches to an incredible turnabout.

1947 World Series: Brooklyn Dodgers vs. New York Yankees

This was a series that had some of the most glorious moments in baseball history. Included among them were Bill Bevens of the Yankees losing a no-hitter (and the game) in the bottom of the ninth with two out in Game Four, and the Dodgers' Al Gionfriddo (who never ever played another game in the big leagues) robbing Joe DiMaggio of a homer with a game-saving catch in Game Six. And it also featured the appearance of Jackie Robinson, the first African-American to ever play in a World Series. Finally, it spotlighted the premier reliever in baseball at the time, Yankees lefty Joe Page of the eventual victors.

Page, who was rescued from obscurity by the opportunity presented to him during the season by Manager Bucky Harris, responded with a sparkling season that got his team to the "Big Dance." The Dodgers had one of the toughest offensive lineups in the game with Robinson, Pete Reiser, Dixie Walker, Peewee Reese, Eddie Stanky, Carl Furillo, Bruce Edwards, Spider Jorgensen and Gene Hermanski. Although he surrendered 12 hits in the 13 innings of the four games in which he pitched, Page delivered when the games were on the line.

The Yankees did not have the kind of starting rotation they had boasted in years past, or in the seasons that lay ahead, hence Page's role as savior was key to their success. Rookie Frank "Spec" Shea was their best pitcher, but Harris called on Page to pitch the last four innings of Game One to maintain the eventual 5–3 triumph. In Game Three, although the Yankees lost 9–8, Page gave the club another three innings after Bobo Newsom, Vic Raschi, Karl Drews and Spud Chandler were lit up for all nine runs before Page could put out the fire. However, another fine reliever at the time, Hugh Casey, shut down the Yankees in the last 2⅔ innings to preserve the win.

With the series tied at three games each, the Yankees got nothing out of starter Shea and reliever Bevens in the first four innings, although they had taken a 3–2 lead in the bottom half of the fourth. Harris once again, as he had all year, turned to Page to come in and save the victory and the series. Page responded by merely giving up one harmless hit over the last five innings and the championship belonged to the Yankees.

At this point in baseball history, there was no such designation as a middle or long reliever, setup man or closer. That was not to happen for years to come. At the time relievers like Casey, Page and Johnny Murphy would come in at any time to put out "fires" and to give their teams as many innings as they were capable of providing to save the starting rotations.

1949 World Series: Brooklyn Dodgers vs. New York Yankees

While both teams had begun to build up solid starting rotations—the Yankees with Allie Reynolds, Vic Raschi and Ed Lopat, and the Dodgers with Don Newcombe, Preacher Roe and Ralph Branca—the series once again would revolve around the fortunes of the bullpen. The Yankees and their new manager, Casey Stengel, had Joe Page and the Dodgers had the proverbial "cast of the thousands." Hugh Casey, who had been traded to the Pittsburgh Pirates in the off-season, obviously was no longer available so the Dodgers' pen was simply no match for the Bronx Bombers. Ironically, Casey wound up with Yankees late that year (his last in the majors) but he did not get the chance to pitch in the World Series against his old team.

The teams split 1–0 victories in the first two games as Newcombe bested Reynolds in Game One and Raschi, with ninth inning help from Page, got the better of it with Roe. The Yankees took Game Three as Page relieved a very wild Tommy Byrne in the third inning and pitched the rest of the way. Page gave his team 5⅔ innings of solid pitching and, despite giving up solo homers to Luis Olmo and Roy Campanella in the bottom of the ninth, held on to give the Yankees a 4–3 win.

Leading the series three games to one and not requiring any assistance from Page in Game Four, the Dodgers got no help at all from starter Rex Barney, who gave up six walks in the first three innings as the Yankees jumped out to a commanding 5–1 lead. When starter Vic Raschi was rocked for four runs by the Dodgers in the bottom of the seventh, Stengel brought in Page, who staved off any further scoring to give the Yankees a 10–6 win and another world championship.

Page, who suffered through an extremely mediocre season in 1950, was never the same pitcher and wasn't even used in that season's World Series sweep over the Phillies. He stayed out of baseball until 1954 when he was signed by the Pittsburgh Pirates, but retired after seven mediocre appearances. He passed away in Latrobe, Pennsylvania, on April 21, 1980.

1958 World Series: New York Yankees vs. Milwaukee Braves

Revenge was on the mind of the Yankees in this year's Fall Classic. Embarrassed by a former farmhand, Lew Burdette, who beat them three times, including the seventh game clincher in 1957, the Bronx Bombers were out to redeem themselves and vanquish their nemesis, Burdette. Unfortunately for the New Yorkers, someone forgot to tell the Braves, who rushed out to a 3–1 games lead including a crushing 13–5 defeat by Burdette in Game Two.

However, in order to become the first team since the 1925 Pittsburgh Pirates to come back from a 3–1 deficit to win it all, Manager Casey Stengel had to call on his bullpen to perform some magic. The "Old Perfesser" pulled a couple of rabbits out of his hat in the remaining three tilts, one of whom was second game starter "Bullet" Bob Turley, who was bombed out by the Braves after a third of an inning while the National Leaguers were scoring seven times in the initial stanza. The other was the bespectacled Ryne Duren, who after two very unspectacular years with the Baltimore Orioles and Kansas City Athletics, had become a star out of the pen for the Yankees with 20 saves during the regular season.

Game Five was a cakewalk for the New Yorkers at Yankee Stadium as Turley shut the Braves out on five hits and finally tagged a defeat on Burdette after four straight Yankee losses. The crucial Game Six in County Stadium had both teams' starters pitching with only two games' rest. Whitey Ford of the Yankees was unable to get anybody out in the second inning and was replaced by Art Ditmar, who gave them 3⅔ innings of shutout ball. The Braves, while they got 9⅔ innings out of Warren Spahn, the veteran lefty could not protect a 2–2 tie in the top of tenth inning. Meanwhile, Duren had shut down the Braves completely for 4⅔ innings until there were two out in the bottom of the tenth with the Yankees leading 4–2. Duren did tire and walked Johnny Logan, who promptly stole second as the big right-hander went into a full windup. Hank Aaron then singled to score Logan and it was now a one-run lead for the Yankees. Joe Adcock's single enabled Aaron to reach third and represent the tying run just 90 feet away. Exit Duren, enter Turley, who got pinch-hitter Frank Torre to line out to Gil McDougald for the final out and tie the series at three games each.

The following day it was Turley's time to shine once again. Starter Don Larsen lasted but 2⅓ innings and the Yankees were up 2–1 when Stengel gave the ball to Turley once again. Although surrendering one run in the sixth inning to tie the game at 2–2, the Yankees rallied for four runs with two out in the eighth thanks to Elston Howard's tie-breaking single and Bill Skowron's homer. Meanwhile, Turley sucked it up and shut down the Braves in the last three innings to give the Yankees their revenge and the 1958 world championship.

1960 World Series: Pittsburgh Pirates vs. New York Yankees

This had to be one of the most bizarre world championship series of all time. The Pirates, who had not won a series since 1925, were matched up against the most successful franchise in the history of the game. And although the Yankees dominated them in every offensive category and pitching ERA as well, the Pirates prevailed in seven games in one of the most dramatic finishes ever.

Losing to the Yankees by such lopsided scores as 16–3, 10–0 and 12–0 (both shutouts courtesy of Whitey Ford), the Pirates were able to scratch out victories in four other contests largely because their bullpen, led by their ace, Elroy Face, stopped the Yankees when they absolutely had to, while the New York relievers were unable to get the job done.

Face was coming off a 10–8 won-lost mark and 26–save season in which he had appeared in a National League–leading 68 games. The diminutive right-hander gained his first save in the opener at Forbes Field, relieving the team's best pitcher, Vern Law, in the last two innings with the Pirates winning 6–4. After being blown out in Game Two, 16–3 and 10–0 in Game Three, Law and Face combined to beat the Yankees, 3–2, at Yankee Stadium as the Buccos' ace reliever held the home

team at bay for the last 2⅔ innings by retiring the final eight opposing batters.

Back at ancient Forbes Field in Pittsburgh, the Yankees blasted the
Pirates, 12–0, to tie the series at three games apiece and set the stage for
the heroics to follow. Game Seven was a classic as the Pirates dispatched
Bob Turley in the second inning on their way to a 4–0 lead. Bobby Shantz
took over for Turley and shut the Pirates down for five straight innings.
The Yankees finally got to Law and knocked him out in the sixth inning.
Face, who had relieved Law as usual, was called on to protect a 4–2 lead.
However, he was touched up for a three-run homer off the bat of Yogi
Berra to give the Yankees a 5–4 header. Face held the Yankees off from
there on until the top of the eighth, when they scored twice more to now
lead 7–4. In the bottom of the eighth, the never-say-die Pirates rallied for
five runs that included a three-run blast by backup catcher Hal Smith to
put the home club in front once again, 9–7.

Bob Friend, who had been chased by the Yankees in a starting role
the day before, was brought in for the top of the ninth to protect the lead.
Friend was unable to get anyone out and the Yankees tied the game at 9–9
before the veteran Harvey Haddix finally was able to get the last three
outs. The rest, as they say, is history as Ralph Terry was called on in the
bottom of the ninth to face Bill Mazeroski, who was only thinking about
one thing—getting on base. Instead, "Maz," not known as a home run hitter—he had only hit 11 that year—got hold of Terry's second pitch and
deposited it over the wall to give the Pirates their third world title ever.
Face, although he did not pitch as effectively in this game as he was capable, his three saves in 10⅓ innings of work was a key element in the Pirates'
first championship in 35 years.

1966 World Series: Baltimore Orioles vs. Los Angeles Dodgers

Few relievers can point to a singular performance in a World Series
that can match that of Baltimore's journeyman right-hander, Moe
Drabowsky, in 1966. Then with his fifth team in 11 years in the big leagues,
the Polish–born Drabowsky established the tone for a four-game sweep
of the defending World Champion Dodgers with one of the most incredible relief stints ever.

Thanks to a two-run homer by Frank Robinson and a solo shot by
Brooks Robinson in the top of the first in the first game, the Orioles led
4–1 going into the bottom of the third inning. However, 23-year-old starter

Dave McNally had control problems and, after getting one out, the 13-game winner proceeded to walk the next three batters. He was given a quick hook by Manager Hank Bauer, who despite the early three-run lead, decided to go to Drabowsky.

The big right-hander, who had saved seven games along with six wins and no losses during the regular season, also had a neat 2.81 ERA in 44 games that year. He had also struck out 98 batters in his 96 innings of work. The 31-year-old veteran immediately fanned the dangerous Wes Parker but walked Jim Gilliam to force in Lou Johnson with the Dodgers' second and last run of not only the game but the entire series. Los Angeles never scored again as Drabowsky mowed them down in the fourth and fifth innings by striking out the side in each inning to tie a series record of six strikeouts in a row. All told, Drabowsky fanned 11 in 6⅔ innings and gave up but one hit. It was a shattering performance.

Thereafter the Dodgers were shut out 6–0 by Jim Palmer, who bested Sandy Koufax; 1–0 by 21-year-old Wally Bunker, who outpitched Claude Osteen; and 1–0 again, this time by the youngster McNally (who outdueled Don Drysdale) to conclude the sweep. But it was Drabowsky's opening game histrionics that helped speed the National Leaguers down the road to defeat.

1972 World Series: Cincinnati Reds vs. Oakland A's

This series spotlighted the latest baseball dynasty to follow the Miller Huggins–Joe McCarthy–Casey Stengel Yankees and Sparky Anderson's "Big Red Machine." It also preceded by a couple of decades Joe Torre's current day Bronx Bombers of the late '90s. Directed on the field by the crafty Dick Williams, and put together personally by Charles O. (for "Owner") Finley, the Oakland A's featured hitters like Reggie Jackson, starting pitchers the likes of Jim "Catfish" Hunter and Ken Holtzman and a bullpen headed by the best in the business at the time, Rollie Fingers.

Destined to go seven games, the series produced an improbable offensive hero like catcher Gene Tenace, who was its MVP and who, among other things, homered in his first two at-bats in Game One to set a series record and contribute to his team's 3–2 win at Cincinnati's Riverfront Stadium. A beautifully pitched 2–1 win by Hunter the next day got Fingers into the act as he saved it by getting the last out. The Reds got a three-hit shutout win by Jack Billingham in the opener at the Oakland-Alameda

Coliseum, 1–0, but the A's came back to take Game Four, 3–2, as Tenace hit yet another home run.

However, the Reds refused to fold and captured the next two games, 5–4 and 8–1, to set up a seventh and deciding game in their home park. With Jackson out of action due to a pulled hamstring, it was the relievers who managed to pull this one out for the victorious A's. Since there was "no tomorrow," as the cliché goes, Williams, who had started John "Blue Moon" Odom, didn't hesitate to bring in his two biggest starters: Hunter, who pitched 2⅔ innings, and Ken Holtzman, to protect a 3–1 Oakland lead going into the bottom half of the eighth. But Holtzman faltered as the Reds closed the gap to 3–2 and Fingers, making his sixth appearance in relief, shut the door to pick up his second save as the franchise won its first world title since 1930.

1973 World Series: New York Mets vs. Oakland A's

The A's were now getting their due as one of the best baseball teams ever and were heavily favored to defeat the Mets, who barely won their division by finishing a scant three games over .500. But the feisty New Yorkers under Manager Yogi Berra had a great pitching staff and acquitted themselves extremely well by defeating the 1972 National League champion Cincinnati Reds in a hard-fought playoff series, three games to two. Manager Dick Williams' 1972 World Champion A's had a tough playoff series against the Baltimore Orioles, too, but they also prevailed three games to two so both teams were primed for what was to be another seven-game clash.

Ken Holtzman got credit for the win in Game One, 2–1, but needed help from relief ace Rollie Fingers, and Darold Knowles, who made the first of a record seven appearances. Fingers relieved Holtzman in the sixth and pitched 3⅓ innings and Knowles got the save based on his two-thirds of an inning of work. The Mets took Game Two, 10–4, with a four-run ninth as Fingers was actually tagged with the loss.

However, the A's got a well-pitched six innings from starter "Catfish" Hunter at Shea Stadium on their way to a 3–2 ,11-inning win in Game Three. Knowles shut out the Mets in the seventh and eighth innings while Paul Lindblad got the win with another two shutout innings. Fingers redeemed himself by picking up a save in shutting down the Mets in the eleventh. Game Four was a 6–1 win for the New Yorkers and Jon Matlack and Game Five also went to the "Amazins" as Jerry Koosman and Tug McGraw combined to blank the A's, 2–0.

Back in Oakland with the Mets now leading the series, the A's behind Hunter bested Tom Seaver 3–1 to knot the series at three games each, and Knowles and Fingers once again made appearances with the latter credited with his second save. With the series squarely on the line in Game Seven, Matlack was driven out in the third inning during a four-run A's outburst as Holtzman held the Mets for the first 5⅓ innings. Leading 5–1 at that point, Williams called on Fingers once again and the bullpen ace came through with 3⅓ excellent innings. With the tying run at the plate in the ninth, Knowles came in for a record seventh time to get the last out and clinch back-to-back championships for the A's.

1974 World Series: Los Angeles Dodgers vs. Oakland A's

All that stood between the A's becoming the first team besides the Yankees to win three straight World Series was Manager Walter Alston's Dodgers, a team that had won 102 regular season games and dispatched the Pittsburgh Pirates in three of four playoff games. Conversely, Dick Williams' A's had only won 90 games but had also taken three of four playoff games from their perennial Eastern Division rival Baltimore Orioles.

The Dodgers had a good starting rotation in Don Sutton, Andy Messersmith and Al Downing to counter the A's staff of "Catfish" Hunter, Ken Holtzman and Vida Blue. The Dodger bullpen was headed by Mike Marshall, who had set a new major league record of 106 appearances accompanied by 14 victories and 21 saves. Oakland's relievers included the omnipresent Rollie Fingers coming off still another solid season.

The A's took Game One in Chavez Ravine, 3–2, when Holtzman was relieved by the durable Fingers in the midst of a Dodger uprising in the bottom of the fifth. Leading 2–1, Fingers pitched into the ninth inning and was the winning pitcher as Dick Williams had Hunter come in to get the last out by striking out catcher Joe Ferguson with the tying run on first. The Dodgers tied the series the next day in a 3–2 game, as Sutton got the best of Blue, but it was to be the one and only L.A. victory. The A's took the next three.

In the third straight 3–2 decision, Downing was knocked out in the fourth in Oakland as the A's took a 3–0 lead into the eighth inning. Hunter, who had held the Dodgers scoreless until Bill Buckner homered, was replaced by Fingers, who despite giving up a ninth inning solo home run to Willie Crawford in the ninth, held on for the save.

Fingers picked up his second save in row the following day when he relieved Holtzman, who had pitched 7⅔ strong innings to get the victory over Messersmith, 5–2. Fingers hurled the final 1⅓ innings. The A's, who desperately wanted to clinch the series at home the next day, did exactly that when, with the game tied 2–2 in the bottom of the seventh against Marshall, who had relieved Sutton in the sixth, Joe Rudi homered into the left-field seats. Naturally the ball was given to Fingers at the beginning of the eighth and he earned his third save to go along with a win and match Larry Sherry's 1959 series record of having a role in all four decisions.

1978 World Series: New York Yankees vs. Los Angeles Dodgers

Two old nemeses faced off one more time. Manager Billy Martin's Yankees had gotten into the playoffs against Kansas City via Bucky Dent's famous home run in a "winner take all" playoff game against the Boston Red Sox in Fenway Park. They easily beat the Royals, three games to one, while the Dodgers, now managed by former longtime coach Tommy Lasorda, had defeated the Philadelphia Phillies, also in four games.

The Dodgers featured Burt Hooten, Tommy John and Don Sutton in the starting rotation with Bob Welch, Terry Forster and Charlie Hough, among others, coming out of the bullpen. The Yankees had free agent signee "Catfish" Hunter, Ron Guidry and Ed Figueroa as their starters and Goose Gossage throwing out of their pen nothing but hard stuff that most hitters just couldn't catch up with.

The Yankees fell behind two games to none in the pair played at L.A.'s Chavez Ravine. John beat Figueroa and three relievers easily, 11–5, while Hooten nipped Hunter, 4–3. Guidry brought the Yankees back to respectability with a 5–1 victory in the opener at New York. The following day the home club tied the series when Ed Figueroa, who had pitched the first five innings, fell behind, 3–0, on the strength of a Reggie Smith home run. Dick Tidrow came in to shut the Dodgers down for three innings as the Yankees rallied for two runs in the bottom of the sixth and another in the bottom of the eighth to tie it against Welch. Meanwhile, Gossage, who took over in the ninth, pitched into the tenth as well and got the victory as Lou Piniella singled in Roy White with the winning run. Relievers Tidrow and Gossage retired 16 of the final 19 Dodgers to gain the victory. The last game at Yankee Stadium was a rout as the home team won it, 12–2, on 18 hits. Rookie Jim Beattie, after being behind 2–0 in the third, pitched six shutout innings with the Yankees setting a new series record on the strength of 16 singles. The Yankees now led the series, three games to two.

In L.A., the Yankees had another easy time of it as Hunter beat Sutton, 7–2. "Catfish" pitched the first seven innings and Gossage the last two and, although not in a save situation, the Coloradan put the icing on the cake by retiring the last six Dodger batters for the team's second consecutive world championship. The Yankees had become the first team in World Series history to get behind two games to none and win it all in six.

1979 World Series: Pittsburgh Pirates vs. Baltimore Orioles

After sweeping the Cincinnati Reds in the playoffs, Manager Chuck Tanner's Pirates were primed to meet Earl Weaver's Orioles, who had easily defeated the California Angels, three games to one. Led by co–National League MVP Willie "Pops" Stargell (he shared the award with the Cardinals' Keith Hernandez), the Buccos had a decent starting rotation, but it was the serviceable Kent Tekulve (94 games, 31 saves, 10 wins, 134 innings) who was their main man to stem any trouble that might develop.

After dividing the first two games in Baltimore (Tekulve pitched a perfect ninth inning to save Game Two), the teams headed to Pittsburgh's Three Rivers Stadium for the next three games. The situation looked pretty bleak for the homestanding Pirates as the Baltimore bats took over and won the next two games rather handily, 8–4 and 9–6, to take a commanding three games to one lead. However, the Pirates bounced back in Game Five and won, 7–1, highlighted by Bert Blyleven's outstanding four shutout innings in relief of Jim Rooker, who had pitched well but was behind 1–0 after five.

Still down three games to two and going back to Baltimore, the "We Are Family" Pirates got tremendous pitching performances out of both starter John "Candy Man" Candelaria and Kent Tekulve to tie the series with a 4–0 victory. Candelaria worked the first six innings and Tekulve chipped in with three innings in which he blanked the home club as well.

Weaver pulled out all of the stops in Game Seven as he tried to quell a Pirate rally in the ninth inning to pad their slim 2–1 lead. Weaver used no fewer than five pitchers in the ninth inning to no avail, as Pittsburgh tallied twice. Meanwhile, Tekulve had come on in the bottom of the eighth with the Pirates leading 2–0, none out and the tying runs in scoring position at second and third. He proceeded to strike out both Gary Roenicke and Doug DeCinces before getting pinch-hitter Pat Kelly to fly out for the final out. He retired the Orioles with little difficulty in the ninth to garner the save and give the Pirates a stunning world championship after all had appeared lost following Game Four.

1980 World Series: Philadelphia Phillies vs. Kansas City Royals

Up until this season, the only teams playing major league baseball in 1903, the former St. Louis Browns (in Baltimore since 1954) and the Phillies, had never won a World Series. That was about to change thanks due in no small measure to free agent signee Pete Rose and relief ace Tug McGraw. Both had been there before, Rose in several series with Cincinnati and McGraw with the 1973 Mets. The only difference was that Rose had won before and McGraw hadn't.

The Royals, under Manager Dick Howser, had swept the New York Yankees in three games to reach the ultimate challenge while Dallas Green's Phillies had to win a tough five-game series against the Houston Astros to get there. Howser's bullpen ace, Dan Quisenberry, had picked up a win and a save against the Yankees in a relatively easy series and was well-rested. McGraw, meanwhile, had to relieve in all five games against Houston, picking up a win and two saves to get his club to the "Big Dance."

The first two games at Veterans Stadium in Philadelphia went to the home club, 7–6 and 6–4, as McGraw pitched two innings and earned a save in the opener while Quisenberry was tagged with the loss in Game Two. McGraw, meanwhile, was not called on by Green for the first time in seven post-season games.

In Kansas City, the Royals managed a victory as a result of a 4–3, 10-inning heart-thumper in Game Three as Quisenberry bested McGraw when Willie Aikens drove in the winning run with one out. The home team tied the series the following day, 5–3, as Aikens, who had homered twice in Game One, became the first player in history to have multiple homers in a World Series when he again hit two out.

The Phillies got their advantage back in Game Five as McGraw, in his third inning of relief, with the bases loaded and two out and his team clinging to a 4–3 lead, struck out pinch-hitter Jose Cardenal for the final out. This time McGraw got the win and Quisenberry was tagged with the loss.

Returning to Philadelphia with 24-game winner and future Hall of Famer Steve Carlton looking for his second series victory, the Phillies prevailed, 4–1, as McGraw twice stopped the Royals with the bases loaded in both the eighth and ninth innings to gain his second save of the series and the Phillies' first-ever world title. In 7⅔ total innings of work, McGraw, although he walked eight, had it when he had to, striking out 10 and pitching to a nifty 1.17 ERA.

1982 World Series: St. Louis Cardinals vs. Milwaukee Brewers

The Cardinals had swept the Atlanta Braves while the Brewers had to win Game Five against the California Angels to cop the American League playoff series. Whitey Herzog's Cardinals had a bullpen that featured 43-year-old southpaw Jim Kaat, the second oldest player to ever appear in a World Series, and ex–Cub Bruce Sutter, who was coming off a 70-appearance, league-leading 36-save season. Manager Harvey Kuenn's Brewers, called "Harvey's Wallbangers" for their home run production (216, the most in 18 years), was forced into a "bullpen-by-committee" situation since free agent signee Rollie Fingers was unavailable due to a disabling injury. But they were determined to make a series out of it and that they did.

At Busch Stadium in St. Louis, the Brewers won the opener easily, 10–0, as Paul Molitor had five hits and Robin Yount added four of the 17 base knocks that the club accumulated. But the Cardinals came on to win Game Two, 5–4, as Sutter worked his split-fingered fastball to near-perfection in the final 2⅓ innings to preserve the victory.

Moving to County Stadium in Milwaukee, the visitors won 6–2 as Sutter once again was called on to pitch the final 2⅓ innings and gain still another save. The home team tied the series in Game Four as they outscored the Cardinals, 7–5, with Sutter now unavailable. The Brewers attained the advantage in Game Five which they won, 6–4, and got a record-breaking performance out of future Hall of Famer Robin Yount, who became the first player in series history to have two four-hit games.

Back in the friendly confines of St. Louis' Busch Stadium, the Cardinals won big, 13–1, as John Stuper became the first rookie ever to start two games in a World Series. The series now stood tied at three apiece. The Cardinals, who trailed 3–1 going into the bottom of the sixth, knotted the game via Keith Hernandez's two-run single and went ahead to stay when George Hendricks delivered a run-scoring single. In came Bruce Sutter to relieve starter Joaquin Andujar and all he did was throw two perfect innings at the Brewers to give the Cardinals their seventh seven-game series win in their fabled history.

1990 World Series: Cincinnati Reds
   ## vs. Oakland A's

No one expected the kind of result that emanated from this series. The Oakland A's, the defending world champions of Manager Tony LaRussa (considered a "genius" by some), held a 10-game post-season winning streak and featured 27-game winner Bob Welch, 20-game winner Dave Stewart and 48-save reliever Dennis Eckersley along with Mark McGwire (39 homers), Jose Canseco (37 homers) and Rickey Henderson (65 stolen bases). How could they miss? But miss they did. The upstart Reds under Manager Lou Piniella who led a young and relatively inexperienced squad whom most people had barely heard of swept the A's in four games. Game One at Riverfront Stadium set the tone as the Reds blanked the A's, 7–0, behind young, hard-throwing Jose Rijo. Rob Dibble and Randy Myers, the forerunners of the "Nasty Boys," worked an inning each to complete the shutout.

In Game Two, the Reds, who trailed 4–2 in the early going, picked up single runs in the fourth and eighth, to send it into extra innings. Over the last seven innings, the Reds' bullpen kept the visitors at bay and the home club ended it against the usually reliable Dennis Eckersley with an RBI single off the bat of catcher Joe Oliver to give Cincinnati a 5–4 win and a two-games-to-none series lead.

The home advantage in Oakland did not guarantee success as the Reds exploded for seven runs in the third inning and won, 8–3, as Tom Browning pitched the first six innings to get the win and—who else—Dibble and Myers mopped up.

The clincher was the proverbial barn-burner as Rijo, after giving the A's a first-inning run, retired the next 20 hitters in succession. Shut out by Stewart until the eighth, the Reds came to life and touched up the veteran for two runs. Meanwhile, Myers shut down the A's (although Carmelo Martinez was robbed of a two-run homer in the ninth by outfielder Glenn Braggs) and got the final two outs by retiring Carney Lansford and Canseco. The Reds, with great help from their pen, picked up their first world championship since 1976.

1996 World Series: New York Yankees
   ## vs. Atlanta Braves

Another improbable end to a world championship took place in this year's Fall Classic. The Yankees of first-year manager Joe Torre came back from a seemingly impossible 2–0 deficit in games in which they were embarrassed in Yankee Stadium, 12–1 and 4–0. The Bronx Bombers proceeded to take four straight, including three in Atlanta, against a team with, arguably, the best starting rotation in the game. And all four Yankee wins were saved by the series MVP, John Wetteland.

Game Three was close until the Yankees burst out with three runs in the eighth and, while setup man Mariano Rivera yielded a run in the bottom of the inning, Wetteland shut them down in the ninth for a 5–2 win. Game Four was an extra-inning affair as the Yankees nearly self-destructed early by getting down 6–0 but, they pecked away and made it 6–3 until the top of the eighth. Jim Leyritz blasted a three-run dinger off the Braves' bullpen ace, Mark Wohlers, to tie it. Reliever Graeme Lloyd kept the shell-shocked Braves out of the scoring column and got the win as Wetteland once again stopped the home club and the visitors scored two more in the tenth to win it, 8–6.

Game Five was a duel to the death as Andy Pettite of the Yankees and John Smoltz of the Braves battled it out. The Yankees had picked up an unearned run in the fifth and held a shaky 1–0 lead going into the bottom of the ninth. Following Pettite's surrender of a leadoff double to Chipper Jones, the southpaw was able to get one man out while Jones advanced to third. Wetteland was again called upon and with the infield in, the reliever succeeded in getting the first batter he faced to ground out on one pitch for the second out as Jones held third. After intentionally walking Ryan Klesko, ex–Yankee Luis Polonia, who was sent up to hit for Jermaine Dye, lined a hard drive into the gap in right-centerfield that Paul O'Neill ran down for the final out for a three-games-to-two series lead.

Back at Yankee Stadium for Game Six, the Braves' ace, Greg Maddux, who had shut the Bombers out in Game Two, was touched up for three runs in the third inning, which turned out to be all the Yankees needed. The Braves trailed 3–1 at the end of six and as usual, Rivera and Wetteland did the rest. Wetteland gave up a run in the top of the ninth to make it interesting and, with runners on first and second with two down, the relief ace closed it out by inducing Mark Lemke to foul out to Charlie Hayes to give the Yankees still another world championship.

1999 World Series: New York Yankees vs. Atlanta Braves

Riding the crest of a ten-game winning streak in World Series play since 1996, the Yankees were to go up against the team they started their run against, the Atlanta Braves. The latter had basically the same starting staff—Greg Maddux, John Smoltz, and Tom Glavine and newcomer Kevin Millwood—and a bullpen now headed by the irascible but effective left-hander John Rocker.

The Yankees still had holdovers Andy Pettite and David Cone from 1996 along with five-time Cy Young Award winner Roger Clemens, who was seeking what he never had a chance to obtain—a championship ring. The Yankees also had one of the best bullpens in the game and, unquestionably, the top reliever around in 1999 in Mariano Rivera. The 29-year-old Panamanian was credited with 45 saves in 49 opportunities and a 1.83 ERA but, more importantly, finished the year by not permitting a run in 30⅔ innings in 28 games while posting 22 consecutive saves since July 21, starting against the very same Braves.

Rivera began things for himself and his team by getting the last four outs of Game One as the Yankees breezed, 4–1, in Atlanta. His services weren't required in Game Two, which the Yankees also won, but he came back in Game Three at Yankee Stadium to pitch two scoreless innings and preserve a 6–5 victory. In the Game Four clincher, Rivera was called upon in the eighth inning with the tying runs on base and soon-to-be National League MVP Chipper Jones at bat. He retired the dangerous Braves' third baseman on a grounder to end the visitors' final chance to score. Rivera put the Braves away easily in the ninth to pick up his third save and a well-deserved series MVP Award as the Yankees won the championship, 4–1. That save lengthened Rivera's scoreless innings total to 12⅓ innings over eight games in three World Series. The victory also enabled five-time Cy Young Award winner Roger Clemens to get what had eluded him throughout his career—a series win, a world championship and a ring. It also confirmed the New York Yankees as the "Team of the Century" as they claimed their twenty-fifth title of the second millennium.

2000 World Series: New York Yankees vs. New York Mets

In the first so-called "Subway Series" played in 44 years, the result remained the same as the Yankees defeated their New York City National League counterparts once again. The 1956 series, which featured the first and only no-hitter in series history, and a perfect game at that, by Don Larsen of the Yankees, had the Brooklyn Dodgers providing the opposition. In the year 2000 it was the New York Mets, who were attempting to keep the Yankees from a "three-peat." No such luck—the Yankees prevailed in five games despite only outscoring the Mets by a mere three runs, 19–16.

As in many World Series, pitching, and particularly relief pitching, played a formidable role in the outcome. The Yankee relievers, led by the man considered to be the dominant closer in the game today, Mariano Rivera, and his cohorts, Jeff Nelson and Mike Stanton, were well nigh unhittable by almost all of the Mets' hitters. Even David Cone contributed in a cameo appearance out of the bullpen.

In Game One, the Mets had taken a 3–2 lead over their hosts at Yankee Stadium into the bottom of the ninth inning by virtue of a pinch-hit two-run single by Bubba Trammell in the top of the seventh. However, the usually reliable Mets closer, Armando Benitez, was unable to protect the lead when he allowed back-to-back singles to Luis Polonia and Jose Vizcaino in the bottom of the ninth to tie the game. Yankee relievers Nelson, Rivera and Stanton pitched shutout ball for the last 5⅓ innings of the 12 inning affair, which was finally won by a single off the bat of Vizcaino. The latter, a surprise starter for the Yankees at second base over the erratic-fielding Chuck Knoblauch, who was the team's DH, ended the longest game played in series history at four hours and 51 minutes.

Game Two was "highlighted" by an implausible incident involving Yankee starter Roger Clemens and Mets catcher Mike Piazza, who had been hit in the head by Clemens during an interleague game back in July. This time Piazza's bat cracked in three places with the barrel end fielded by Clemens and thrown by the right-hander in Piazza's direction. Clemens was not ejected but he was fined $50,000 a couple of days later by Major League Baseball. "The Rocket" proceeded to mow down the Mets for eight innings on the way to a 6–0 lead. However, Nelson and Rivera were uncharacteristically touched up five runs in the top of the ninth off home runs surrendered to Jay Payton and Piazza to make it close but not enough. The Yankees won it, 6–5.

Game Three belonged to the Mets as they hosted the Yankees at Shea Stadium. The home team became the first club to ever defeat Yankee starter Orlando "El Duque" Hernandez in the post-season. The right-hander had accumulated a post-season record of 8–0 entering the game. The Mets broke a 2–2 tie in the bottom of the eighth after 40-year-old John Franco held the Yankees at bay in the top half of the inning. Benitez closed it out in the ninth and Franco thus became the second oldest man in history to win a World Series game. Dolph Luque of the Giants, at 43 in 1933, is the oldest pitcher in series history to gain a victory. The Mets' win also ended the Yankees' consecutive World Series winning streak at 14 games.

Game Four was another cliffhanger but the Yankees triumphed, 3–2, as Cone, Nelson, Stanton and Rivera blanked the Mets over the last 4⅓ innings with Rivera notching the save. Cone only pitched to one batter but it was the dangerous Piazza, who had homered earlier off starter Denny Neagle and had barely missed another off the southpaw. Cone got ahead of Piazza in the count at 1–2, then tied him up with an inside slider, enticing the slugger to pop up to second base to end the bottom of the fifth.

In Game Five, the score was tied at 2–2 in the top of the ninth when Luis Sojo, a late-inning replacement, singled up the middle off starter Al Leiter and scored Jorge Posada, who had been walked. Scott Brosius scored on the same play as Payton's throw hit Posada and bounced away from Piazza and into the Mets' dugout. Enter Rivera, who gained his second save of the series and record-breaking seventh save in the post-season to give the Yankees their 26th world championship and fourth in the last five years.

♦ *Chapter 11* ♦

Evaluating the
Relief Corps

Assessing the performances of relief pitchers either over the course of a season or throughout their entire careers has never been, and doubtless will never be, an exact science. Although several formulas have been created and developed over time from variety of sources, consideration has to be given to such intangibles as the era in which a particular pitcher is being judged. That is to say, what rules were in effect at the time, what were the playing surfaces and equipment like, what were the dimensions of each of the ballparks, how was the bullpen managed and a host of other variables almost too numerous to mention. It is well nigh impossible to factor in such vastly different ingredients, and yet each plays a role in how we evaluate any athlete.

Dick Bosman, former pitching coach of the Texas Rangers, put it this way: "You need more reinforcements now because of all of the offense. Smaller parks, smaller strike zones, harder balls, harder bats—[frequent pitching changes are] a reaction to all of it. Now it takes more pitches, more effort, to get through a lineup, especially in our league [American]."

Having said that, it would seem to be a futile attempt to consider all of these elements to figure out, say, how the Doc Crandall of the '20s could possibly be evaluated against the Mariano Rivera of the new millennium, for example. Then, too, why should they even be pitted against one another by means of a formula that cannot possibly take into account all of the variables necessary for a meaningful conclusion?

Suffice it to say, the only way to judge one player against another, be it a position player or pitcher, is to measure them by the times or eras in which they performed. That is precisely why this book is divided into specific periods in baseball history that have relevance. True, there is some overlapping, but not enough to make that much of a difference.

The late Ralph Horton, in his 1994 monograph, *Rating Relief Pitchers,* came up with a concept called the "Relative Performance System" (RPS) that measured pitchers from 1946 through 1993 in their respective leagues. Most baseball historians would concur that the post–World War II period represented a point in time when relief specialists came into vogue in greater numbers than ever before.

In RPS, point totals in 11 statistical categories are the summation of points earned each season by relievers as follows: innings pitched (10), games won (10), winning percentage (15), games pitched (20), saves (20), earned run average (20), hits per nine innings (20), bases on balls per nine innings (20), strikeouts per nine innings (20), wins (plus saves) as a percentage of team wins (25), and earned run differential (25). The latter represented the difference between a pitcher's ERA and his team's ERA. The highest number of points a pitcher can earn in a given year is 205, provided he would be the leader in all 11 categories.

Qualifiers had to pitch at least one inning for each three scheduled games (at the time 54 innings), or had to have recorded ten or more saves. Occasional starters had to have begun fewer than ten games and the total number of starts had to be less than one-third of a pitcher's appearances.

What makes RPS so unique is that the top rated pitcher is often not the one with the most saves. As a matter of fact, the Top Ten list in a particular season would include middle relievers and setup men in the groupings. A look at the list of the greatest relievers of all time using this method of evaluating performance shows that relievers with lengthy careers are at the head of the class. In other words, as Horton wrote, "While Ellis Kinder and Dick Radatz may have been the best ever based on average points per year, their career totals put them only 38th and 39th on the all-time list."

Hoyt Wilhelm with 1,849 RPS points ranks as the greatest reliever ever, utilizing this system. He is followed by Rollie Fingers, Goose Gossage, Lindy McDaniel, Elroy Face, Sparky Lyle, Lee Smith, Don McMahon, Tug McGraw and Bruce Sutter to round out the Top Ten.

Horton himself was quick to acknowledge that although Firpo Marberry and Johnny Murphy pitched prior to 1946, they probably should be on the list or ranked in at least the Top Twenty. Both pitched in a time when there were not enough relief specialists around to rate them under the RPS. It should also be noted that some pitchers on the list who had not yet ended their careers, such as Dennis Eckersley (No. 20), John Franco (No. 28) and Jesse Orosco (No. 50), could easily move up on that list once they were to call it a day, as Eckersley did in 1999.

A gentleman named Doug Drinen recently came up with an interesting new method by which to judge how well a relief pitcher performs that bears consideration too. He calls it "Win Probability Added," or WPA for short. It's a new wrinkle on a sabermetric approach first introduced in a 1969 book titled *Player Win Averages* by Harlan and Eldon Mills.

Drinen's WPA theory takes into account the following: the number of outs and runners on base when the reliever enters; the score of the game at the time; the number of runs he allows; and the number of outs and runners on base when he leaves. By evaluating all of these factors, he hypothesizes that the data provides a better understanding of the tenuous situations that the reliever encounters and just how successful he is at improving them or not. Then, too, it's his belief that such information can tell how well (or not so well) managers use their relievers and exactly who in the bullpen is best equipped to handle tough circumstances with the game hanging in the balance.

Probably the first category by which relief pitchers were judged that had any kind of significance was the "save" statistic. And, as was pointed out earlier, even that designation has been changed since its introduction by one of the most distinguished sportswriters of all time, Jerome Holtzman, who is also the historian for Major League Baseball (MLB). Holtzman, who was inducted into the Hall of Fame in 1990, was appointed the historian of MLB by Commissioner Allan H. "Bud" Selig in June 2000. He has been writing about baseball for more than 44 years.

Up until the time he created his formula for *The Sporting News* in 1960, the only way in which relievers were evaluated was either by their earned run average or their won-lost mark, neither of which could give these specialists a true picture of their worth. As he pointed out in an article in the *Chicago Tribune* on July 7, 1999, "The ERA wasn't a good index because many of the runs scored off a reliever are charged to the previous pitcher; the reliever's ERA should be at least one run less than a starter. The W-L record was equally meaningless; the reliever, particularly the closer, is supposed to protect a lead, not win the game…. Initially, to earn a save, the reliever had to come in with the tying or winning run on base or at the plate and finish the game with the lead. The following season the degree of difficulty lessened: a two-run lead was sufficient."

Although he had been keeping unofficial figures for nine years and writing a weekly article for *The Sporting News* along with a list of the leaders, Holtzman relinquished the feature when the majors approved the save as an official statistic in 1969. Thus it became the first new consequential statistic in the game since the "run batted in" was added in 1920. Some say that when the save was created it gave regular occupants of the bullpen a sense of dignity in their role instead of considering themselves constantly auditioning for a start.

Unfortunately, Major League Baseball lessened the value of the save statistic when it modified the rule and allowed a reliever who just finished a game, no matter the score, credit for a save. This change infuriated the game's followers so much that in 1973, as noted in an earlier chapter, the rule was again redefined whereby a reliever had to put in either three innings or come into a game with the tying or winning run either on base or at bat. Two years later the rule was again eased to permit the tying run to be on deck, thus allowing the reliever the luxury of putting a base runner on.

Today, of course, the rule permits a save to be recorded for any reliever who enters a game with his team leading by three or fewer runs. The number of innings or parts of an inning has nothing whatever to do with it. The problem with this is that a pitcher who comes in with, say, two outs in the ninth inning to protect a three-run lead will get a save just the same as someone who, perhaps, relieved as early as the seventh and held on to a one-run edge.

Saves in and of themselves are no real indicators of a reliever's effectiveness. Some are literally a "slam dunk." A perfect example of this is Cleveland's ace closer in 1995 and 1996, Jose Mesa. During both years, he had to hold on to a one-run lead only 26 times and there were only a total of 16 men on base when he made his 131 appearances.

As good a reliever as John Wetteland has been over the years, his record when he won the 1996 World Series MVP award for the New York Yankees, if examined closely, may not be as herculean an effort as one might imagine. In the first place, he faced only 19 of the 232 Atlanta hitters who came to bat against all Yankee pitchers. Then, too, in three of the four saves with which he was credited, Wetteland came into games with no one on and a lead of at least two runs, and he only needed to get either two or three outs.

The foregoing is in no way meant to denigrate the left-hander's performance because he was called on to get the job done. He accomplished the task he was given and his achievements were very instrumental in helping his team win the world championship that year. The point is that one can easily get carried away by the "save" statistic in and of itself, when it should be given its proper weight against the totality of the situation that the reliever faces.

Actually, the premium that was once put on a save per se has been growing more and more cloudy. If one harkens back to the time when relievers were called "firemen"—Johnny Murphy, Joe Page, Hoyt Wilhelm, even Goose Gossage of more recent vintage—you would discover men who would come in well before the seventh inning to do their stuff and actually put out fires. Now the flames are extinguished, hopefully, early in the contest by middle or long relievers and setup men well before the ninth inning, when most closers are brought into a game.

Take John Franco of the New York Mets, the current active leader in saves, for instance. Through September 20, 1999, the left-handed veteran reliever had picked up only 12 of his 205 saves over the previous eight years with the tying run on base. In 171 of those save opportunities that he ultimately captured, no one was on base. And of his 416 total saves up until that time, Franco was asked to hold a one-run lead only 148 times. More often than not—138 game appearances to be exact—he had a lead of three or more runs when he took the mound.

Again, Franco, as in the example cited earlier of John Wetteland in the 1996 World Series, does not ask his manager when to come in and what the situation has to be when he is summoned. All he can do is try to help his team win and his record shows he has been more successful at doing just that than any southpaw reliever in history.

As Doug Melvin, general manager of the Texas Rangers, puts it: "First you needed a closer, then it was the setup guy, then it was right- and left-setup guys. Then you needed a left-handed specialist [like Paul Assenmacher and Mike Stanton] and now you need a long man, because you don't want to have to use a setup guy in long relief and not have him available for the next couple of games."

As a matter of fact, setup men have become so invaluable to the fortunes of a ball club that many who actually possess the most outstanding arms on a team are put into the starting rotation. Scott Williamson of the Cincinnati Reds, Steve Karsay of the Cleveland Indians and Ramiro Mendoza of the New York Yankees are the most recent examples of this line of thinking. Consequently, setup men are now among the most desired commodities in baseball. And if you're left-handed, so much the better. Witness the fact that southpaws represented the four biggest paychecks among relief pitchers in the game who did not come on board a team as its predominant closer.

To illustrate just how prominent setup men have become, from 1987 to 1998 the number of pitchers who came in to a game to pitch to just one batter nearly doubled—from 532 to 978. While the expansion years of 1993 and 1998 probably contributed somewhat to this inflated number, the trend would have been significant without the additional teams.

As major league baseball moves forward, the numbers clearly illustrate that although closers are accumulating more and more saves, they are working fewer and fewer innings each year. Going back to 1969 when the save became an official stat, the leading ten closers that season were averaging 22.2 saves in 64.1 appearances in 1.54 innings per game. By 1996, those same stats showed that the average number of saves for the "Top Ten" had increased to 39.2 but the average number of innings pitched to attain 17 more saves was accomplished in 69.3 appearances in only 1.08 innings per game.

When you examine these numbers against the makeup of the 1971 Baltimore Orioles relief corps, for example, you get to see how spectacular the changes have been over the last three decades alone. That season the Orioles boasted four 20-game winners—Mike Cuellar, Pat Dobson, Jim Palmer and Dave McNally. With the way baseball is now played, we'll likely never see a repeat of that caliber of starting rotation ever again or anything close to it. Since those four pitched well into each of their starts— an average of 7.6 innings per game—Pete Richert and Eddie Watt, who led the team in relief stints, averaged only 35 appearances each or fewer than every starter except McNally. My, my has the game has changed. Indeed.

A constantly raging argument today is how relievers should be stacked up against starters and their respective overall values to their clubs. First off, the standard relief pitcher will only work about one-third the number of innings in which a starter operates over the length of a season. Consequently, some have advanced the theory that a starter with a 3.90 ERA, for example, in 200 or more innings of work, would equate to a reliever with a 2.50 ERA in 75 or more innings. This belief stems from the number of runs that relievers are "expected" to save in a given year.

Some people reason that the value of relief pitchers and their contributions to a team's success are massive because their work often comes at times when games are on the line. It is generally felt that runs scored at this juncture of a game have greater merit than those scored earlier so that the reliever's role in winning or losing the contest is huge. With this kind of pressure placed upon them, relievers are thought to have a lopsided impact on the ultimate outcome and this results in the undervaluing of closers. Therefore, it is believed that although ERA is generally superior to saves as a gauge by which to judge relievers, it too is fraught with difficulties. Again due to the fewer innings that a reliever works as opposed to starters, if he has one or two poor performances, his ERA will suffer immensely when viewed at the end of the year. Then again, the reliever's ERA might come out of a game unscathed even though he permits inherited runners to score, which, of course, would be charged to the starter or middle reliever whom he was expected to bail out. The fact is,

ERA is and always has been the norm by which all pitchers are judged and will likely remain so in the foreseeable future.

What must be kept in mind is that the role of relief pitchers is one that is still developing. Their won-lost marks are even less critical than they were even a decade or more ago because of the point at which they enter games. As Pete Palmer and John Thorn pointed out in their article, "Relief Pitching," in *Total Baseball*: "A reliever may pick up a win with as little as a third of an inning's work, if he is lucky, while a starter must go five innings; a reliever may also pick up a loss more easily, for if he allows a run there may be little opportunity for his teammates to get it back, as they can for a starter. Earned run average is meaningful for the reliever, but it must be .15 to .25 lower to equate with that of a starter of comparable ability; a reliever frequently begins his work with a man or two already out, and thus can put men on base and strand them without having to register three outs.

"Ratios of hits-to-innings, strikeouts-to-innings, strikeouts-to-walks—all of these have their interest, but none is sufficient by itself to measure relief pitcher effectiveness. Relievers may also have an edge in these ratios because they generally face each batter only once in a game, thus leading to fewer hits and more strikeouts per inning."

Since Herman Franks managed the Chicago Cubs from 1977 to 1979 and had the incomparable Bruce Sutter and his demon split-fingered fastball as his closer, the question before the house was always and still is: Is the best way to use a closer in games when the starter has departed and the reliever is charged with protecting a razor-thin lead late in the game? Franks believed that was the only way to utilize a closer, and in his case it was Sutter, who was the best around for several years. Up to that time many, if not most, managers would bring in their relief aces from the seventh inning on regardless of what the score might have been. Franks, who never managed again after 1979, was of a mind that his team's best chance to achieve victory was when it held a slim lead and the closer was brought in toward the end of the game to hold down the opposition.

Yet at the same time, closers like Goose Gossage of the 1978 world champion New York Yankees pitched 134 innings that year. "I'd come in the seventh inning of a tie game," says Gossage of a time in the history of baseball when the club's stopper was called on not just to extinguish fires but to impede them. "I remember being used by (Manager) Billy Martin in the fifth inning with the bases loaded."

Herman Franks, on the other hand, could have been accused of coming up with his method purely as a result of circumstance. In his first two years as the Cubs' skipper, Sutter was never as good in the second half of the season as he was in the first half. Franks reasoned that overwork was responsible and told anyone who would listen that the only time they would see his bullpen ace was with the issue in serious doubt late, like in the ninth inning.

This theory took off in the '80s and even up until recent years has held sway among most managers. Tony LaRussa was certainly a disciple and utilized Dennis Eckersley almost exclusively in this manner after making him his closer in Oakland, much to the southpaw's annoyance. After all, hadn't he been a starter for seven seasons and given his teams lots of innings? Also, hadn't he thrown a no-hitter and won 20 games one year in the process?

But guess what? Since then not a single team has ever won a world championship with a closer who pitched as much as 90 innings. Before that, in fact for 14 consecutive years, every closer for a series winner put in at least that many innings of work.

It should be noted that pre-war and immediate post-war managers like Joe McCarthy and Leo Durocher, as well as John McGraw before them, would bring in their star reliever early in the contest when their starters would falter and had to be replaced. Today there seems to be a trend in the direction of having some closers actually being called on either at the beginning or partway through the eighth frame until the end of the ninth inning, representing somewhat of a departure from Herman Franks' pattern.

All in all, a foolproof system for evaluating the work of relief pitchers over various time periods, be it a game, a season or a career, has not yet touched down to earth and perhaps never will. Those who have attempted to offer some semblance of methods by which to judge the merits of these specialists—Jerome Holtzman, Ralph Horton and Bill James, to name but three—are to be commended for trying and giving us some guiding measurements.

One person who's convinced that relievers are the major contributors to the results of ball games is former Dodgers' manager Tom Lasorda, who's spent more than a half century with that organization and who coached the USA baseball team to a gold medal in the 2000 Summer Olympics. "I've said it many, many times," he says. "And people don't seem to believe me when I say that pennants, playoffs and World Series are won or lost in the bullpen. I've been saying that for a long time. And it's a proven fact."

◆ *Chapter 12* ◆

Inside the Bullpen

It's anybody's guess as to how the expression "bullpen" was actually conceived. One speculation espoused by Jonathan Fraser Light in his book, *The Cultural Encyclopedia of Baseball*, is that in the early days of the National League, fans were allowed into the games for only 10 cents if they arrived after the first inning. These latecomers were penned in like "bulls" behind ropes in foul territory beyond first and third base.

Relief pitchers would warm up along the sidelines adjacent to these areas, hence the name "bullpen" was applied. Sounds logical. Although the designation really didn't come into popular baseball terminology until around 1915, the first formal bullpen area had been installed at the Polo Grounds in New York ten years earlier.

Another theory that has been advanced by a number of baseball historians is that the phrase was derived from the Bull Durham Tobacco Company signs that adorned the outfield fences in many of the first ballparks. Since the area near these advertising billboards was used by pitchers to warm up either before or during the game, the name supposedly grew out of this practice. Of course, since in those days many ballplayers chewed Bull Durham tobacco and "shot the bull," it was another seemingly logical reason to label that particular area "The Bullpen." Could also be. As they say (whoever "they" are): "You pay your money and you take your chances."

Today as always, the bullpen represents the worst possible place in the stadium to view the game. It's usually located in the farthest reaches of the ballpark in most cities and its inhabitants tend to get bored and even downright lonely at times. What this leads to are situations whereby the bullpen's denizens can get a little stir crazy were it not for the scintillating conversations they have among themselves on a variety of topics or, better yet, the pranks they play on each other.

Nowadays with most pitching staffs up to about 12 in number, of which at least five are starters, the bullpen maintains about seven pitchers, a catcher and a coach once the ball game begins. That's a very substantial group of people with divergent personalities and interests. By the same token, it makes for some intriguing sets of bedfellows who are together constantly not just in the "pen" but in the clubhouse, as roommates on the road or just hanging out and "chilling" together for long periods of time. It makes for a camaraderie that is difficult for the rest of the team to duplicate.

Many relievers are famed for their—shall we say—idiosyncrasies. Hollywood–born Jim Gott, who at one time or another toiled for the Toronto Blue Jays, San Francisco Giants and Pittsburgh Pirates during the 1980s, would aptly fit that description. According to Mike Lavalliere, who caught him in Pittsburgh, Gott would arrive at the mound after running in from the bullpen actually snorting like a horse. "He's huffing and puffing, so the first thing I want to do before I go back to warm him up is let him catch his breath a little bit," said Lavalliere. The adrenaline flowing through his veins would make it difficult for Gott to maintain his mechanics properly. "That is one reason why he has to throw from a stretch even when he is starting an inning. He gets so excited he really couldn't keep all the body parts going in the same direction enough to throw strikes," claimed Lavalliere.

Yet Gott would be as affable an individual as you could ever find before it came time for him to go to work. "You can talk to him in the bullpen until up around the seventh inning," declared Lavalliere. "Then he goes into a kind of trance. When he finally gets the phone call, he works himself up. He has to be in fourth gear when he comes in. Countered Gott: "We're little kids playing a kid's game. Why shouldn't we show emotion?" No reason, Jim.

One of the most notorious free spirits of all time was reliever Moe Drabowsky, whose exploits in the 1966 World Series for the Baltimore Orioles were incredible, as related earlier. It is said that one of his favorite pranks was to taunt his teammate, Paul Blair, by buying snakes in a pet shop, sneaking them into the clubhouse and tossing them on the unsuspecting outfielder, who was deathly afraid of them. One time he put a five-foot boa constrictor in another teammate's locker.

One of Drabowsky's other tricks was to tie a long, thin black thread to a $50 bill and place it in the middle of the lobby of a hotel where his team was staying. Someone would come along and try to snare it by placing his foot on the bill and Drabowsky would move it ever so slightly out of the person's foot range and continue to do so for as long as the individual would be fooled by it. He even went so far as to give the bill a jerk every so often so that it would rise in the air, just to see how folks would react in an attempt to snatch it out of the air.

Since he had played earlier in his career with Kansas City, Drabowsky knew that one could call the home team's bullpen from that of the visitors. He would imitate the voice of the club's manager and tell the bullpen coach to get a particular pitcher to start warming up which, obviously, infuriated the skipper. The next day or night, he would call down to the pen again and pretend to be the owner and ask for an explanation to the previous game's mixup.

Drabowsky's hotfoots were not of the usual variety either. Instead of just lighting a match on the sole of a player's spiked shoe, he would leave a long trail of lighter fluid from around a corner so as to be completely out of sight.

When Drabowsky was ultimately traded back to Kansas City from Baltimore, he initiated a "war" of sorts between the opposing bullpens during which the participants would prowl underneath the stands with paint for redecoration purposes, an arsenal of cherry bombs, small rocks to toss at one another and goldfish to float in the respective water coolers. Traded back to Baltimore prior to the 1969 World Series, he actually hired an airplane to fly over the stadium with a sign that read: "Beware of Moe."

Other characters deserving of note include another Baltimore Oriole reliever, and a very good one at that for a couple of years, named Don Stanhouse. The right-hander, who recorded 21 and 24 saves respectively in the 1978 and 1979 campaigns, was given the nickname "Stan the Man Unusual" for obvious reasons. For example, once in a while he would hang upside down in the bullpen to—as he put it—"get a new perspective on the game." He did it once too often, though, and fell on his head, effectively ending his career altogether.

Tug McGraw not only grew tomatoes and other vegetables in the bullpen, he also sat on flagpoles. Marty Pattin, who pitched for five different American League teams over a 13-year period and could also do a mean imitation of Donald Duck, would bring his barbecue grill to the bullpen and charcoal some nifty steaks every now and again for his fellow relievers. Ken Brett (George's big brother) pitched for ten clubs in his 14 years in the big leagues and was a teammate of Pattin's at Kansas City in 1980. Brett would actually prance around like a horse and zig zag his way to the mound sometimes when getting the call in from the pen.

If you've ever sat near a bullpen at any one of the major league ballparks, you may have noticed how some of the relief staff reacts to some of the music blaring out of the stadium loudspeakers. It's not uncommon to see some of these guys "boogieing" to the tunes being played. You might also see some others using the pins that are used to hold down the tarpaulin as darts for a variety of targets. Not confined to the bullpen—it is sometimes even tried in the dugout when the manager isn't looking—is a game similar to pitching pennies, only played by spitting out sunflower seeds.

Undoubtedly, one of the reasons why a lot of the bullpen's occupants turn to such diversions is that on many occasions throughout the season they have the most stressful of positions on a team. This is particularly true for the closer, who is being counted upon usually to hold on to the club's lead. It is not a job for the faint-hearted.

The ordeals placed on a relief staff—again especially the closer—are so heavy at times that it consumes many of them and sometimes leads to an early departure from the game. In other words, they simply can't handle the pressure imposed upon them.

The mindset that relievers must possess is that of being able to put aside one bad performance and be prepared to do the job another time. The manager's cooperation and confidence in his staff is necessary as well. He has to demonstrate it by running a pitcher out there again almost immediately after a failure.

In short, one has to be a certain type of individual to succeed in the bullpen over time. Norm Charlton, a veteran left-hander who enjoyed success over a period of years, says: "If closing was easy, a whole lot of people would do it, and there aren't that many that can do it well. There are guys out there who have great stuff who flat out do not want to be closers because they can't handle the stress and the grind of the job."

Today, with closers being asked to pitch fewer and fewer innings in a game, finding people who can take the heat almost on a daily basis places a huge load on general managers. Former Chicago Cubs General Manager Ed Lynch put it this way: "On a staff of 10 pitchers you might have five or six with the stuff to be a closer, but one, if you're lucky, who has the mental approach. The good ones have guts and a short memory. If we have someone we think could be a closer and the reports say he's an [expletive deleted], I think, good. The traits that serve you well in society, like humility, don't serve you well on the mound."

Houston Astros' General Manager Gerry Hunsicker couldn't agree more: "Closers become more problematic because of the demands of that position and the lack of pitchers that are capable of becoming closers ... constantly in the back of your mind (you) have to be looking for a closer and anticipating that you may need to fill that void at any time. It's very difficult to count on a closer."

Weighing heavily on a club's stopper is that the life of a closer is relatively short when compared to starting pitchers and even long relief and setup men. There's no comparison to the average career of a closer versus a position player. "The shelf life of someone [closing] is normally short," says Brian Cashman, general manager of the New York Yankees. "Closers don't have a margin for error. If they lose something, whether it's because of injury or just giving it your 110 percent over a three-, four-year period, maybe the gas tank gets a little low, and all of a sudden you're not the same pitcher. I would expect maybe every four years you have to recycle a guy and find someone new."

Sometimes, though, rather than recycling, developing a new pitch to add to one's arsenal might do the trick. San Diego Padres closer Trevor Hoffman, who is the all-time leader in saves percentage at .882, feels that adding a pitch has lengthened his successful stay in the majors. "I was basically a hard thrower," says Hoffman. "But I also knew after watching Brian Harvey in Florida that I needed kind of an equalizer pitch, something that really kept guys off balance. And for me, it wasn't going to be the split-finger—I didn't have a good feel for it, nor did I want to put that pressure on my arm. And I came up with the changeup. When they were leaning on the fastball, I needed to rely on something else."

Hoffman attributes much of his success to his manager in San Diego and a former catcher, Bruce Bochy, for not letting him pitch more than one inning a game. "I can't put a price tag on that," says Hoffman. "Bochy is following the premise that he's going to have me ready to go every night. He knows that if he sticks to that game plan, I'm not limited to three or four days in a row. If I monitor my pitches and keep the pitch counts low, I can go every day until we don't have an opportunity [to save]."

A pitcher who was being groomed to be a closer by the Atlanta Braves, Kerry Ligtenberg, knows full well that adding a pitch to one's repertoire once the season has begun can be hazardous to a person's health. His usefulness as a closer had to be put on hold in 1999 when he started employing a split-fingered fastball. The first thing he knew was that he needed elbow surgery and would be shelved temporarily. Fortunately for the Braves, John Rocker (since known as "The Mouth of the South") was brought along to take over the closer's role and helped them reach the World Series once again. For Ligtenberg it was back to the drawing board and a role as a setup man and occasional closer.

"When you're a closer and you pitch in games, it's usually do or die, and you can't be out there messing around," says Ligtenberg. "If you're a starter, you can mess around with certain hitters up at different times. But if you're a closer, you need to go hard all the time."

Closers also must have an understanding manager who will give them a much-needed rest between appearances, especially late in the year when their arms get tired. When it comes to times like this, Trevor Hoffman can't say enough good things about his manager, Bruce Bochy, whom he will approach for a day off when his arm is almost dangling at his side. Why be forced to come into a game when you don't have your best stuff and you'll just prove to be ineffective? Makes no sense.

A pitching coach who knows a thing or two about closers and their psyches is Leo Mazzone, Manager Bobby Cox's longtime sidekick in Atlanta. It's his contention that the reason many closers do not stay around the game very long is "because (they) are throwing now with such violence. With the exception of Hoffman," adds Mazzone, "or even (Mariano) Rivera, who throws extremely hard but is smooth, there's a whole bunch of 'em that get erratic and overthrow, try to blow guys out and end up with two on and two out before they save the game.

"They think they've got to grow a goatee, look mean, start firing balls all over the place, grunt when they throw, stare down somebody and act like they're going to macho their way through. I don't even like to look at that as a pitching coach."

A closer who is more apt to be the type that Leo Mazzone would rather see operating is Danny Graves of the Cincinnati Reds. He has the kind of smooth delivery Mazzone talks about, combined with a variety of pitches that he learned while honing his craft as a closer in both college and in the minor leagues. Graves thinks he may be one of those elite closers now coming into the game who aren't just fireballers but are complete pitchers.

"A lot of the closers were guys that threw 95-plus," Graves says. "They just came in and threw as hard as they can. Nowadays you've got guys like me and Trevor Hoffman and Keith Foulke [of the Chicago White Sox], Derek Lowe [of the Boston Red Sox]. We're not guys that are just going to blow people away. I think since we know how to pitch, and we know how to change speeds, that's going to help keep us in the game longer, keep us as a closer. You don't have to throw 99 miles an hour to be a closer."

Danny Graves might just be on to something because as Brian Cashman believes, most closers have a pretty good "career" for three years or so and then run down hill rapidly in the next couple of seasons thereafter. It's not a pretty sight. But if they were to come up with another pitch along the way, they have a real chance to stay around a bit longer.

Former Kansas City Royals closer Jeff Montgomery agrees that the closer's job is physically intense. "If you look at closers who have one or two dynamite years—Mark Davis, Bobby Thigpen, Duane Ward, Jeff Brantley—they're usually going above and beyond what their normal load has been physically," he was quoted as saying after he had lost his closer's spot occasionally due to being either disabled or ineffective. "They've been in more games, more intense situations, and thrown more pitches. I know the season after I had my big year (in '93 with 45 saves), I started having shoulder problems. You're just asked to go out there and do a little more than what your body is accustomed to doing. It's usually a year or two afterward that your performance tapers off."

As has been either been stated or implied here by reputable pitching coaches, closers who fire the ball as hard as possible for as long as they can do not tend to last long in major league baseball. Yet most teams have leaned more to using the so-called "strikeout" pitchers than the more sophisticated relievers. But Boston Red Sox pitching coach Joe Kerrigan had this to say of former Cincinnati Reds flamethrower Rob Dibble: "He was a time bomb waiting to go off."

In 1993, Dibble, Duane Ward, Gregg Olson, Bryan Harvey and Mitch Williams had a total of 181 saves among them. But each of them came apart at the seams, and from then on and through late 1997, the five had only accumulated a total of 25 saves.

If you want dramatic turnarounds, try Mark Davis and Bobby Thigpen on for size. Davis went from Cy Young (he won the award in 1989) to "Sayonara" by saving 44 games for the San Diego Padres that year to only six in the following season. Thigpen, who set a record for saves, which still stands at 57 for the Chicago White Sox in 1990, went on to record 30, 22, one and zero saves in the years that followed.

As Kansas City bullpen coach Guy Hansen put it back in 1997: "Williams, Olson and Davis are pretty much all-effort pitchers. They're trying to make people swing and miss. That causes wear and tear on the arm." Enough said.

Tom Verducci, noted baseball writer for *Sports Illustrated*, wrote a piece for the magazine's August 18, 1997, issue called "No Relief In Sight" and raised a marvelous point. "What these test-tube closers of the '90s are missing out on," he wrote, "especially when they are pampered by starting the ninth inning with no one on base—is the experience of learning how to pitch out of jams. [Troy] Percival [of the Anaheim Angels], for instance, worked only 295⅔ innings in six pro seasons before this year. Not once did he start a game. [Dennis] Eckersley, on the other hand, had logged 1,077 innings—almost all of them as a starter—on his odometer as he entered his seventh year and didn't become a closer until three seasons later. Ultimately the best tool against burning out from the nightly rush of adrenaline and all-you've-got fastballs is a good head rather than a good arm. Says [Norm] Charlton, 'In this job you have to learn from failure.'"

One of the most unheralded members of any ball club, yet an integral part of the team, is the bullpen catcher. Few fans even know the name of their own favorite team's bullpen catcher. However, to say that his role is any less than that of other members of the coaching staff would be to underestimate his true value.

Take a look at what the bullpen catcher's responsibility is. Most fans think all he does is warm up the incoming relief pitchers. That's only a small part of what he gets paid to do. First of all, during batting practice he has to catch pitchers who want to get their "side" work in. Then he warms up the starting pitcher. When the game begins, he has to catch at least two pitchers and as many as seven others who want to get some work in. That includes some of the starters who want to remain sharp between starts.

If the starting pitcher for that day or night is "on," he may have an easy time of it. Doug Witt, a one-time bullpen catcher for the Texas Rangers and brother of pitcher Bobby Witt, recalls having such a night a few years ago.

"Kenny Rogers' perfect game," says Witt. "He didn't have anything warming up. In the bullpen, he had some of the worst stuff I've ever seen. You can see by a guy's facial expressions and body movements that they don't feel they have it, and he was that way."

But there are other days and nights when a bullpen catcher like Doug Witt can spend the last two hours of a game in a crouch while the manager is trying to find the right man to come out of the bullpen to stop the hemorrhaging. In Witt's case, with the temperature running in the 90-degree range in Texas and 90-mph balls bouncing in the dirt, the job can get to be pretty demanding.

"I get nailed all the time," said Witt. "Chest, shoulder, everywhere. But the pain goes away. It hurts a couple of minutes, then goes away. I get mad at them but they're not trying to do it."

Not every pitcher is as wild as this though, according to Witt. "There are guys you enjoy catching because they make my job easier. I love catching John Burkett's side work. He's always five (pitches) on the corner, five in, five out. He gets his work in and everything is pinpoint. That's fun.

"I'm there every day doing what needs to be done," continued Witt. "I get tired, but it's a job to me, and I've got to do it. As long as we win, it doesn't bother me."

Like most bullpen catchers, Doug Witt put in long hours, worked hard and didn't get paid a lot of money when he was the bullpen catcher for the Rangers. Most pitchers will also tip the bullpen catchers at the end of a season for just that reason. "I'm going to keep doing this until something else comes up," Witt said. "I want to stay in the game of baseball, and scouting would be good. I think I've got the knowledge of what it takes to play at this level. I don't want to catch forever. There's not much money in scouting, but it's a chance to move up."

Most fans think that the bullpen is strictly for the use of the relief staff and nothing could be further from the truth. Of course, it is mainly used for that purpose, but starters often throw two "bullpens" a week, each in the middle of the usual five-man rotation. By doing so the pitcher keeps himself fine-tuned by throwing from a mound and permitting himself to work on his mechanics, pitch command and other precise disciplines in his repertoire that he and the pitching coach feel may need attention in between starts.

One of the two bullpens is thrown from the regular pitching distance while the other is from a shorter distance. The latter doesn't place as much stress on his arm and the pitcher can still work on what needs to be worked on at the shorter distances. Even throwing from flat ground will help him accomplish the same objectives.

How hard or easy the pitcher works in each of these bullpens will rest on just how many pitches he may have thrown in his last appearance, and if he is arm-weary at all. Most pitching coaches believe that younger pitchers on a staff should not throw at all if they are experiencing any sort of soreness or tiredness. Overextending one's self can only lead to poor mechanics and perhaps even risk of injury. The best method of determining when the session is to end is if the pitcher's mechanics begin to turn sour or if he should tire. All in all, depending upon how a pitcher feels, 15 minutes to a half hour should do it. Finally, some pitching coaches stress working from 50 to 60 percent of the time from the stretch since it is felt that the most critical pitches in a game are thrown from the stretch position.

The main purpose of each bullpen is to have pitchers get comfortable with their mechanics, release points, the feel of specific pitches and their mental approach to the game. Most pitching coaches urge their pitching staff to use their bullpen work to achieve a particular goal, like working on a pitcher's command for a certain portion of home plate, for example, or keeping the ball down. It's better to have a plan at the ready before heading down there to get their work in.

Last, but far from least, bullpen activity must simulate game conditions in order to be effective. Pitchers need to work on their mental approach using a direct pre-pitch routine that will enable them to enter a game in both the proper frame of mind and physical form.

John Wetteland of the Texas Rangers has been a premier reliever in the majors for a long time, going back to his days with the Montreal Expos and New York Yankees. The man who was voted Rolaids Reliever of the Decade for the 1990s believes that to stay on top for as long as possible, relievers, and especially today's closers, have to work hard every day. Wetteland will spend an hour on the treadmill after concluding his usual pregame workout, which also includes lifting weights. Then he will go into the bullpen and throw under the careful observation of his pitching coach. "To me there's no substitute for work," claims Wetteland.

"He does that kind of stuff every day," says his former pitching coach, Dick Bosman. "Not a lot of relievers can put out that kind of effort, then close a game."

It's Wetteland's contention that closers can only stay around only as long as they labor continuously. And he has more than 300 career saves and an ERA under 3.00 to prove his point.

According to Sammy Ellis, pitching coach for the Baltimore Orioles, what separates dominant closers from the rest of the breed is a good delivery. "When most guys break down early, that's not caused by an act of God or poor conditioning or bad eating habits," says Ellis. "It's usually a poor delivery. A pitcher's arm is not designed to throw over a long period if the other body parts aren't going in the right direction. Success, longevity, location all go hand in hand with a good delivery. You get a pitcher who can throw the baseball where he wants to, he's going to succeed. And to throw the baseball where he wants to, he needs to have a good delivery that he can repeat. It all ties in."

So how are closers created anyhow? They can come from all sorts of differing backgrounds. Some of the best ever—Dennis Eckersley and Goose Gossage—actually began as starting pitchers while some of the most successful closers in the business, like John Franco and Rod Beck, never started a game in their lives.

Dick Bosman certainly doesn't profess to have an answer. "I don't know if there's any ideal way to do it," he says. "I've seen closers come from both directions. Some guys have been halfway decent starters who've come to closing because they just can't maintain it that long. We've seen guys come out of the minor leagues as closers, gone to the big leagues as setup men and more or less gathered experience doing that. Armando Benitez [of the New York Mets] is a guy who comes to mind as a guy who did it that way.

"You need the experience to develop your pitches and to develop your confidence in pitching under pressure in ballgames. On the other end of it, not everyone can handle the ninth inning. That's a mental thing more than it is a physical thing. About the only way you're going to find out is by running them out there in the ninth inning."

Sammy Ellis doesn't necessarily agree with Bosman's assessment. "Almost all guys who have been good closers were starters," says Ellis. "Lee Smith was a starter in the minor leagues. Eckersley was a starter in the big leagues. Gossage was a starter. [Dave] Righetti was a starter. They learned how to pitch, then somebody put them in that closer role because they had the fortitude and the aptitude to handle it. That's why Righetti was put out there [the bullpen]. It wasn't his stuff. It was what was in his stomach.

"I think it's hard to earmark a guy in the minor leagues and say, 'you're going to be a reliever. You're going to be a closer,' unless he's proven to you that he runs out of gas consistently. I'd rather see all the good arms start, especially at an early age in the minor leagues."

Tom Grieve, former vice president and general manager of the Texas Rangers, presents still another view of how closers are generated: "What seems to be as good a way as any is for them to come into the minor leagues as a high draft choice—or at least with a great arm—and pitch as a starter for a couple of years to develop their control, develop their pitches. It seems like nowadays, in this age of specialization, they're starting to come out of college.

"I guess there's no set way of doing it, but I've always thought the best way to develop a young pitcher was as a starter. As a starter, in the minor leagues they can let you give up six, seven, eight runs, get your four or five innings in at least, and you throw all your 90 pitches. You develop them. Then, if you've got the kind of arm that bounces back and you look like you might be that kind of guy, you're more apt to have more than one pitch and the ammunition to get hitters out."

Right-handed reliever Mike Timlin, a ten-year veteran now with the St. Louis Cardinals, contends that when a pitcher first hits the big leagues he's usually put into middle relief. "They can groom you either way from there. Some guys come up and they're straight into the starting rotation. Middle relievers can go either way. Obviously, if you're versatile enough to pitch three or four days a week and your arm's strong enough to do that, you gradually kind of fall into a more defined role toward the end of the game. [Closers] kind of graduate toward that."

Former setup man Mariano Rivera of the New York Yankees claims that when he first became a closer he didn't know how to get ready. "Now I have a routine," he says. "I watch the game, after the seventh inning I start stretching, throw a weighted ball, get loose, and wait for the call."

John Wetteland came into the majors as a starting pitcher for the Los Angeles Dodgers although he asked to be a closer in his final year in the minors. "The only reason I switched over was because I was sick and tired of being a mediocre starter," he says. "I think what starting taught me most was to use all my pitches in all kinds of situations. When you're closing and that's all you're doing, you're facing one particular situation. I think what starting does is put you in a myriad of circumstances where you need to learn how to pitch. You're more apt to get more innings in a year. You get more time at your craft." Wetteland believes that closers should talk to each other about their profession. "A lot of closers would talk—more so in the earlier days," he says, "and it wasn't so much about how to do this, how to do that. [Closers] understand the ninth inning. It was always kind of like 'How are you doing?' Emotional support."

However, he believes that the situation has changed. "The problem is nowadays a lot of closers are very young and I see a lot of pride and ego out there," says John Wetteland. "Maybe they don't want to [share information]. That's fine. But I encourage it. I'll try to prepare someone to take my job. I think that's part of my responsibility to this organization, because at some point, for whatever reason, I'm not going to be able to do this."

♦ *Chapter 13* ♦

Relief Pitching in the 21st Century

With the arrival of the third millennium, it is only natural to look at just where the craft of relief pitching has taken the game of baseball, and to speculate on where exactly it might it be heading. First off, we only have to look at the post–World War II era to see that whereas big league teams were averaging about one reliever a game over the course of a season, that figure has now climbed to around three.

The rationale behind this nearly 300 percent upward swing is, as has been pointed out repeatedly here: bigger, stronger hitters throughout the lineup; the smaller ballparks now being built; and the trend away from the single "fireman" and toward the specialists, be they middle or long relievers, setup men or closers. For these and other reasons, and like it or not, the relief specialist is now counted on to play a major role in the ultimate outcome of nearly every ball game played today. There is absolutely no good reason to believe that this movement will not continue. On the contrary, fans should only look for it to grow. In fact, it's been reported that more than one manager or two (Tony LaRussa is alleged to be one) foresees the day when there may be a different pitcher on the mound in almost every inning. Imagine it—a bullpen with pitchers working constantly to get ready to come into games at a moment's notice.

As it stands now, the complete game is approaching the dinosaur stage. Whereas only 30 years ago, the best pitchers in the game were averaging more than 300 innings a season and finishing the bulk of what they started, today's starters are considered extraordinary if they pitch more than 200 innings and complete 20 percent of their starts. Of course, there was a four-man starting rotation back then that accounted for a lot of these numbers, which some look at with fondness now. It wasn't until the 1971 San Francisco Giants switched to a five-man rotation that the number of pitches a starter threw and the number of innings he worked over the course of a season started to decrease. By the late 1970s, almost every team had gone to the five-man starting rotation.

Believe it or not, apart from some overmanaging, there are good reasons why this change has taken place. First of all, the number of strikeouts per game has been on the increase since the 1970s and early 1980s when they averaged fewer than five per nine innings. That figure has jumped up to nearly seven a game, which simply translates into more pitches thrown. Coupled with more base runners (from 12 to 13 a game) and the number of pitches goes up once again. Runs, too, have been on the increase (from fewer than four a game in the 1970s to more than five now) and the pitch count continues to grow. All in all, more pitchers per batter, more batters per game, more runners on base, more runs scored and more "pressure" pitches overall have led starting pitchers to work harder and simply run out of gas earlier than they did in the past. The upshot? An increasing reliance on more and specialized relievers to get the job done.

Of course, the game as it has evolved with the proliferation of relief pitchers is not without its critics. What seems like interminable games are not that popular with many of baseball's staunchest followers. The purists among us cannot see why a manager insists on changing pitchers simply because, for instance, a left-handed hitter is coming up to bat against the starting right-hander at a critical juncture of the game. With the computer age in full flower now, the skipper can look down on his printout sheets and see instantly who hits or doesn't hit against every pitcher on his roster. The pitcher he elects to bring in may only be there long enough to face that one hitter before being replaced himself. And on it goes. Overmanaging? Perhaps, but don't look for it to go away anytime soon.

Right now every big league team, almost without exception, carries a minimum of 12 pitchers as opposed to just eight or nine 30 or 40 years ago. Some have even carried as many as 13 at a given time during the season. Position players like a third catcher or extra outfielder or infielder who may also double as pinch-hitters may have to be either traded or sent to the minors to make room for today's inflated pitching staff. There has been talk of late of trying to remedy the situation by increasing the rosters to 26 from the age-old 25, the number that has been in existence since before 1920. Don't hold your breath on that one, though.

No less an expert than Bill James, in his *Guide to Baseball Managers From 1870 to Today,* opines that "the bullpen of the future may consist of six men, but each of those six men may pitch 80 to 120 times per season, as opposed to the 50 or 80 which is standard now. A pitcher pitching 100 games a season, but facing two or three batters per outing, thus pitching only 50 to 70 innings in those 100 games ... that probably is going to be *part* of the future bullpen."

James goes on: "[T]here are two other elements of the 1990s bullpen that I feel strongly are going to break up, simply because the world is ultimately logical, and what major league managers are doing now *isn't* logical. Those two elements are: (1) the constant use of left-handed relievers to get out one or two hitters, and (2) the construction of nearly all save opportunities onto a single reliever."

To prove that it really doesn't matter how a bullpen is constituted, in his book James cites the case of Felipe Alou's 1994 Montreal Expos with five right-handers and no left-handers in his pen that year. Alou contended that these were the best pitchers he had available to relieve and that he could and would live with that. In the final analysis, the Expos had the best record in baseball (74–40) when that infamous work stoppage took place late that year. James reasoned mathematically that Alou's lack of a lefty out of the bullpen could have cost him a platoon advantage in less than 100 matchups over the course of a season. Since "the normal platoon advantage is about .025, twenty five points," wrote James, "the lack of a left-hander in the bullpen probably cost him less than three hits."

Bill James is of a mind that Alou's use of an all-right-handed bullpen enabled him "to *schedule* the work of his relievers to a much greater extent. The left-handed one-out man—he's got to pitch when the opportunity arises. If everybody's right-handed, you can just set up a schedule and rotate them. And he did." It certainly worked for Felipe Alou that year. And James believes teams could actually free up two or three roster spots if they did not subscribe to theory of the need for one or two lefties to populate and counterbalance the bullpen. He says he's seen too many failures as a result of this strategy simply because "*managers like to control the flow of the action.*"

What we are seeing right now in major league baseball is the relatively short careers of today's closers. In the year 2000, only five of the closers of the 30 major league teams now in existence were the same ones that were finishing games for their clubs back in 1997: Detroit's Todd Jones, Florida's Antonio Alfonseca, San Diego's Trevor Hoffman, the Yankees' Mariano Rivera and, before he was lost for the year early in the season, Montreal's Ugueth Urbina. Burnout? Possibly. More likely is the fact there just aren't enough good ones around to pitch in that role like the Eckersleys, Gossages and Fingers of years past. Could expansion be rearing its ugly head by the lack of experienced, fundamentally sound players of every stripe not being readily available?

True, there have been injuries, as in the case of the aforementioned Urbina, in addition to Mike Jackson of the Philadelphia Phillies and Tom Gordon of the Boston Red Sox early in the year 2000. But it goes beyond that sometimes. As Dick Bosman, the former pitching coach of the Texas Rangers, ventured to say on the subject not too long ago: "Some of them may get the 'yips' and some of them may get a little fried, mentally. There are contract issues, there are expectations, there are fans. You factor all that in with somebody who's got a fragile ego or who's not as strong mentally as you'd like, and you've got all the factors involved for a breakdown."

Matt Mantei, an unhittable closer when Arizona pried him loose from Florida in the middle of the 1999 pennant race, lost his job to the fireballing sidearmer Byung-Hyun Kim early in the 2000 season. "It's all mental," says Mantei.

Billy Wagner of the Houston Astros tends to agree. "When the team doesn't have confidence in you, that's not a good feeling," he says. "I don't like the thought of sitting [in the bullpen] knowing that other guys are having to do my job."

Wagner, who saved 39 games in 42 chances for the Astros and pitched to a 1.57 ERA in 1999, had no location on his pitches in 2000 and attempted to pitch through a torn flexor tendon, which affected him both physically and mentally. Out for the season, he worried about the future: "When your livelihood is a fastball, of course you are concerned," he says. "Next year I have to come back and probably prove myself all over."

Pressure? Of course, it's part of a reliever's and, especially, a closer's existence. "Obviously, we're expected to go out and close the game, every game," says St. Louis Cardinals reliever Mike Timlin. "You've got to be perfect, otherwise you get booed. It's part of the job. You've got to deal with it."

Former Texas Ranger vice president and general manager Tom Grieve definitely thinks that some closers could easily end up burnt out if they don't have the right frame of mind. "There's pressure and that builds up day after day, year after year," he says. "It seems like it almost burns the concentration. To take that job, it's obvious that you have to be able to put things behind you ... you can only put someone in that role who has a short memory, a lot of courage and a lot of confidence in himself. Even some of the good ones—it seems after four, five or six years, they just get burned out on the job."

The noted baseball author and commentator Bill James doesn't think it's necessary to deem one man as a team's closer and put your fortunes in his hands. "Is it more effective to use your best pitcher only in save situations, or more effective to use him the way Elroy Face was used?" he asks. "[T]he belief that only The Closer can finish games is a shibboleth [idiosyncracy], just like the belief that all of your best pitchers had to be starting pitchers was a shibboleth, and sooner or later it will dissolve into the nothingness of which it is made."

In his book, *The Bill James Guide to Baseball Managers,* he seems to imply that it's really not the manager's job to worry about getting as many saves as he can for his one and only closer. Nor should he treat his bullpen unequally because all of his relievers are probably as good as his designated closer. So why not use them in that role as well once in awhile? A fair question.

Bill James concludes his book with a statement that I think bears repeating here and is good enough to close with here also: "Relief strategy has been in constant motion for a hundred years. It is very clear, to me, that we are nowhere near a stopping point."

Bibliography

Adomites, Paul, and Saul Wisnia. *Best of Baseball*. Publications International, Ltd., 1997.

Alexander, Charles. *Our Game*. Fine Communications, 1997.

Bowman, John S., and Joel Zoss. *The Pictorial History of Baseball*. Gallery Books, 1986.

Brosnan, Jim. *The Long Season*. Ivan R. Dee, 2002.

DiGiovanna, Mike. "Rivera: A Cut Above Most Relievers." *Los Angeles Times*, October 21, 1999.

Duren, Ryne, and Robert F. Drury. *The Comeback*. Lorenz Company, 1998.

Felber, Bill. "The Changing Game: Strategy After 1920; Recent Strategy; The Changing Game: Pitching." *Total Baseball*. Total Sports, 1999.

Gallagher, Mark, and Neil Gallagher. *Baseball's Great Dynasties—The Yankees*. Gallery Books, 1990.

Gilman, Dan. *The Way Baseball Works*. Richard Ballantine Books, Simon & Schuster, 1996.

Grosshandler, Stanley. "The Brewers' Best." *Exclusively Yours*, May 1972.

Grosshandler, Stanley. "Do You Remember Jim Konstanty?" *Sports Digest*, July 1973.

Grosshandler, Stanley. "Relief Pitchers: Specialists in Crisis." *Baseball Digest*, May 1972.

Heinz, W.C. *Once They Heard the Cheers*. Doubleday, 1979.

Horton, Ralph L. *Rating Relief Pitchers*. Horton, 1994.

James, Bill. *The Bill James Guide to Baseball Managers from 1870 to Today*. Scribner, 1997.

James, Bill. *The New Bill James Historical Abstract*. Simon & Schuster, 2001.

Lahman, Sean. *A Brief History of Baseball*. The Baseball Archive.

Leibowitz, Kerry. "A Vanishing Art: Why Complete Games Are Going the Way of the Dodo." www.orioleshangout.com, 2000.

Light, Jonathan Fraser. *The Cultural Encyclopedia of Baseball*. McFarland, 1997.

Livingstone, Seth. "Few Can Answer Closer's Call." *Baseball Weekly*, June 28, 2000.

Lyle, Sparky, and Peter Golenbock. *The Bronx Zoo*. NY Crown Publishing, 1979.

Marx, Doug. *Relief Pitchers*. The Rourke Corporation, Inc., 1991.

Mathewson, Christy, and John N. Wheeler. *Pitching in a Pinch*. Madison Books, 1977.

McCullough, Bob. "Closers Can't Live on Fastballs Now." NBC Sports with *The Sporting News*, August 3, 2000.

Mote, James. *Everything Baseball*. Prentice Hall Press, 1989.

Rader, Benjamin. *Baseball: A History of America's Game*. University of Illinois Press, 1994.

Reichler, Joseph L., editor. *The Baseball Register*. Macmillan, 1988.

Ritter, Lawrence S. *The Story of Baseball*. William Morrow, 1983.

Seymour, Harold. *Baseball: The Early Years; Baseball: The Golden Years; Baseball: The People's Game*. Oxford University Press, 1989.

Shapiro, Milton J. *Heroes of the Bullpen*. Julian Messner, 1967.

Sullivan, T.R. "Catcher Doug Witt Stays Cool Warming Up Rangers Pitchers." *Fort Worth Star-Telegram*, July 28, 1998.

Total Sports. *Total Baseball*, sixth edition, 1999.

TSN Archives. "The History of the World Series." *The Sporting News*, 1999.

Verducci, Tom. "No Relief in Sight." *Sports Illustrated*, August 18, 1997.

Verducci, Tom. "The Pen Is Mightier." *Sports Illustrated*, September 20, 1999.

Ward, Geoffrey C. *Baseball: An Illustrated History*. Alfred A. Knopf, 1994.

Index